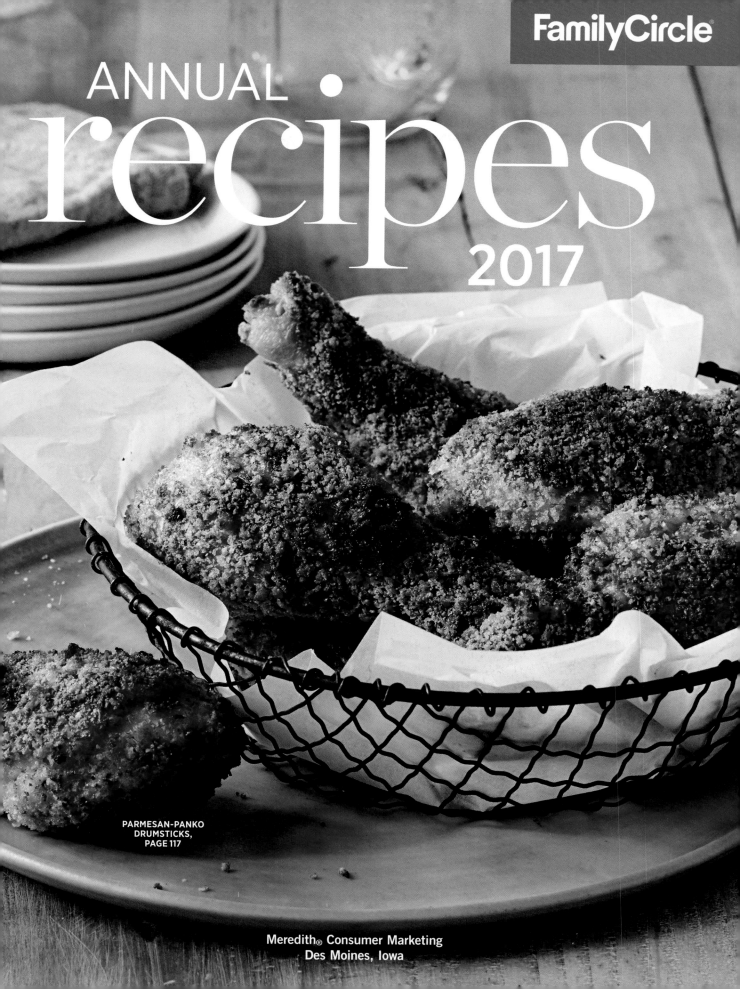

FamilyCircle®

ANNUAL
recipes
2017

Meredith® Consumer Marketing
Des Moines, Iowa

PARMESAN-PANKO
DRUMSTICKS,
PAGE 117

FROZEN RASPBERRY-
CHOCOLATE CAKE, PAGE 110

A YEAR'S WORTH OF FABULOUS *FAMILY CIRCLE*® FOOD AT YOUR FINGERTIPS!

Whether it's a speedy weeknight meal before dashing off to the rest of the day's activities or a once-a-year celebration during which we slow down and savor the specialness of the occasion, feeding our families well is important to all of us. At *Family Circle*, we carefully consider the recipes we include in our magazine. We know that the quick recipes need to be easy, health- and budget-conscious, and—it goes without saying—delicious. The company-worthy recipes need to be spectacular in some way but still simple enough to make at home. You'll find both kinds of recipes—and everything in between—in this one volume: an at-your-fingertips collection of every recipe that appeared in the 2017 issues of the magazine. It's organized by month, so you can easily find just the kind of recipe you're looking for—and can take advantage of whatever produce is at peak season.

For Valentine's Day, indulge in chocolate treats such as Chocolate Raspberry Cups (page 37) or No-Bake Chocolate Ganache Tart (page 38). Grillside, up your burger game with innovative takes on this summer staple. (The Million Dollar Burger [page 155] features a ground chicken patty infused with truffle oil and shallot and topped with goat cheese and arugula, all served on a toasted brioche bun. Yum!) When back-to-school schedules kick into high gear, turn to a jar of marinara sauce as a base for quick, family-pleasing recipes such as Spaghetti and Meatball Skillet Pie (page 216) and Chicken Tikka Masala (page 217).

We know that busy weeknights present cooking challenges, so in every issue—in regular features such as Healthy Family Dinners—we bring you ways to get delicious, nutritious food on the table any night of the week.

Food and family are interconnected. We hope the recipes in this book help you enjoy them both every day.

Cheryl E. Brown, Editor in Chief
Family Circle Magazine

Family Circle. *Annual Recipes 2017*

Meredith Consumer Marketing
Consumer Marketing Product Director: Heather Sorensen
Consumer Marketing Product Manager: Tami Perkins
Consumer Products Marketing Manager: Wendy Merical
Business Manager: Diane Umland
Senior Production Manager: Al Rodruck

Waterbury Publications, Inc.
Editorial Director: Lisa Kingsley
Associate Editor: Tricia Bergman
Creative Director: Ken Carlson
Associate Design Director: Doug Samuelson
Graphic Designer: Mindy Samuelson
Contributing Copy Editors: Angela Renkoski, Carrie Truesdell
Contributing Indexer: Mary Williams

Family Circle. **Magazine**
Editor in Chief: Cheryl E. Brown
Food Director: Regina Ragone, M.S., R.D.
Executive Food Editor: Julie Miltenberger
Associate Food Editor: Melissa Knific
Assistant Food Editor: Sarah Wharton

Meredith National Media Group
President: Jon Werther

Meredith Corporation
Chairman and Chief Executive Officer: Stephen M. Lacy

In Memoriam: E.T. Meredith III (1933–2003)

Copyright © 2017
Meredith Corporation.
Des Moines, Iowa.
First Edition.
Printed in the United States of America.
ISSN: 1942-7476
ISBN: 978-0696-30257-2

All of us at Meredith Consumer
Marketing are dedicated to providing
you with information and ideas to
enhance your home. We welcome
your comments and suggestions.
Write to us at: Meredith Consumer
Marketing, 1716 Locust St.,
Des Moines, IA 50309-3023.

LET'S EAT! Coming together around the family table at the end of the day to enjoy a home-cooked meal soothes away the day's stresses and satisfies on so many levels. This collection of recipes from the 2017 issues of *Family Circle* magazine makes it easier than ever to serve tasty food you cook yourself—whether it's a 30-minute dinner, a holiday celebration or a special evening with friends. Recipes are organized by month to take advantage of what's in season and to make it easy to find the perfect recipe for any occasion.

Rice Pudding with Almonds and Cider Syrup (page 269) is part of the "10 Totally Totable Treats" story that appeared in the November issue. Other sweet treats from that issue include Salted Caramel Blondie Bites, Chocolate-Peanut Butter Mousse Cups, and Pumpkin Whoopie Pies.

40-CLOVE GARLIC
CHICKEN, PAGE 221

CONTENTS

SHRIMP AND
VEGGIE ROLLS,
PAGE 15

JANUARY

21

26

30

RING IT IN

Easy apps paired with perfect drinks mean less fuss and more fun.

BLACK-EYED PEA
HUMMUS

CURRIED POPCORN
AND CASHEWS

KOREAN
MEATBALLS

Black-Eyed Pea Hummus

MAKES 12 servings **PREP** 15 minutes

- 2 cans (15.5 oz each) black-eyed peas, drained and rinsed
- 1 small clove garlic, roughly chopped
- ½ cup tahini paste
- ½ cup extra-virgin olive oil, plus more for drizzling
- ⅓ cup plus 1 tsp lemon juice
- ¾ tsp salt
- ¼ tsp cayenne pepper
- 2 vine tomatoes, diced
- 2 scallions, sliced
- 1 tbsp chopped fresh cilantro or parsley
   Salsa
   Tortilla chips or sliced raw vegetables

■ In a food processor, combine black-eyed peas, garlic, tahini, oil, ⅓ cup lemon juice, the salt and cayenne until very smooth, 3 to 5 minutes.

■ In a small bowl, toss tomatoes, scallions, cilantro, 1 tsp lemon juice and a pinch of salt.

■ Transfer hummus to a bowl and make a well in the middle; fill with salsa. Drizzle with more oil and serve with tortilla chips or sliced raw vegetables.

PER SERVING 190 **CAL**; 14 g **FAT** (2 g **SAT**); 6 g **PRO**; 12 g **CARB**; 1 g **SUGARS**; 3 g **FIBER**; 348 mg **SODIUM**

Korean Meatballs

MAKES 48 meatballs **PREP** 30 minutes
COOK 17 minutes

- 1½ lb ground beef
- 1 small shallot, minced
- 3 garlic cloves, finely minced
- 2 tbsp gochujang (Korean hot chile paste)
- 3 tsp grated ginger
- 2 tsp sesame oil
- ¾ tsp salt
- 2 tbsp vegetable oil
- 1 cup ketchup
- ¼ cup packed brown sugar
- 2 tbsp rice vinegar
   Toasted sesame seeds and scallions (optional)

■ In a bowl, combine beef, shallot, 2 minced garlic cloves, 1 tbsp gochujang, 2 tsp ginger, 1 tsp sesame oil and the salt. Roll into forty-eight 1-inch meatballs.

■ In a large skillet, heat 1 tbsp vegetable oil over medium-high. Add half the meatballs. Cook 2 minutes; turn and cook 1 minute, until browned (meatballs don't need to be cooked all the way through). Remove to a paper-towel-lined plate. Add 1 tbsp vegetable oil and repeat with remaining meatballs.

■ Reduce heat under the same skillet to medium. Add 1 minced garlic clove and 1 tsp ginger; cook 30 seconds. Add ketchup, brown sugar, vinegar, 1 tbsp gochujang and 1 tsp sesame oil. Whisk until blended. Bring to a simmer, then reduce heat to medium-low and simmer 5 minutes.

■ Return meatballs to skillet. Simmer in sauce for 5 minutes. Transfer to a serving bowl and, if using, scatter sesame seeds and scallions on top. Serve with toothpicks or cocktail forks.

PER SERVING (4 meatballs) 150 **CAL**; 7 g **FAT** (3 g **SAT**); 11 g **PRO**; 12 g **CARB**; 11 g **SUGARS**; 0 g **FIBER**; 490 mg **SODIUM**

Curried Popcorn and Cashews

MAKES 24 cups **PREP** 10 minutes
BAKE at 375° for 10 minutes **COOK** 2 minutes

- 8 tbsp unsalted butter
- ¼ cup sweet Indian curry powder
- 2 tsp sugar
- 1½ tsp salt
- ¼ tsp cayenne pepper
- 2 cups raw unsalted cashews
- 2 tbsp coconut or vegetable oil
- 1 cup popcorn kernels
- 1 cup golden raisins

■ Heat oven to 375°. In a large skillet, melt 2 tbsp unsalted butter over medium. Stir in 2 tbsp curry powder, 1 tsp sugar, ½ tsp salt and ⅛ tsp cayenne. Cook 1 minute, then stir in cashews. Transfer to a large rimmed baking sheet in a single layer and bake 8 to 10 minutes. (Set aside skillet to use later.) Let cool on baking sheet while preparing popcorn.

■ In the same skillet, melt 6 tbsp unsalted butter over medium. Stir in 2 tbsp curry powder, 1 tsp sugar, 1 tsp salt and ⅛ tsp cayenne. Cook 1 minute and remove from burner. Cover to keep warm.

■ In a very large lidded pot, stir oil and popcorn kernels over medium. Cover with lid slightly off-center to release steam. Cook as per package directions until most of the kernels have popped.

■ Pour butter into a large bowl, add popcorn and raisins, and toss until coated. Stir in cashews until well mixed.

PER CUP 150 **CAL**; 9 g **FAT** (4 g **SAT**); 3 g **PRO**; 14 g **CARB**; 6 g **SUGARS**; 2 g **FIBER**; 150 mg **SODIUM**

Manchego and Marcona Almond Cheese Balls

MAKES 36 cheese balls **PREP** 25 minutes
REFRIGERATE 1 hour

- **8** oz cream cheese, at room temperature
- **1** cup shredded Manchego cheese
- **1** tbsp honey
- **½** tsp freshly cracked black pepper
- **1** cup finely chopped Marcona almonds
- **36** pretzel sticks

■ Combine first 4 ingredients in a bowl with a spatula. Scoop out 36 generous teaspoonfuls and place on a parchment-lined baking sheet. Form into balls, then roll in almonds. Insert a pretzel stick in center of each ball. Refrigerate 1 hour before serving.

PER SERVING (3 cheese balls) 210 **CAL**; 19 g **FAT** (7 g **SAT**); 7 g **PRO**; 5 g **CARB**; 3 g **SUGARS**; 2 g **FIBER**; 150 mg **SODIUM**

Bacon-Cheddar Cheese Balls

MAKES 36 cheese balls **PREP** 25 minutes
REFRIGERATE 1 hour

- **8** oz cream cheese, at room temperature
- **1** cup shredded sharp cheddar
- **¼** cup finely chopped fresh chives
- **¾** tsp smoked paprika
- **8** oz smoked bacon, cooked until crispy, very finely chopped
- **36** pretzel sticks

■ Combine first 4 ingredients in a bowl with a spatula. Scoop out 36 generous teaspoonfuls and place on a parchment-lined baking sheet. Form into balls, then dip bottom half of each in chopped bacon. Insert a pretzel stick in center of each ball. Refrigerate 1 hour before serving.

PER SERVING (3 cheese balls) 180 **CAL**; 17 g **FAT** (8 g **SAT**); 6 g **PRO**; 1 g **CARB**; 7 g **SUGARS**; 1 g **FIBER**; 250 mg **SODIUM**

Kalamata Olive and Dill Cheese Balls

MAKES 36 cheese balls **PREP** 25 minutes
REFRIGERATE 1 hour

- **10** oz soft goat cheese, at room temperature
- **⅓** cup crumbled feta
- **¼** cup finely chopped Kalamata olives
- **1** tsp lemon zest
- **36** pretzel sticks
- **2** tbsp finely chopped fresh dill

■ Combine first 4 ingredients in a bowl with a spatula. Scoop out 36 generous teaspoonfuls and place on a parchment-lined baking sheet. Form into balls, then insert a pretzel stick in center of each ball. Refrigerate 1 hour. Just before serving, sprinkle with dill.

PER SERVING (3 cheese balls) 110 **CAL**; 9 g **FAT** (6 g **SAT**); 6 g **PRO**; 1 g **CARB**; 0 g **SUGARS**; 0 g **FIBER**; 210 mg **SODIUM**

Lemony Baked Ricotta

MAKES 8 servings **PREP** 10 minutes
BAKE at 400° for 25 minutes **BROIL** 3 minutes

- **1** lb whole-milk ricotta
- **1** egg
- **1** tbsp chopped fresh thyme
- **1** tbsp lemon juice
- **1** tsp zest
- **¾** tsp salt
- **¼** tsp black pepper
  Extra-virgin olive oil (optional)
  Crackers

■ Heat oven to 400°. In a bowl, beat ricotta, egg, thyme, lemon juice, ½ tsp lemon zest, the salt and pepper until well mixed.

■ Transfer to a 2-cup oven-safe dish. Bake 25 minutes, until set and starting to brown. Broil 2 to 3 minutes, until lightly browned. Scatter ½ tsp lemon zest on top and drizzle with olive oil, if desired. Serve with crackers.

PER SERVING 110 **CAL**; 8 g **FAT** (5 g **SAT**); 7 g **PRO**; 2 g **CARB**; 0 g **SUGARS**; 0 g **FIBER**; 270 mg **SODIUM**

MANCHEGO AND
MARCONA ALMOND
CHEESE BALLS

KALAMATA
OLIVE AND
DILL CHEESE
BALLS

BACON-CHEDDAR
CHEESE BALLS

LEMONY BAKED
RICOTTA

SHRIMP AND
VEGGIE ROLLS

Asian food and hard cider are a great match, but Sauvignon Blanc is also a winner.

Shrimp and Veggie Rolls

MAKES 16 rolls (32 halves) **PREP** 30 minutes

- 1 **cup coconut milk**
- 2 **tbsp creamy peanut butter (such as Jif)**
- 2 **tbsp packed light brown sugar**
- 2 **tbsp soy sauce**
- 2 **tsp Thai red curry paste**
- 1 **tsp fresh lime juice, plus wedges for squeezing**
- 16 **8- or 9-inch rice paper wrappers**
- 1 **lb cooked and peeled medium shrimp (about 24), sliced in half lengthwise**
- ½ **English cucumber, thinly sliced and cut into half-moons**
- 1 **cup shredded carrots**
- 1 **cup shredded red cabbage**
- ½ **cup fresh cilantro leaves**
- ½ **cup fresh mint leaves**

■ In a bowl, whisk coconut milk, peanut butter, brown sugar, soy sauce, curry paste and 1 tsp lime juice until smooth. Set aside.

■ Fill a shallow bowl or pie plate with warm water. Dunk a rice paper wrapper in water, flip, then remove and drain on a paper towel. Place on a cutting board and arrange 3 pieces of shrimp; a bit of the cucumber, carrots and cabbage; and a few cilantro and mint leaves on bottom third of wrapper, leaving a 1-inch border. Squeeze some fresh lime juice on top. Fold bottom of wrapper over filling, then fold in ends and roll tightly. Repeat with remaining wrappers and filling. Slice in half on the bias and serve with coconut-peanut sauce.

PER SERVING (2 rolls) 240 **CAL**; 9 g **FAT** (6 g **SAT**); 18 g **PRO**; 23 g **CARB**; 6 g **SUGARS**; 1 g **FIBER**; 910 mg **SODIUM**

HEALTHY FAMILY DINNERS

Try these 10 easy recipes on crazy-busy nights.

STEAK FAJITA
BOWLS

Steak Fajita Bowls

MAKES 4 servings **PREP** 10 minutes
COOK 40 minutes

- ¾   **cup brown rice**
- ¾   **tsp salt**
- 1   **can (15.5 oz) low-sodium black beans**
- 1¼   **lb sirloin steak**
- 1   **tsp black pepper**
- 1   **tsp ancho chile powder**
- 1   **tsp ground cumin**
- 2   **tbsp vegetable oil**
- 2   **medium poblano or green bell peppers, thinly sliced**
- 1   **medium red onion, thinly sliced**
- 4   **tbsp crumbled queso blanco or Cotija cheese**
- **Lime wedges and tomatillo salsa (optional)**

▪ Bring 1¾ cups water to a boil. Add rice and ¼ tsp salt. Cover and reduce heat to low; cook 40 minutes. Drain and rinse beans; stir into rice. Keep warm.

▪ Meanwhile, rub steak with black pepper, chile powder, cumin and ½ tsp salt. Heat 1 tbsp oil in a large cast-iron skillet over medium-high. Add steak to pan and cook 10 to 12 minutes, turning once. Transfer to a cutting board and loosely cover with foil. Reduce heat to medium. Add 1 tbsp oil and stir in the peppers and onion. Cook 5 minutes, stirring occasionally.

▪ Slice steak into thin strips across the grain. Toss with vegetables in a pan. Divide rice and beans among 4 bowls. Divide steak mixture among bowls. Top each with 1 tbsp of the cheese. Serve with lime wedges and tomatillo salsa, if desired.

PER SERVING 470 **CAL**; 15 g **FAT** (5 g **SAT**); 39 g **PRO**; 51 g **CARB**; 3 g **SUGARS**; 11 g **FIBER**; 770 mg **SODIUM**

CORNMEAL-CRUSTED
FLOUNDER WITH BLISTERED
GREEN BEANS

Cornmeal-Crusted Flounder with Blistered Green Beans

MAKES 4 servings **PREP** 30 minutes **COOK** 16 minutes

- 1   **large egg white**
- ½   **cup cornmeal**
- 2   **tbsp all-purpose flour**
- 1   **tsp salt**
- ¼   **tsp black pepper**
- ⅛   **tsp cayenne pepper**
- 4   **flounder fillets (4 oz each)**
- 2   **lb sweet potatoes, cut into chunks**
- 5   **tbsp unsalted butter**
- ¾   **lb green beans, trimmed**
- ¼   **cup milk**
- 1   **tbsp sugar**

▪ Place egg white in a shallow dish and whisk lightly. In another shallow dish, combine cornmeal, flour, ½ tsp salt, black pepper and cayenne pepper. Dip flounder in egg white to coat. Coat flounder completely with cornmeal mixture and place on a plate.

▪ Peel potatoes and cut into chunks. Place in a large pot and add salted water to cover. Bring to a boil; cook 12 minutes.

▪ Meanwhile, heat 2 tbsp butter in a large stainless skillet over medium-high. Add 2 flounder fillets and cook 2 minutes per side. Remove to a plate and repeat with 2 tbsp butter and remaining flounder. Melt 1 tbsp butter in same skillet and add green beans. Cook 2 minutes without stirring. Continue to cook 6 minutes, stirring occasionally. Drain sweet potatoes and mash with milk, sugar and ½ tsp salt. Serve flounder with potatoes and beans.

PER SERVING 460 **CAL**; 17 g **FAT** (10 g **SAT**); 19 g **PRO**; 58 g **CARB**; 15 g **SUGARS**; 6 g **FIBER**; 790 mg **SODIUM**

PENNE WITH CHICKEN AND SQUASH

Chicken Burgers with Roasted Broccoli

MAKES 4 servings **PREP** 15 minutes
COOK 10 minutes
ROAST at 425° for 25 minutes

1	lb broccoli florets
1	tbsp olive oil
½	tsp salt
½	tsp black pepper
1	lb ground chicken
6	oz (about 7 medium) white mushrooms, grated
2	tbsp plain dry bread crumbs
1	tsp chopped fresh thyme
4	thin slices cheddar
4	burger buns
1	cup shredded lettuce

■ Heat oven to 425°. Toss broccoli with olive oil and ¼ tsp each salt and pepper. Spread onto a baking sheet and roast 20 to 25 minutes, turning once.

■ Meanwhile, in a large bowl, combine chicken, mushrooms, bread crumbs, thyme and ¼ tsp each salt and pepper. Form mixture into four 5-inch patties (about 5 oz each). Heat a large nonstick skillet over medium-high. Add burger patties and cook 4 to 5 minutes. Flip over; add a cheddar slice to each burger. Cook 4 to 5 more minutes, until temperature reaches 160°. Place cheddar-topped burger patties on buns. Top each with ¼ cup lettuce. Serve with roasted broccoli.

PER SERVING 475 **CAL**; 24 g **FAT** (9 g **SAT**); 34 g **PRO**; 34 g **CARB**; 6 g **SUGARS**; 4 g **FIBER**; 780 mg **SODIUM**

Penne with Chicken and Squash

MAKES 6 servings **PREP** 15 minutes **COOK** 15 minutes

1¼	lb butternut squash, cubed
¾	lb penne pasta
1	cup chicken broth
¾	cup heavy cream
1	lb boneless, skinless chicken breasts
1	tsp salt
2	tbsp unsalted butter
3	cloves garlic, sliced
2	tbsp all-purpose flour
¼	tsp black pepper
⅛	tsp nutmeg
½	cup grated Parmesan
½	cup chopped fresh basil

■ Bring a large pot of salted water to a boil. Add squash; cook 5 minutes. Add penne and cook 5 more minutes; drain.

■ Meanwhile, heat broth and ¼ cup heavy cream in a large lidded skillet over medium-low. Season chicken with ¼ tsp salt. Add to skillet; cover and poach 10 minutes, turning once. Remove chicken and pour broth-cream mixture into a bowl. Melt butter in skillet over medium. Add garlic; cook 1 minute. Whisk in flour; cook 1 minute. Whisk in broth mixture, ¼ tsp salt, pepper and nutmeg. Simmer 3 minutes. Remove from heat and add ½ cup heavy cream and ¼ cup Parmesan. Slice chicken. Toss penne and squash with sauce, chicken, basil and ½ tsp salt. Top with ¼ cup Parmesan.

PER SERVING 529 **CAL**; 20 g **FAT** (11 g **SAT**); 29 g **PRO**; 58 g **CARB**; 5 g **SUGARS**; 4 g **FIBER**; 695 mg **SODIUM**

SHRIMP PAELLA

Shrimp Paella

MAKES 6 servings **PREP** 10 minutes
COOK 50 minutes

- 4   slices turkey bacon, diced
- 1   tbsp vegetable oil
- 1   tbsp canola oil
- 1   medium red onion, chopped
- 1   sweet red pepper, chopped
- 1   green bell pepper, chopped
- 1   tbsp garlic, minced
- 1   tsp saffron threads
- ½   tsp black pepper
- 2   cups brown basmati rice
- 4   cups seafood stock
- 1½ lb shrimp, peeled and cleaned
- 1   cup frozen peas, thawed
- ¼   tsp salt
-     Chopped fresh parsley

■ In a heavy 3-quart lidded sauté pan, cook bacon in vegetable oil over medium-high until crisp, about 4 minutes. Remove with a slotted spoon and place in a small paper-towel-lined bowl; set aside. Add canola oil, onion and the red and green peppers; cook over medium 5 minutes. Stir in garlic, saffron threads and black pepper. Cook 1 minute. Add rice and cook, stirring, 1 minute. Stir in stock and bring to a boil. Reduce heat and simmer, covered, 35 minutes. Stir in shrimp and peas; re-cover and cook 3 minutes, until shrimp are opaque. Stir in bacon and salt. Sprinkle with parsley.

PER SERVING 431 **CAL**; 10 g **FAT** (2 g **SAT**); 34 g **PRO**; 53 g **CARB**; 4 g **SUGARS**; 5 g **FIBER**; 772 mg **SODIUM**

SKEWERED MOROCCAN
SALMON WITH COUSCOUS

Skewered Moroccan Salmon with Couscous

MAKES 6 servings **PREP** 15 minutes **COOK** 7 minutes **BROIL** 8 minutes

- 2   tsp curry powder
- 2   tsp ground ginger
- 2   tsp ground cinnamon
- ½   tsp black pepper
- 1¼ tsp salt
- 1½ lb skinless salmon fillets, cut into 1-inch chunks
- 1½ cups pearl couscous
- ½   cup dried apricots, chopped
- ½   cup dried figs, chopped
- 1   can (15.5 oz) chickpeas, drained and rinsed
- 1   tbsp olive oil
- ½   cup toasted slivered almonds
-     Kale or other green vegetable (optional)

■ In a small bowl, stir curry powder, ginger, cinnamon, black pepper and 1 tsp salt. Toss 1 tbsp spice mixture with salmon. Thread onto 4 wooden or metal skewers and set on broiler pan.

■ Bring a medium pot of lightly salted water to a boil. Add couscous to pot and cook 5 minutes. Add dried fruit and cook 2 minutes. Drain couscous and combine in a serving bowl with chickpeas. Toss with olive oil, almonds, ¼ tsp salt and remaining spice mixture.

■ Broil salmon skewers 4 inches from heat 8 minutes, turning frequently. Serve over couscous with sautéed kale or other green vegetable, if desired.

PER SERVING 534 **CAL**; 17 g **FAT** (2 g **SAT**); 37 g **PRO**; 59 g **CARB**; 12 g **SUGARS**; 10 g **FIBER**; 749 mg **SODIUM**

SIZZLING PINEAPPLE BEEF

Pork Tenderloin with Herbed Farro

MAKES 6 servings **PREP** 10 minutes
ROAST at 425° for 40 minutes
COOK 25 minutes

1½	lb thin carrots, scrubbed
4	tbsp extra-virgin olive oil
1¾	tsp salt
1¼	tsp pepper
1½	cups quick-cooking farro (such as Nature's Earthly Choice)
1¾	lb pork tenderloin
½	tsp cumin
2	tbsp olive oil
½	cup chopped fresh herbs (such as parsley or basil)
3	scallions, sliced
2	tbsp white wine vinegar

■ Heat oven to 425°. Place carrots on a rimmed baking sheet with ¼ cup water. Cover tightly with foil; roast 20 minutes. Uncover, drizzle with 2 tbsp extra-virgin olive oil, and sprinkle with ¼ tsp each salt and pepper. Roast 20 minutes.

■ While carrots roast, bring 3 cups water to a boil. Add farro and ½ tsp salt. Reduce heat; cover and simmer 25 minutes. Meanwhile, slice pork tenderloin on the bias into ½-inch-thick slices. Season with cumin and ½ tsp each salt and black pepper. Heat 1 tbsp olive oil in a large stainless skillet over medium-high. Add half the pork and cook 5 minutes, turning once. Remove to a plate. Repeat with remaining 1 tbsp olive oil and pork. Stir ⅓ cup water into pan, scraping up any browned bits. Drain farro if water remains in pot. In a bowl, toss farro with 2 tbsp extra-virgin olive oil, fresh herbs, scallions, white wine vinegar and ½ tsp each salt and black pepper. Serve pork with carrots and farro.

PER SERVING 462 **CAL**; 17 g **FAT** (3 g **SAT**); 35 g **PRO**; 43 g **CARB**; 5 g **SUGARS**; 7 g **FIBER**; 783 mg **SODIUM**

Sizzling Pineapple Beef

MAKES 6 servings **PREP** 20 minutes **COOK** 10 minutes

⅓	cup reduced-sodium soy sauce
¼	cup packed brown sugar
2	tbsp cornstarch
2	tbsp rice vinegar
¾	lb rice noodles
2	tbsp vegetable oil
1	lb skirt steak, diced into ¾-inch pieces
4	cloves garlic, sliced
1¼	lb (3 small heads) baby bok choy, chopped
2	cups fresh pineapple, diced
3	scallions, chopped
⅓	cup roasted salted cashews, chopped
	Sriracha or chili sauce

■ In a bowl, whisk 1 cup water, soy sauce, brown sugar, cornstarch and rice vinegar. Set aside. Bring a large pot of salted water to a boil. Add noodles and cook 4 to 6 minutes. Drain and rinse well.

■ Meanwhile, heat vegetable oil in a large stainless skillet over high. Add steak and cook 3 minutes. Remove to a plate with a slotted spoon. Add garlic and cook 1 minute. Stir in bok choy and pineapple. Stir-fry 4 minutes, until bok choy leaves are wilted. Add reserved sauce to skillet and cook 2 minutes, until thickened. Stir in beef and cooked noodles. Toss to combine and coat with sauce. Sprinkle with scallions and cashews. Serve with sriracha or chili sauce on the side.

PER SERVING 536 **CAL**; 16 g **FAT** (4 g **SAT**); 22 g **PRO**; 77 g **CARB**; 18 g **SUGARS**; 3 g **FIBER**; 772 mg **SODIUM**

PORK TENDERLOIN
WITH HERBED FARRO

EGGPLANT PARM
STACKS

Eggplant Parm Stacks

MAKES 6 servings **PREP** 25 minutes
COOK 9 minutes **MICROWAVE** 3 minutes
BAKE at 400° for 20 minutes

- ¾ **cup all-purpose flour**
- 5 **egg whites, lightly beaten**
- 1⅓ **cups seasoned bread crumbs**
- 2 **large eggplants (2¼ lb total)**
- 6 **tbsp olive oil**
- 1 **can (28 oz) Red Pack crushed tomatoes in puree with basil, garlic and oregano**
- 3 **tbsp balsamic vinegar**
- 9 **thin slices provolone**
- 6 **tbsp grated Parmesan**

■ Place flour in a shallow dish. Place egg whites in a second dish and the bread crumbs in a third dish. Peel eggplants. Cut each eggplant into 9 slices. Dip in flour, egg whites and bread crumbs to coat, then place on a sheet of wax paper. Heat 2 tbsp olive oil in a large nonstick skillet over medium-high. Place 6 slices in skillet and cook 1½ minutes. Carefully flip and cook 1½ minutes more. Repeat twice, using 2 tbsp olive oil each time.

■ Place crushed tomatoes in a glass bowl. Stir in balsamic vinegar. Microwave 3 minutes to heat.

■ Heat oven to 400°. To assemble stacks, line a large rimmed baking sheet with foil and fit a rack into baking sheet. Place 6 large eggplant slices on rack. Spoon 1 cup tomato mixture over slices. Top with 6 more eggplant slices and 1 cup tomato mixture. Top with provolone (1½ slices per stack). Finish with 6 eggplant slices, 1 cup tomato mixture and Parmesan (1 tbsp per stack). Secure with toothpicks. Bake 20 minutes.

PER SERVING 450 **CAL**; 24 g **FAT** (8 g **SAT**); 19 g **PRO**; 39 g **CARB**; 11 g **SUGARS**; 7 g **FIBER**; 812 mg **SODIUM**

TURKEY ROLL-UPS

Turkey Roll-Ups

MAKES 4 servings **PREP** 25 minutes **COOK** 11 minutes

- 4 **thinly sliced (1 lb total) turkey cutlets**
- 4 **thin slices (½ oz) smoked turkey**
- 12 **fresh basil leaves**
- 4 **thin slices (¾ oz) mozzarella**
- ½ **tsp salt**
- ½ **tsp black pepper**
- 3 **tbsp vegetable oil**
- 8 **oz wide egg noodles (4¼ cups)**
- 1 **large or 2 small zucchini (9 oz total)**
- 2 **tbsp grated Romano**

■ Bring a large pot of lightly salted water to a boil. Pound turkey cutlets to ⅛ inch thick. Top each cutlet with 1 thin slice smoked turkey, 3 basil leaves and 1 thin slice mozzarella. From a short side, roll up tightly to enclose filling. Secure with a toothpick if it looks like it will unroll when cooked. Season roll-ups with ¼ tsp each salt and pepper. Heat 2 tbsp vegetable oil in a large, lidded stainless skillet over medium-high. Add roll-ups and cook, covered, 8 minutes, turning every 2 minutes.

■ Meanwhile, add egg noodles to boiling water and cook 8 minutes; drain. Shred zucchini on a box grater. Remove roll-ups from skillet and reduce heat to medium. Stir shredded zucchini into same skillet. Season with ¼ tsp each salt and pepper, and sauté 3 minutes. Remove from heat. Add egg noodles to skillet and toss with 1 tbsp vegetable oil and Romano. Slice roll-ups, removing toothpicks if used. Serve with noodles.

PER SERVING 499 **CAL**; 16 g **FAT** (3 g **SAT**); 47 g **PRO**; 41 g **CARB**; 3 g **SUGARS**; 3 g **FIBER**; 785 mg **SODIUM**

FOUR WAYS WITH GRAPEFRUIT

Citrus fruits are at peak season during the winter months. Get your grapefruit on with these fresh recipes.

Grapefruit Upside-Down Cake

MAKES 8 servings **PREP** 20 minutes
BAKE at 350° for 40 minutes **COOL** 15 minutes

- ¼ **cup unsalted butter**
- ¼ **cup brown sugar**
- 2 **pink grapefruits, peeled and thinly sliced**
- 1½ **cups baking mix (such as Bisquick)**
- ½ **cup sugar**
- ⅓ **cup milk**
- ¼ **cup mascarpone cheese**
- 1 **egg**
- 2 **tbsp vegetable oil**
- 1 **tsp vanilla extract**

■ Heat oven to 350°. In a 9-inch cake pan, melt butter in oven; sprinkle brown sugar evenly over butter. Fan grapefruit over bottom of pan.

■ Combine baking mix, sugar, milk, mascarpone, egg, oil and vanilla. Beat on low to combine, then on medium 4 minutes, occasionally scraping down sides of bowl. Pour over grapefruit. Bake 40 minutes or until toothpick inserted in center comes out clean. Turn out onto a serving plate. Leave pan in place a few minutes so that sugar mixture drizzles over cake. Remove pan and cool 15 minutes.

PER SERVING 335 **CAL**; 20 g **FAT** (9 g **SAT**); 4 g **PRO**; 39 g **CARB**; 22 g **SUGARS**; 4 g **FIBER**; 302 mg **SODIUM**

Grapefruit Margarita Granita

MAKES 8 servings **PREP** 15 minutes
FREEZE 6 hours

- 3 **red grapefruits**
- 2 **cups grapefruit juice**
- ⅓ **cup tequila**
- 1 **lime**
- 1 **cup Simple Syrup (recipe below)**
  Fresh mint

■ Peel and section grapefruits. Add to a food processor along with grapefruit juice, tequila, zest and juice of lime, and Simple Syrup. Process until smooth. Pour into a freezer-safe shallow dish and freeze 6 hours, stirring from the center outward every hour. Place in food processor and pulse 5 seconds. Serve with a sprig of fresh mint.

Simple Syrup: Combine 1 cup each water and sugar in a small saucepan. Bring to a boil and stir until sugar dissolves. Let cool.

PER SERVING 98 **CAL**; 0 g **FAT**; 1 g **PRO**; 21 g **CARB**; 17 g **SUGARS**; 5 g **FIBER**; 0 mg **SODIUM**

GRAPEFRUIT UPSIDE-DOWN CAKE

GRAPEFRUIT MARGARITA GRANITA

Grapefruit-Thyme Marmalade

MAKES 4 cups **PREP** 10 minutes
COOK 25 minutes

- **3   large pink grapefruits**
-     **Pinch of baking soda**
- **½   pkg (from a 1.75 oz pkg) powdered pectin (such as Sure-Jell)**
- **3¼ cups sugar**
- **2   tsp chopped fresh thyme**

■ Thinly slice rind from 1 grapefruit; cut crosswise into smaller pieces. Place in a medium saucepan with 1 cup water and a pinch of baking soda; simmer 15 minutes. Section 2 grapefruits, coarsely chop sections and add to saucepan. Simmer 10 minutes. Add pectin and bring to a boil. Add sugar and bring to a boil; boil 1 minute. Remove from heat and stir in thyme. Cool slightly and pour into four 1-cup lidded jars. When cool, secure lids; refrigerate overnight to set. Can be refrigerated for up to 2 weeks.

PER TBSP 29 **CAL**; 0 g **FAT**; 0 g **PRO**; 9 g **CARB**; 8 g **SUGARS**; 0 g **FIBER**; 3 mg **SODIUM**

Grapefruit Mousse

MAKES 6 servings **PREP** 10 minutes
BROIL 5 minutes

- **3   red grapefruits**
- **3   white grapefruits**
- **¼   cup turbinado sugar**
- **1   cup cold heavy cream**
- **1   tbsp sugar**
- **¼   tsp lime extract**
-     **Lime zest**

■ Peel and section red and white grapefruits. Place on a rimmed baking sheet and sprinkle with turbinado sugar. Broil 5 minutes, until slightly caramelized. Cool.

■ Meanwhile, whip heavy cream, sugar and lime extract to medium-soft peaks. Gently fold in grapefruit, saving a few sections for garnish. Top with strips of lime zest.

PER SERVING 300 **CAL**; 15 g **FAT** (9 g **SAT**); 3 g **PRO**; 44 g **CARB**; 32 g **SUGARS**; 12 g **FIBER**; 15 mg **SODIUM**

GRAPEFRUIT MOUSSE

GRAPEFRUIT-THYME MARMALADE

VEG OUT

No one will wonder "Where's the beef?" with these boldly flavored vegetarian slow cooker suppers.

3-BEAN SLOPPY JOES

3-Bean Sloppy Joes

MAKES 12 servings **PREP** 15 minutes
SLOW COOK on LOW for 6 hours

- ½ green bell pepper, chopped
- ½ onion, chopped
- 3 cloves garlic, chopped
- 1 can (15.5 oz) red kidney beans, drained
- 1 can (15.5 oz) pink beans, drained
- 1 can (15.5 oz) small white beans, drained
- 1 can (15 oz) no-salt-added tomato sauce
- ½ cup ketchup
- 2 tbsp cider vinegar
- 2 tbsp chili powder
- 2 tbsp brown sugar
- 1 tsp ground cumin
- ¼ tsp salt
- ½ cup scallions, sliced
- 1 tsp hot sauce
- 12 potato rolls
- 1 tbsp shredded cheddar
  Bread-and-butter pickle slices
  Potato chips (optional)

■ Coat slow cooker with nonstick cooking spray. Add first 13 ingredients (through salt). Cover and cook on LOW for 6 hours. Stir in scallions and hot sauce. On each of the potato rolls, spoon about ½ cup bean mixture, sprinkle with shredded cheddar, and top with a few pickle slices. Serve with potato chips, if desired.

PER SERVING 373 **CAL**; 5 g **FAT** (2 g **SAT**); 17 g **PRO**; 66 g **CARB**; 12 g **SUGARS**; 10 g **FIBER**; 754 mg **SODIUM**

Vegetarian Lasagna Alfredo

MAKES 8 servings **PREP** 30 minutes
SLOW COOK on LOW for 4 hours
COOL 30 minutes

- 1 container (15 oz) ricotta
- 1 egg
- 3 cups shredded mozzarella
- ¼ cup plus 3 tbsp grated Parmesan
- 1 pkg (12 oz) veggie crumbles (such as MorningStar Farms)
- 1 lb frozen kale
- 1 jar (14.5 oz) Alfredo sauce
- 12 traditional lasagna noodles

■ Fit slow cooker bowl with a disposable liner and coat lightly with nonstick cooking spray. Combine ricotta, egg, 1 cup mozzarella and ¼ cup Parmesan.

■ Microwave veggie crumbles and kale following package directions. Combine crumbles, kale and Alfredo sauce.

■ Break 3 noodles into thirds and spread over bottom of slow cooker. Spread half of crumble mixture evenly over noodles and top with 3 more broken noodles. Spread with ricotta mixture and top with 3 more broken noodles. Layer with remaining crumble mixture and 3 more broken noodles. Sprinkle 2 cups mozzarella and 3 tbsp Parmesan over top. Cover and cook on LOW for 4 hours.

■ Remove bowl from slow cooker and cool 30 minutes. Use liner bag to lift out lasagna. Remove slow cooker liner and cut lasagna into pieces.

PER SERVING 499 **CAL**; 26 g **FAT** (14 g **SAT**); 37 g **PRO**; 33 g **CARB**; 3 g **SUGARS**; 4 g **FIBER**; 953 mg **SODIUM**

VEGETARIAN LASAGNA ALFREDO

RED LENTIL THAI CURRY

Red Lentil Thai Curry

MAKES 8 servings **PREP** 15 minutes **SLOW COOK** on HIGH for 3 hours

- 2 cups red lentils
- 2 cups diced onions
- 3 tbsp green curry paste (such as Thai Kitchen)
- 6 cloves garlic, chopped
- 2 tbsp soy sauce
- 2 tbsp ginger, chopped
- 2 tsp sugar
- ⅛ tsp cayenne pepper
- 1½ cups carrot juice
- 1 cup yellow cherry tomatoes, halved
- 1 cup coconut milk
- ¼ cup chopped fresh cilantro
- 4 cups cooked jasmine rice
  Lime wedges

■ Coat a slow cooker with nonstick cooking spray. Add first 8 ingredients (through cayenne). Stir in 2 cups water, carrot juice and cherry tomatoes. Cover and cook on HIGH for 3 hours. Stir in coconut milk and cilantro. Serve with jasmine rice and lime wedges.

PER SERVING 372 **CAL**; 6 g **FAT** (5 g **SAT**); 16 g **PRO**; 62 g **CARB**; 7 g **SUGARS**; 4 g **FIBER**; 466 mg **SODIUM**

CREAM OF TOMATO
TORTELLINI SOUP

Adding quinoa is a quick way to pump up the protein and iron in any vegetarian recipe.

Black Bean and Quinoa Enchilada Casserole

MAKES 8 servings **PREP** 15 minutes
SLOW COOK on HIGH for 4 hours or LOW for 6 hours

1	can (15.5 oz) black beans, drained
2	cups frozen corn kernels, thawed
2	cans (10 oz each) diced tomatoes and green chilies (such as Ro-Tel)
2	cans (15 oz each) mild enchilada sauce
1¼	cups uncooked quinoa
½	tsp salt
¼	tsp black pepper
4	oz chive and onion cream cheese spread
1½	cups shredded Tex-Mex cheese blend
	Chopped fresh cilantro, diced avocado, diced red onion and sour cream (optional)

■ Coat slow cooker with nonstick cooking spray. Add black beans, corn, diced tomatoes, 1 can enchilada sauce, quinoa, 1 cup water, salt and pepper. Stir in cream cheese spread. Top with 1 more can enchilada sauce and Tex-Mex cheese. Cover and cook on HIGH for 4 hours or LOW for 6 hours. If desired, top with cilantro, avocado, red onion and dollops of sour cream.

PER SERVING 364 **CAL**; 15 g **FAT** (7 g **SAT**); 16 g **PRO**; 41 g **CARB**; 5 g **SUGARS**; 6 g **FIBER**; 1,112 mg **SODIUM**

Cream of Tomato Tortellini Soup

MAKES 8 servings **PREP** 15 minutes
SLOW COOK on HIGH for 3 hours or LOW for 5 hours, plus 15 minutes

1½	cups carrots, diced
1½	cups onions, diced
4	cloves garlic, chopped
2	tbsp olive oil
4	cups reduced-sodium vegetable broth
2	cans (28 oz each) San Marzano plum tomatoes
½	cup chopped fresh basil plus more for garnish
1	tsp sugar
½	tsp salt
¼	tsp black pepper
2	pkg (9 oz each) fresh cheese tortellini
⅔	cup heavy cream
1	bag (6 oz) baby spinach
	Shaved Parmesan

■ Coat slow cooker with nonstick cooking spray. Add first 10 ingredients (through black pepper) and 1 cup water. Cover and cook on HIGH for 3 hours or LOW for 5 hours.

■ Puree mixture and return to slow cooker; add tortellini and cook 15 minutes. Add heavy cream and spinach. Stir until spinach wilts. Sprinkle with shaved Parmesan and additional basil.

PER SERVING 338 **CAL**; 12 g **FAT** (7 g **SAT**); 12 g **PRO**; 48 g **CARB**; 12 g **SUGARS**; 7 g **FIBER**; 571 mg **SODIUM**

**BLACK BEAN AND QUINOA
ENCHILADA CASSEROLE**

BRAIDED CINNAMON BUNS

These delicious sweet rolls feature a twist—literally—on the classic spiral shape.

BRAIDED CINNAMON BUNS

Braided Cinnamon Buns

MAKES 12 buns **PREP** 25 minutes **KNEAD** 5 minutes **LET RISE** 2 hours **BAKE** at 350° for 20 minutes

- 1 **cup buttermilk**
- 12 **tbsp (1½ sticks) unsalted butter, softened**
- 1 **pkg (0.25 oz) active dry yeast**
- 3 **tbsp warm water (110° to 115°)**
- 2 **tsp plus ⅔ cup granulated sugar**
- 1 **large egg plus 1 egg yolk, white reserved**
- 4 **tsp ground cinnamon, plus more for sprinkling**
- ½ **tsp salt**
- 4½ **cups all-purpose flour**
- ⅓ **cup packed dark brown sugar**
  Brown Sugar Glaze (optional) (recipe follows)

■ Combine buttermilk and 6 tbsp butter in a small saucepan. Heat over medium-low until butter melts. Cool to 110°.

■ In a small bowl, sprinkle yeast over 2 tbsp warm water and 1 tsp granulated sugar. Let stand 5 minutes, until foamy.

■ When buttermilk mixture reaches 110°, stir in yeast mixture. In a stand mixer, combine egg, egg yolk, ⅓ cup granulated sugar, 1 tsp cinnamon and the salt. Beat on medium speed until blended. Beat in yeast mixture, followed by flour. Turn dough out onto a floured surface and knead 5 minutes, adding more flour if dough is very sticky.

■ Oil a large bowl and add dough, turning to coat with oil. Cover with plastic wrap and let rise until doubled, 2 hours.

■ Heat oven to 350°. Punch down dough and divide into thirds. In a medium bowl, mix 6 tbsp butter, ⅓ cup granulated sugar, 3 tsp cinnamon, 1 tbsp warm water and the brown sugar until smooth.

■ Cut one piece of dough in half. With your hands, roll into a long rope. Lay on work surface and, with a rolling pin, roll out to an 18 x 4-inch rectangle. Spread with 2 tbsp filling and sprinkle with cinnamon. Cut in half crosswise to create two 9 x 4-inch pieces. Starting from a long side, roll up to enclose filling and pinch seam shut. With a sharp knife, cut through dough lengthwise, leaving one end attached (see steps, below). Twist dough over itself to resemble a braid, pinching end together. Roll dough on itself and tuck end under. Transfer to a parchment-lined baking sheet, spacing 2 inches apart. Repeat with remaining dough and filling.

■ Brush buns with egg white and sprinkle with 1 tsp granulated sugar. Bake 18 to 20 minutes, until golden brown. Brush with Brown Sugar Glaze, if using.

Brown Sugar Glaze Combine ¼ cup each packed dark brown sugar and granulated sugar in a saucepan with 3 tbsp water and 1 tbsp unsalted butter. Heat over medium until glaze is smooth. Brush over buns.

PER BUN 412 **CAL**; 14 g **FAT** (9 g **SAT**); 7 g **PRO**; 64 g **CARB**; 28 g **SUGARS**; 2 g **FIBER**; 138 mg **SODIUM**

Do the Twist

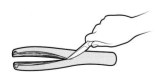

1. Once you've rolled up dough to enclose filling, cut through with a sharp knife, leaving one end attached.

2. Twist dough over itself to resemble a braided rope. Tightly pinch end together so pieces don't separate while baking.

3. Starting at attached end, roll up braid onto itself, like the shell of a snail. Tuck end under center of roll and place on pan.

Wet your hands with a little water to make working with dough a lot easier.

CHOCOLATE
RASPBERRY CUPS,
PAGE 37

FEBRUARY

43

52

57

YOU HAD ME AT COCOA

Snuggle up with your sweetheart and *Chocolate: A Love Story* this Valentine's Day.

BUTTERMILK CHOCOLATE LAYER CAKE

Buttermilk Chocolate Layer Cake

MAKES 24 servings **PREP** 35 minutes
MICROWAVE 2 minutes
BAKE at 350° for 45 minutes **COOL** 30 minutes
REFRIGERATE 1 hour

CAKE

- **6** oz bittersweet chocolate, chopped
- **1** tbsp vegetable oil
- **3** cups all-purpose flour
- **2¼** tsp baking soda
- **½** tsp salt
- **2¼** sticks (18 tbsp) unsalted butter, softened
- **2¼** cups sugar
- **1** tbsp vanilla extract
- **6** eggs
- **2¼** cups buttermilk

FROSTING

- **12** oz milk chocolate, chopped
- **12** oz bittersweet chocolate, chopped
- **2** sticks (1 cup) unsalted butter, cut into pieces
- **16** oz sour cream
- **4** tsp vanilla extract
- **2** boxes (16 oz each) confectioners' sugar

■ **Cake.** Heat oven to 350°. Coat two 9 x 2-inch round cake pans with nonstick cooking spray. Line bottoms with wax paper; coat with spray. Microwave bittersweet chocolate and vegetable oil 1 minute. Stir until smooth. Cool slightly.

■ In a medium bowl, combine flour, baking soda and salt. In a large bowl, beat butter, sugar and vanilla until fluffy. Add eggs, one by one, beating after each addition. Beat in chocolate.

■ On low speed, beat flour mixture into butter mixture in 3 additions, alternating with buttermilk and ending with flour; beat 1 minute. Divide batter between pans.

■ Bake 45 minutes or until toothpick inserted in center of layers comes out clean. Cool 15 minutes on wire racks. Invert pans and turn out cakes onto racks. Remove paper; cool completely.

CHOCOLATE RASPBERRY CUPS

■ **Frosting.** In a large microwave-safe bowl, combine milk and bittersweet chocolates with butter. Microwave 1 minute; stir until smooth. Cool slightly, then with hand mixer, beat in sour cream and vanilla. On low speed, beat in confectioners' sugar until fluffy and easy to spread. Refrigerate 10 minutes if too soft.

■ Insert toothpicks halfway up side of one cake layer. Using picks as a guide, slice cake in half horizontally. Repeat with other layer.

■ Set aside 3 cups frosting. Place one cake layer, cut side down, on serving platter. Spread with 1¾ cups frosting. Repeat with remaining cake layers and frosting, ending with one cake layer, cut side down. Spread reserved 3 cups frosting over top of cake. Refrigerate 1 hour before slicing and serving.

PER SERVING 675 **CAL**; 34 g **FAT** (21 g **SAT**); 6 g **PRO**; 92 g **CARB**; 75 g **SUGARS**; 2 g **FIBER**; 246 mg **SODIUM**

Chocolate Raspberry Cups

MAKES 12 servings **PREP** 30 minutes
MICROWAVE 1 minute **REFRIGERATE** 6 hours

- **12** oz semisweet baking chocolate
- **1** tsp vegetable oil
- **12** foil cupcake liners
- **8** oz good-quality white chocolate, chopped
- **1½** cups heavy cream
- **6** tsp seedless raspberry jam
- **2½** pints fresh raspberries
- **2** tbsp confectioners' sugar

■ Place semisweet chocolate and oil in a microwave-safe bowl. Microwave 1 minute. Stir until smooth, microwaving in additional 15-second intervals if needed.

■ Spoon 2 tbsp melted chocolate into each liner and swirl until inside is completely coated. Place on a baking sheet and refrigerate 1 hour.

■ Place white chocolate in a bowl; heat 1 cup cream until steaming. Pour over white chocolate and whisk until smooth. Refrigerate 1½ to 2 hours.

■ Beat ½ cup cream on medium-high until semi-firm peaks form. Add white chocolate mixture and beat on medium for 4 minutes or until mousse-like consistency.

■ Gently peel liners away from chocolate cups. Fill with white chocolate mixture. Swirl ½ tsp jam into each cup and refrigerate 3 hours.

■ To serve, top each cup with raspberries and lightly dust with confectioners' sugar.

PER SERVING 396 **CAL**; 28 g **FAT** (17 g **SAT**); 5 g **PRO**; 36 g **CARB**; 28 g **SUGARS**; 5 g **FIBER**; 32 mg **SODIUM**

WHOOPIE PIE BUNDT CAKE

and let cool in pan 15 more minutes. Gently run a spatula in between cake and pan and invert again.) Cool completely.

■ When cool, slice cake level in half horizontally.

■ Beat cream cheese with ½ cup sugar, ¼ cup heavy cream and a pinch of salt until smooth. In a separate bowl, whip ½ cup heavy cream. Fold whipped cream into cream cheese mixture and spread into middle of cake. Refrigerate 1 hour. Finely chop 4 oz chocolate and place in a small bowl. Microwave ½ cup heavy cream for 40 seconds and pour over chocolate. Let stand 5 minutes. Whisk until smooth. Remove cake from refrigerator. Pour chocolate ganache over cake, letting it drip down the sides.

PER SERVING 541 **CAL**; 31 g **FAT** (18 g **SAT**); 8 g **PRO**; 64 g **CARB**; 42 g **SUGARS**; 3 g **FIBER**; 280 mg **SODIUM**

Whoopie Pie Bundt Cake

MAKES 16 servings PREP 25 minutes MICROWAVE 2 minutes, 40 seconds
BAKE at 350° for 55 minutes REFRIGERATE 1 hour LET STAND 5 minutes

Flour-and-oil spray (such as Baker's Joy)

12 oz semisweet chocolate baking bars

2 sticks (1 cup) unsalted butter, softened

2½ cups sugar

5 large eggs

1 tbsp vanilla extract

3 cups all-purpose flour

⅓ cup unsweetened cocoa powder

1 tbsp baking powder

¾ tsp plus a pinch salt

1 cup milk

4 oz cream cheese, softened

1¼ cups heavy cream

■ Heat oven to 350°. Liberally coat a 12-cup Bundt pan with spray. Set aside.

■ Chop 8 oz chocolate. Microwave 2 minutes, stirring halfway. Cool while starting cake batter.

■ In a stand mixer, beat butter until smooth and creamy. Add 2 cups sugar, beating until smooth, about 3 minutes, scraping down sides of bowl. Beat in eggs, one by one, until blended. On low speed, beat in melted chocolate and vanilla.

■ In a medium bowl, whisk flour, cocoa, baking powder and ¾ tsp salt. On low speed, beat in half the flour mixture followed by milk and then remaining flour mixture. Spread into prepared Bundt pan.

■ Bake 55 minutes, until cake springs back when lightly pressed. Cool in pan 15 minutes. Invert onto a cooling rack and remove pan. (If cake sticks to pan, don't force it. Flip back over

No-Bake Chocolate Ganache Tart

MAKES 12 servings PREP 15 minutes
REFRIGERATE 2 hours or overnight

1 pkg (9 oz) chocolate wafers (such as Nabisco Famous)

1 stick (½ cup) unsalted butter, melted

9 oz milk chocolate, chopped

4 oz bittersweet chocolate, chopped

¾ cup heavy cream

6 strawberries, sliced

■ Break up wafers and place in a food processor; blend until fine crumbs. Add butter and process until blended. Press into bottom and up sides of a 5 x 14-inch removable-bottom tart pan. Freeze while preparing filling.

■ Place 8 oz milk chocolate and the bittersweet chocolate in a bowl. Heat cream to just steaming and pour over chocolate. Whisk until smooth.

■ Pour chocolate mixture over crust and top with strawberries. Refrigerate 2 hours or overnight. Melt remaining milk chocolate and drizzle over tart.

PER SERVING 356 **CAL**; 24 g **FAT** (15 g **SAT**); 3 g **PRO**; 35 g **CARB**; 24 g **SUGARS**; 2 g **FIBER**; 177 mg **SODIUM**

NO-BAKE CHOCOLATE GANACHE TART

GLUTEN-FREE
HAZELNUT CAKE

Gluten-Free Hazelnut Cake

MAKES 12 servings **PREP** 20 minutes
BAKE at 375° for 37 minutes
REFRIGERATE 2 hours

CAKE

8	oz semisweet baking chocolate, coarsely chopped
1½	sticks (¾ cup) unsalted butter, cut into small pieces
1¼	cups sugar
5	eggs
1	tsp vanilla extract
¼	tsp salt
1½	cups finely ground toasted hazelnuts
⅓	cup unsweetened cocoa powder

TOPPING

1	cup heavy cream
1	tbsp sugar
½	tsp vanilla extract
¼	cup toasted hazelnuts, coarsely chopped

■ **Cake.** Heat oven to 375°. Coat a 9-inch springform pan with nonstick cooking spray.

■ Place chocolate and butter in a large metal bowl over a pot of simmering water. Stir occasionally until melted. Remove bowl from pot and cool slightly. Beat in sugar until combined; beat in eggs, one by one, incorporating each before adding the next. Beat 2 minutes.

■ Beat in vanilla and salt. Gradually add hazelnuts while beating on low speed. Sift cocoa into bowl and beat until incorporated and batter is smooth. Pour into pan.

■ Bake 35 to 37 minutes. Cool on a wire rack to room temperature. Refrigerate 2 hours. Remove side of pan.

■ **Topping.** Whip cream, sugar and vanilla to soft peaks. Spoon onto cake and sprinkle with hazelnuts.

PER SERVING 391 **CAL**; 35 g **FAT** (17 g **SAT**); 7 g **PRO**; 18 g **CARB**; 13 g **SUGARS**; 3 g **FIBER**; 88 mg **SODIUM**

CHALLAH CHOCOLATE
BREAD PUDDING

Challah Chocolate Bread Pudding

MAKES 10 servings **PREP** 20 minutes **LET STAND** 30 minutes **BAKE** at 350° for 40 minutes

5	eggs
⅔	cup plus 2 tbsp sugar
3½	cups half-and-half
2	tsp vanilla extract
¼	tsp salt
16	oz challah bread, cut into 1-inch cubes (about 12 cups)
8	oz milk chocolate chips
¾	tsp ground cinnamon
2	tbsp unsalted butter, melted
2	tbsp cocoa powder
	Espresso Mascarpone Cream (recipe follows)

■ Heat oven to 350°. Butter a 13 x 9 x 2-inch baking dish.

■ In a large bowl, whisk eggs, ⅔ cup sugar, the half-and-half, vanilla and salt. Stir in 8 cups bread and the chocolate chips. Add to prepared baking dish and let stand 30 minutes.

■ Combine 2 tbsp sugar with the cinnamon. Combine 4 cups bread with the butter and cinnamon sugar. Scatter evenly over pudding and press to partially submerge. Bake 40 minutes. Let cool slightly. Dust with cocoa and serve with Espresso Mascarpone Cream.

Espresso Mascarpone Cream
Dissolve 2 tbsp espresso powder in 2 tbsp half-and-half; beat with 8 oz mascarpone and 1 tbsp sugar until smooth.

PER SERVING 573 **CAL**; 35 g **FAT** (19 g **SAT**); 14 g **PRO**; 54 g **CARB**; 30 g **SUGARS**; 2 g **FIBER**; 400 mg **SODIUM**

SOUPED-UP SUPPERS

Tuck into comfort in a bowl.

MEXICAN PORK AND
HOMINY CHOWDER

Mexican Pork and Hominy Chowder

MAKES 4 servings **PREP** 15 minutes
COOK 17 minutes

- **3 tbsp extra-virgin olive oil**
- **1¼ lb trimmed pork tenderloin, cut into ¾-inch pieces**
- **1 medium yellow onion, chopped**
- **1 to 2 jalapeños, seeded and chopped**
- **2 cloves garlic, peeled and chopped**
- **¾ tsp salt**
- **¼ tsp black pepper**
- **3 cups low-sodium chicken broth**
- **1 russet potato, peeled and cut into ½-inch dice**
- **1 can (15 oz) white hominy, drained and rinsed**
- **1 cup heavy cream**
- **1 cup whole milk**
-   **Sliced scallions, chopped tomato, sliced avocado and tortilla chips, for serving**

■ In a wide-bottom pot, heat oil over medium-high. Add pork and cook, stirring occasionally, until browned, about 5 minutes. Reduce heat to medium and add next 3 ingredients. Cook, stirring occasionally, until onion is translucent, about 4 minutes. Season with ¼ tsp each salt and pepper.

■ Add broth and bring to a simmer. Add potato and hominy, and simmer, partially covered, until potato is tender, about 8 minutes. Stir in cream and milk, and return to a simmer. Stir in ½ tsp salt and remove from heat. Divide among 4 bowls and serve with scallions, tomato, avocado and tortilla chips.

PER SERVING 608 **CAL**; 39 g **FAT** (18 g **SAT**); 36 g **PRO**; 30 g **CARB**; 8 g **SUGARS**; 4 g **FIBER**; 977 mg **SODIUM**

HARVEST FRENCH ONION SOUP

Harvest French Onion Soup

MAKES 4 servings **PREP** 15 minutes
COOK 46 minutes **BROIL** 5 minutes

- **4 tbsp unsalted butter**
- **3 medium sweet yellow onions (1¼ lb), thinly sliced lengthwise**
- **¾ tsp salt**
- **¾ tsp black pepper**
- **½ cup water**
- **1 large Cortland or Granny Smith apple, peeled, cored and grated**
- **4 cups low-sodium chicken broth**
- **2 sprigs fresh thyme**
- **2 cups shredded or chopped cooked chicken**
- **8 ½-inch-thick slices baguette, lightly toasted**
- **8 slices sharp white cheddar**

■ In a wide-bottom pot over medium-high, heat butter until melted and foamy. Add onions and cook, stirring occasionally, until they begin to brown, 6 minutes. Reduce heat to medium, season with ¼ tsp each salt and pepper, and add water. Cook, stirring often, until water evaporates, about 10 minutes. Add apple and cook, stirring occasionally, until onions are golden brown and apple has softened, about 15 minutes.

■ Heat broiler. Add broth and thyme to onion mixture. Bring to a simmer and cook, partially covered, 12 minutes. Add chicken and cook until heated through, about 3 minutes. Arrange 4 broiler-proof bowls or crocks on a foil-lined rimmed baking sheet. Remove and discard thyme sprigs; stir in ½ tsp each salt and pepper. Divide soup among 4 bowls and top with 2 slices each baguette and cheese. Broil until cheese is bubbling and browned, 3 to 5 minutes. Carefully—they will be extremely hot—transfer bowls to plates and serve.

PER SERVING 528 **CAL**; 22 g **FAT** (14 g **SAT**); 35 g **PRO**; 51 g **CARB**; 14 g **SUGARS**; 4 g **FIBER**; 630 mg **SODIUM**

MEATBALL, MUSHROOM AND BARLEY SOUP

Italian Chicken and Gnocchi Soup

MAKES 4 servings
PREP 20 minutes **COOK** 16 minutes

- 2 **tbsp extra-virgin olive oil**
- 1 **medium onion, chopped**
- 1 **medium carrot, peeled and chopped**
- 1 **large rib celery, chopped**
- 2 **cloves garlic, peeled and chopped**
- ½ **tsp salt**
- ½ **tsp black pepper**
- 4 **cups low-sodium chicken broth**
- 2 **cups shredded or chopped cooked chicken**
- 3 **plum tomatoes, chopped**
- 1 **pkg (12 oz) shelf-stable or frozen gnocchi**
- ¾ **cup chopped fresh basil**
  Grated Parmesan, for serving (optional)

■ In a wide-bottom pot, heat oil over medium. Add next 4 ingredients and cook, stirring occasionally, until onion is translucent, about 5 minutes. Season with salt and pepper.

■ Add chicken broth, bring to a simmer and cook 5 minutes. Add chicken and tomatoes, and return to a simmer. Add gnocchi and simmer per package directions, about 6 minutes. Stir in basil and divide among 4 bowls. Top with Parmesan, if using.

PER SERVING 310 **CAL**; 9 g **FAT** (2 g **SAT**);
24 g **PRO**; 36 g **CARB**; 4 g **SUGARS**; 3 g **FIBER**;
747 mg **SODIUM**

ITALIAN CHICKEN AND GNOCCHI SOUP

Meatball, Mushroom and Barley Soup

MAKES 4 servings **PREP** 25 minutes **COOK** 19 minutes

- ¾ **lb ground chuck**
- ¾ **tsp salt**
- ½ **tsp black pepper**
- 3 **tbsp extra-virgin olive oil**
- 8 **oz sliced cremini mushrooms**
- 1 **medium yellow onion, chopped**
- 1 **large rib celery, chopped**
- 2 **cloves garlic, peeled and chopped**
- 2 **sprigs fresh thyme**
- 4 **cups low-sodium chicken broth**
- 2 **cups water**
- ⅓ **cup quick-cooking barley**
- 3 **cups baby spinach**

■ In a medium bowl, season beef with ½ tsp salt and ¼ tsp pepper. Gently mix to combine. Do not overmix.

■ In a wide-bottom pot, heat oil over medium-high. Add mushrooms and cook, stirring occasionally, until golden, 5 minutes. Reduce heat to medium and add next 3 ingredients. Cook, stirring occasionally, until onion is translucent, about 4 minutes. Season with ¼ tsp each salt and pepper. Add thyme, broth and water; bring to a simmer.

■ Stir in barley and partially cover. Simmer 5 minutes. Meanwhile, roll slightly rounded teaspoonfuls of seasoned beef into balls; you should have at least 32. Drop into simmering broth and continue to cook 5 minutes, until meatballs are cooked through and barley is tender. Remove thyme stems and stir in spinach. Cook until wilted.

PER SERVING 358 **CAL**; 23 g **FAT** (7 g **SAT**);
21 g **PRO**; 17 g **CARB**; 2 g **SUGARS**; 3 g **FIBER**;
608 mg **SODIUM**

SMOKY WHITE BEAN AND
WINTER VEGETABLE SOUP

Smoky White Bean and Winter Vegetable Soup

MAKES 4 servings **PREP** 25 minutes **COOK** 27 minutes

- **3** tbsp extra-virgin olive oil
- **1** small onion, chopped
- **1** large stalk celery, chopped
- **3** cloves garlic, chopped
- **1** small bunch kale, ribs removed, leaves roughly chopped
- **½** tsp salt
- **½** tsp freshly ground black pepper
- **6** cups low-sodium vegetable broth
- **½** small butternut squash, peeled and cut into ½-inch pieces
- **¼** to ½ tsp smoked paprika
- **1** can (15 oz) cannellini beans, drained and rinsed
- Grated Parmesan, for serving

■ In a wide-bottom pot, heat oil over medium. Add next 3 ingredients and cook, stirring, until onion is translucent, 5 minutes. Add kale and cook, stirring until wilted, about 3 minutes. Season with ¼ tsp each salt and pepper. Add broth, bring to a simmer and cook 10 minutes.

■ Add squash and paprika, and simmer until squash is almost tender, 6 minutes. Add beans and simmer 3 minutes; stir in ¼ tsp each salt and pepper. Divide among bowls; top with Parmesan.

PER SERVING 324 **CAL**; 12 g **FAT** (2 g **SAT**); 11 g **PRO**; 46 g **CARB**; 10 g **SUGARS**; 12 g **FIBER**; 812 mg **SODIUM**

HEALTHY FAMILY DINNERS

Try these 10 easy recipes on crazy-busy nights.

CHICAGO-STYLE
ITALIAN BEEF

MAPLE-GINGER
SALMON AND
CARROTS

*To switch things up,
serve over pasta, rice
or baked potatoes.*

Chicago-Style Italian Beef

MAKES 8 servings **PREP** 10 minutes
SLOW COOK on HIGH for 6 hours

- 1½ **tsp kosher salt**
- 2 **tsp dried minced onion**
- 1 **tsp dried basil**
- 1 **tsp dried oregano**
- ½ **tsp crushed red pepper flakes**
- ½ **tsp black pepper**
- 3 **lb beef chuck**
- 1 **cup beef stock**
- 4 **cloves garlic, sliced**
- **Hoagie rolls**
- **Green bell pepper**
- **Giardiniera (pickled sliced mixed vegetables)**

■ In a bowl, combine first 6 ingredients (through black pepper). Rub onto beef chuck.

■ Place in slow cooker with beef stock and garlic. Cook on HIGH for 6 hours. Shred beef with a fork and stir back into liquid. Serve on sliced hoagie rolls with sautéed green pepper and giardiniera.

PER SERVING 524 **CAL**; 26 g **FAT** (10 g **SAT**); 40 g **PRO**; 36 g **CARB**; 4 g **SUGARS**; 3 g **FIBER**; 770 mg **SODIUM**

Maple-Ginger Salmon and Carrots

MAKES 4 servings **PREP** 10 minutes **COOK** 15 minutes **ROAST** at 425° for 12 minutes

- ¼ **cup maple syrup**
- 4 **tsp grated fresh ginger**
- ½ **tsp ground coriander**
- ½ **tsp black pepper**
- 1½ **lb carrots, peeled and cut into 1-inch pieces**
- 1 **tbsp unsalted butter**
- ¾ **tsp salt**
- 4 **(5 oz each) salmon fillets**
- **Sliced scallions**
- **Buttered edamame (optional)**

■ Mix syrup, ginger, coriander and black pepper. Bring a pot of water to a boil; add carrots. Simmer 15 minutes; drain, reserving ½ cup liquid. Mash carrots and liquid until semi-smooth; stir in half the maple syrup mixture, the butter and ½ tsp salt. Cover and set aside.

■ Heat oven to 425°. Place salmon on a foil-lined baking sheet. Season with ¼ tsp salt and brush with remaining maple syrup mixture. Roast 12 minutes. Serve with mashed carrots, sliced scallions on top, and, if desired, a side of buttered edamame.

PER SERVING 380 **CAL**; 13 g **FAT** (4 g **SAT**); 34 g **PRO**; 30 g **CARB**; 22 g **SUGARS**; 4 g **FIBER**; 590 mg **SODIUM**

LATIN POACHED EGGS

Latin Poached Eggs

MAKES 4 servings **PREP** 10 minutes **COOK** 20 minutes **STAND** 5 minutes

- 1 tbsp extra-virgin olive oil
- 2 cloves garlic, sliced
- 2 tsp Mexican chili powder
- ¾ tsp ground cumin
- 1 (28 oz) can crushed tomatoes
- 1 (4 oz) can diced fire-roasted green chilies
- ¼ tsp salt
- ¾ cup scallions, sliced, plus more for serving
- ½ cup chopped fresh cilantro, plus more for serving
- ¼ cup plus 2 tbsp diced queso blanco
- 8 eggs
  Sliced avocado, tomatillo salsa, sour cream, and rice and beans (optional)

■ In a deep-sided 12-inch skillet, heat olive oil over medium. Add garlic, chili powder and cumin. Cook 1 minute. Add tomatoes, green chilies, ½ cup water and salt. Simmer 10 minutes. Stir in scallions, cilantro and ¼ cup queso blanco.

■ One by one, crack eggs into a small dish and carefully pour them into sauce, evenly spaced apart. Scatter 2 tbsp queso blanco on top and simmer 10 minutes. Cover and remove from heat. Let stand 5 minutes, until eggs reach desired doneness. Scatter more scallions and cilantro on top. If desired, serve with avocado, salsa, sour cream, and rice and beans.

PER SERVING 370 **CAL**; 24 g **FAT** (6 g **SAT**); 20 g **PRO**; 23 g **CARB**; 10 g **SUGARS**; 8 g **FIBER**; 820 mg **SODIUM**

Smoked Apple Sausage and Spinach Pizza

MAKES 6 servings **PREP** 15 minutes
STAND 1 hour **COOK** 8 minutes
BAKE at 450° for 18 minutes

Extra-virgin olive oil
- 1 lb refrigerated pizza dough
- 1 tbsp extra-virgin olive oil
- ½ small red onion, thinly sliced
- 3 cloves garlic, sliced
- ¼ tsp red pepper flakes
- 1 pkg (10 oz) baby spinach
- 1 tbsp cornmeal
- 2 cups shredded Gouda
- 2 sliced precooked smoked chicken apple sausages (such as Aidells)
  Fresh lemon
  Sliced plum tomatoes
  Balsamic dressing

■ Rub extra-virgin olive oil on pizza dough; place in a bowl, cover with plastic wrap and leave on the counter in a warm spot for at least 1 hour.

■ In a large skillet, heat 1 tbsp extra-virgin olive oil over medium. Stir in red onion, garlic and red pepper flakes. Cook 2 minutes. Stir in spinach and cook until wilted and water is gone, about 6 minutes.

■ Heat oven to 450°. Sprinkle cornmeal on a standard round pizza pan, then stretch dough to fit. Scatter ¾ cup Gouda on top, followed by spinach mixture, sausage and 1¼ cups Gouda. Bake 15 to 18 minutes, until crust is browned. Squeeze half a fresh lemon on top. Serve with a salad of sliced plum tomatoes tossed with balsamic dressing.

PER SERVING 399 **CAL**; 19 g **FAT** (7 g **SAT**); 18 g **PRO**; 45 g **CARB**; 6 g **SUGARS**; 5 g **FIBER**; 792 mg **SODIUM**

SMOKED APPLE
SAUSAGE AND
SPINACH PIZZA

**SPICE-RUBBED PORK
WITH QUINOA**

COCONUT-LIME
SHRIMP NOODLES

*Avoid mushy noodles—
rinsing them in cold water
stops the cooking process.*

Spice-Rubbed Pork with Quinoa

MAKES 4 servings **PREP** 15 minutes
COOK 20 minutes
ROAST at 400° for 20 minutes
STAND 5 minutes

- 1 **cup red quinoa**
- 8 **oz yellow grape tomatoes, halved**
- ¼ **cup parsley, chopped**
- ¼ **cup pecans, chopped**
- 2 **tbsp lime juice**
- 1 **tbsp plus 1 tsp extra-virgin olive oil**
- 1 **tsp salt**
- ½ **tsp black pepper**
- 2 **tbsp brown sugar**
- 2 **tbsp chili powder**
- ½ **tsp garlic powder**
- 1¼ **lb pork tenderloin**

■ Combine quinoa with 2½ cups water and bring to a boil. Reduce to a simmer, cover and cook 20 minutes. Remove from heat, let stand 5 minutes, then fluff with a fork. Stir in tomatoes, parsley, pecans, lime juice, 1 tbsp oil, ½ tsp salt and ¼ tsp pepper.

■ Heat oven to 400°. In a small bowl, combine brown sugar, chili powder, garlic powder, ½ tsp salt and ¼ tsp pepper. Place the pork on a foil-lined baking sheet. Brush 1 tsp oil on pork, then coat with spice rub. Roast 18 to 20 minutes, until pork reaches 145°. Let rest 5 minutes before slicing. Serve over quinoa.

PER SERVING 440 **CAL**; 16 g **FAT** (2 g **SAT**); 36 g **PRO**; 40 g **CARB**; 12 g **SUGARS**; 6 g **FIBER**; 730 mg **SODIUM**

Coconut-Lime Shrimp Noodles

MAKES 4 servings **PREP** 10 minutes **COOK** 12 minutes

- 1 **pkg (8 oz) brown rice pad thai noodles (such as Annie Chun's)**
- 1 **tbsp extra-virgin olive oil**
- 1 **shallot, thinly sliced**
- 3 **cloves garlic, sliced**
- 1 **can coconut milk**
- 2 **tbsp fish sauce**
- 2 **tbsp brown sugar**
- 3 **tbsp lime juice**
- 1 **tbsp balsamic vinegar**
- 1 **lb raw shrimp, peeled and deveined**
- 8 **oz sugar snap peas, halved on the bias**
- ¾ **cup fresh basil, chopped**
- ⅓ **cup fresh mint, chopped**

■ Bring a pot of salted water to a boil. Cook noodles according to package directions (about 5 minutes). Drain, rinse with cold water and drain again.

■ In a large skillet, heat oil over medium. Add shallot and garlic. Cook 2 minutes. Whisk in coconut milk, fish sauce, brown sugar, 2 tbsp lime juice and balsamic vinegar. Bring to a simmer and cook 2 minutes. Stir in shrimp and peas. Simmer 2 to 3 minutes, until shrimp are cooked. Stir in cooked noodles, basil, mint and 1 tbsp lime juice.

PER SERVING 410 **CAL**; 19 g **FAT** (14 g **SAT**); 19 g **PRO**; 44 g **CARB**; 8 g **SUGARS**; 5 g **FIBER**; 800 mg **SODIUM**

CHEESY CHICKEN AND BROCCOLI SKILLET

Kick up the heat with a dash of harissa—a spicy sauce made of chiles, garlic, cumin, coriander, caraway and olive oil.

Chicken and Hummus Bowl

MAKES 4 servings **PREP** 10 minutes **COOK** 8 minutes

- 1 tsp ground turmeric
- ¾ tsp salt
- ½ tsp ground cumin
- ¼ tsp cinnamon
- ¼ tsp cayenne pepper
- 1 lb boneless, skinless chicken breasts, diced into ½-inch cubes
- 2 tbsp extra-virgin olive oil
- 1 large zucchini, diced
- Rice
- Hummus
- Tomato, diced
- Cucumber, sliced
- Harissa and whole wheat pitas (optional)

■ Blend first 5 ingredients (through cayenne). Toss chicken with half the spice blend. Heat 1 tbsp oil in a large skillet. Add chicken and sauté 3 minutes, until cooked through. Remove with a slotted spoon. To the same skillet, add 1 tbsp oil, zucchini and remaining spice mixture. Cook 5 minutes, until softened. Serve chicken and zucchini in a bowl over rice with a scoop of hummus, tomato, cucumber and, if desired, harissa and whole wheat pitas.

PER SERVING 420 **CAL**; 15 g **FAT** (2 g **SAT**); 32 g **PRO**; 37 g **CARB**; 2 g **SUGARS**; 5 g **FIBER**; 630 mg **SODIUM**

Cheesy Chicken and Broccoli Skillet

MAKES 6 servings **PREP** 15 minutes **COOK** 9 minutes **BAKE** at 375° for 20 minutes **BROIL** 3 minutes

- 1 cup orzo
- 1 large head broccoli (about 6 cups), cut into florets
- 1¼ lb boneless, skinless chicken thighs, diced into 1-inch pieces
- 1 tsp salt
- ¾ tsp pepper
- 2 tbsp unsalted butter
- 1 small shallot, minced
- 2 cloves garlic, minced
- 2 tbsp all-purpose flour
- 3 cups 2% milk
- 1¼ cups shredded sharp white cheddar
- ½ cup grated Parmesan

■ Bring a large pot of salted water to a boil. Add orzo and cook 9 minutes. After 6 minutes, add broccoli florets. Drain.

■ Heat oven to 375°. Season chicken with ½ tsp each salt and pepper. In a 12-inch cast-iron skillet, heat 1 tbsp butter over medium-high. Add chicken; cook 2 to 3 minutes, until lightly browned. Remove with a slotted spoon to a plate. Reduce heat to medium and add 1 tbsp butter, shallot and garlic. Stir in flour; cook 1 minute. Whisk in milk, ½ tsp salt and ¼ tsp pepper. Bring to a simmer; cook 3 minutes, until thickened. Stir in 1 cup cheddar and ¼ cup Parmesan. Stir until cheese is melted. Fold in orzo, broccoli and chicken. Scatter ¼ cup cheddar and ¼ cup Parmesan on top. Bake 20 minutes. Broil 3 minutes, until browned and bubbly.

PER SERVING 498 **CAL**; 23 g **FAT** (11 g **SAT**); 36 g **PRO**; 37 g **CARB**; 9 g **SUGARS**; 4 g **FIBER**; 780 mg **SODIUM**

CHICKEN AND
HUMMUS BOWL

STEAK AND CAULIFLOWER-POTATO MASH

Steak and Cauliflower-Potato Mash

MAKES 6 servings **PREP** 15 minutes
COOK 15 minutes

- 1 **large head cauliflower, trimmed and cut into florets**
- 1 **lb Yukon gold potatoes, peeled and cut into 2-inch pieces**
- ½ **cup milk**
- 1 **tbsp unsalted butter**
- 1 **tsp salt**
- ½ **tsp black pepper**
- 1½ **lb tri-tip steak, cut into 1-inch pieces**
- 2½ **tbsp all-purpose flour**
- 2 **tbsp extra-virgin olive oil**
- 1 **small onion, diced**
- 1 **clove garlic, sliced**
- 1 **tsp chopped fresh thyme**
- ¼ **cup Marsala wine**
- 1 **can (14.5 oz) beef broth**
- ¼ **cup chopped fresh parsley**
  Asparagus (optional)

- Place cauliflower and potatoes in a pot and cover with 2 inches cold water. Bring to a boil and cook 15 minutes, until fork-tender. Drain and add to a food processor with milk, butter, ½ tsp salt and ¼ tsp pepper. Blend until smooth. Transfer to a bowl and cover with foil to keep warm.

- Meanwhile, toss steak with 1 tbsp flour, ½ tsp salt and ¼ tsp pepper. In a large skillet, heat 1 tbsp oil over medium-high. Add steak; sear 2 minutes to brown, turning once. Remove to a plate with a slotted spoon. Add 1 tbsp oil to the same skillet. Reduce heat to medium. Stir in onion, garlic and thyme. Cook 2 minutes. Stir in 1½ tbsp flour; cook 30 seconds. Pour in wine; cook 30 seconds, scraping bottom of skillet to remove browned bits. Whisk in beef broth; simmer 5 minutes, until thickened. Stir in parsley and the beef. Stir to warm. Serve with mash and, if desired, steamed asparagus.

PER SERVING 400 **CAL**; 19 g **FAT** (6 g **SAT**); 30 g **PRO**; 25 g **CARB**; 5 g **SUGARS**; 4 g **FIBER**; 770 mg **SODIUM**

BBQ CHICKEN PASTA

BBQ Chicken Pasta

MAKES 6 servings **PREP** 15 minutes **COOK** 13 minutes

- 1 **lb rotini**
- 1 **bag (8 oz) frozen chopped collard greens, thawed**
- 1 **tbsp unsalted butter**
- 1 **cup diced red onion**
- 2 **cloves garlic, chopped**
- 1 **plum tomato, diced**
- 1¼ **cups ketchup**
- 2 **tbsp molasses**
- 1 **tbsp cider vinegar**
- 1 **tbsp yellow mustard**
- ½ **tsp black pepper**
- 4 **cups shredded rotisserie chicken**
- 1 **cup frozen fire-roasted corn, thawed**
  Shredded Monterey Jack (optional)

- Bring a large pot of salted water to a boil. Add rotini and collard greens; cook 7 minutes. Drain and return to pot.

- Meanwhile, melt butter in a medium pot. Add onion and garlic. Cook over medium 3 minutes. Whisk in tomato, ketchup, molasses, vinegar, mustard and pepper. Bring to a simmer and cook 10 minutes, stirring every few minutes. Pour into pot with pasta, chicken and corn. Stir to combine. Serve with shredded Monterey Jack, if desired.

PER SERVING 580 **CAL**; 9 g **FAT** (3 g **SAT**); 39 g **PRO**; 85 g **CARB**; 24 g **SUGARS**; 4 g **FIBER**; 790 mg **SODIUM**

FOR THE WIN

Go-to game-day eats

FRIED MAC AND
CHEESE BITES

Fried Mac and Cheese Bites

MAKES 30 bites **PREP** 45 minutes
CHILL overnight **COOK** 3 minutes per batch

- **12** oz macaroni
- **2** tbsp unsalted butter
- **2** tbsp all-purpose flour
- **1½** cups milk
- **½** tsp salt
- **¼** tsp black pepper
- Pinch of cayenne pepper
- **2** cups shredded cheddar
- **4** oz thinly sliced deli American cheese, cut into strips
- **1** cup shredded mozzarella
- **2** large eggs
- Italian-seasoned panko bread crumbs (8 oz box)
- **6** cups peanut or vegetable oil, for frying

■ Bring a large pot of lightly salted water to a boil. Add macaroni and cook 7 minutes or per package directions; drain.

■ Meanwhile, melt butter in a saucepan over medium. Whisk in flour, cooking until bubbly. While whisking, add 1¼ cups milk in a thin stream. Season with salt, black pepper and a pinch of cayenne. Bring to a simmer and cook 2 minutes. Remove from heat and mix in 1 cup cheddar and the American cheese. In a large bowl, fold cheese sauce into macaroni. Cool slightly, then stir in 1 cup each mozzarella and cheddar. Spread mac and cheese onto a rimmed sheet. Cover with plastic and refrigerate overnight.

■ Use a scoop to measure about ¼ cup of the mixture at a time and shape into 2- to 3- inch balls, compressing slightly. Whisk eggs with ¼ cup milk. Dip balls in egg mixture, then coat in bread crumbs. Heat oil in a deep 4-quart pot to 360° on a deep-fry thermometer. Fry 6 or 7 mac and cheese bites at a time 3 to 4 minutes per batch, until golden. Serve warm.

PER SERVING 200 **CAL**; 14 g **FAT** (5 g **SAT**); 6 g **PRO**; 13 g **CARB**; 1 g **SUGARS**; 0 g **FIBER**; 255 mg **SODIUM**

FRICKLES

Frickles

MAKES 16 servings **PREP** 15 minutes **COOK** 3 minutes per batch

- **3** cups canola oil
- **¾** cup cornmeal
- **⅓** cup all-purpose flour
- **¼** tsp black pepper
- **¼** tsp cayenne pepper
- **⅛** tsp salt
- **⅔** cup milk
- **1** large egg
- **1** 32 oz jar whole dill pickles
- **½** cup all-purpose flour
- **1** bottle ranch dressing

■ In a deep pot, heat oil over medium until it registers 375° on a deep-fat fry thermometer. Mix cornmeal, ⅓ cup flour, black pepper, cayenne and salt in a large resealable plastic bag.

■ In a medium bowl, whisk milk and egg. Drain pickles and cut each into spears (about 8 per pickle). Blot dry on paper towels and toss in a bowl with ½ cup flour. Dip 8 to 10 spears in egg mixture, then add to bag with cornmeal mixture and shake to coat. Spread spears onto a rack and continue with all spears (in batches of 8 to 10). Fry one batch of pickles for 3 minutes, until golden. Transfer to a paper towel and repeat, returning oil to 375° before adding each batch. Serve with ranch dressing for dipping.

PER SERVING 142 **CAL**; 9 g **FAT** (2 g **SAT**); 2 g **PRO**; 12 g **CARB**; 2 g **SUGARS**; 1 g **FIBER**; 595 mg **SODIUM**

4 WAYS WITH GROUND BEEF

Turn this staple into a variety of pleasing dishes.

EASY BOLOGNESE

Three-Alarm Chili

MAKES 6 servings **PREP** 20 minutes
COOK 25 minutes

- 2 **lb ground beef**
- 1 **tbsp canola oil**
- 1 **red onion, diced**
- 1 **large green bell pepper, diced**
- 3 **cloves garlic, diced**
- ¼ **cup chili powder**
- 2 **chipotle chiles in adobo, seeded and chopped**
- 1 **can (28 oz) fire-roasted crushed tomatoes**
- ¼ **cup packed brown sugar**
- 2 **cans (15 oz each) beans (your choice), drained and rinsed**
- ¾ **tsp salt**
     Sour cream
     Scallions, sliced

■ In a large pot, brown ground beef over high 5 to 7 minutes. Remove to a bowl; drain off fat. Reduce heat to medium and add oil, onion, green pepper and garlic. Cook 5 minutes. Add chili powder and chiles. Cook 2 minutes. Return beef to pot with tomatoes, 1 cup water and brown sugar. Cover, reduce heat to medium-low and simmer 25 minutes, stirring occasionally. Stir in beans and salt. Serve with sour cream and scallions.

PER SERVING 569 **CAL**; 21 g **FAT** (7 g **SAT**); 44 g **PRO**; 56 g **CARB**; 17 g **SUGARS**; 16 g **FIBER**; 997 mg **SODIUM**

Easy Bolognese

MAKES 6 servings **PREP** 25 minutes
COOK 30 minutes

- 2 **tbsp butter**
- 1 **tbsp olive oil**
- 1 **cup finely chopped carrots**
- 1 **rib celery, finely chopped**
- 1 **yellow onion, finely chopped**
- 2 **cloves garlic, sliced**
- 1 **tsp salt**
- ½ **cup dry white wine**
- 1 **can (28 oz) whole peeled tomatoes in puree**
- 2 **lb ground beef**
- 1 **tbsp sugar**
- 1 **lb fettuccine**
- ½ **cup heavy cream**
     Grated Parmesan

■ In a large pot, heat butter and olive oil over medium. Add carrots, celery, onion and garlic. Cook 7 minutes, stirring often, until onions are translucent. Sprinkle with ½ tsp salt and stir in wine. Cook 1 minute. Add tomatoes, breaking tomatoes apart. Stir in ground beef, sugar and ½ tsp salt. Simmer 20 minutes.

■ Meanwhile, cook fettuccine. Drain. Stir heavy cream into sauce. Toss half the sauce (4 cups) with fettuccine and serve with grated Parmesan. Save remaining half for another meal.

PER SERVING 526 **CAL**; 17 g **FAT** (7 g **SAT**); 27 g **PRO**; 63 g **CARB**; 7 g **SUGARS**; 4 g **FIBER**; 454 mg **SODIUM**

THREE-ALARM CHILI

CURRIED BEEF

Diner-Style Patty Melt

MAKES 4 servings **PREP** 10 minutes
COOK 25 minutes

4	**tbsp butter**
2	**medium onions, sliced**
	Salt
1¼	**lb ground beef**
	Black pepper
8	**slices marbled or regular rye bread**
4	**slices cheddar**

■ In a large stainless skillet, melt 2 tbsp butter. Add onions and cook over medium 10 minutes, stirring occasionally. Sprinkle with salt.

■ Meanwhile, shape ground beef into 4 oval patties. Season liberally with salt and pepper. Remove onions to a bowl; increase heat under skillet to medium-high. Add beef patties and cook 6 to 8 minutes, turning once. Divide onions among 4 slices bread. Top each with a patty and a slice of cheddar. Spread 4 more slices bread with 1 tbsp softened butter and stack on sandwiches, buttered side up. Carefully flip over and spread bottom slices of bread with another 1 tbsp softened butter. Heat a large nonstick skillet over medium-high. Add sandwiches and cook 2 minutes on each side.

PER SERVING 620 **CAL**; 35 g **FAT** (17 g **SAT**); 40 g **PRO**; 37 g **CARB**; 5 g **SUGARS**; 5 g **FIBER**; 945 mg **SODIUM**

Curried Beef

MAKES 6 servings **PREP** 15 minutes
COOK 35 minutes

1	**tbsp curry powder**
1	**tbsp sugar**
1½	**tsp salt**
1	**tsp ground cumin**
1	**tsp turmeric**
1	**tsp ground ginger**
½	**tsp black pepper**
3	**tbsp oil**
1	**onion, sliced**
2	**cloves garlic, chopped**
1¼	**lb ground beef**
4	**cups cauliflower florets**
1	**large potato, peeled and diced (scant 2 cups)**
1	**cup vegetable broth**
¾	**cup golden raisins**
1	**cup frozen peas, thawed**
	Chopped fresh cilantro
	Cooked couscous

■ Combine first 7 ingredients (through pepper). Heat oil in a large stainless skillet over medium. Add onion and garlic. Cook 3 minutes. Add spice mixture and cook 1 minute. Stir in ground beef and cook 5 minutes, stirring occasionally. Mix in cauliflower, potato, broth and raisins. Cover and cook 25 minutes, stirring halfway. Uncover and stir in peas. Serve over couscous and top with cilantro.

PER SERVING 518 **CAL**; 22 g **FAT** (6 g **SAT**); 25 g **PRO**; 56 g **CARB**; 21 g **SUGARS**; 7 g **FIBER**; 841 mg **SODIUM**

DINER-STYLE PATTY MELT

BISON STEAK
SALAD, PAGE 74

MARCH

67

77

82

HEALTHY FAMILY DINNERS

Try these 10 easy recipes on crazy-busy nights.

TOMATO SOUP

GRILLED CHEESE
PANINI

Up the ante on this comfort-food combo with a homemade tomato soup and grilled cheese and tomato sandwiches slathered with pesto. With a little prep the night before and slow-cooking all day, the soup is almost as easy to make as the canned stuff.

Tomato Soup and Grilled Cheese Panini

MAKES 6 servings **PREP** 20 minutes **REFRIGERATE** overnight **SLOW COOK** on HIGH for 6 hours or LOW for 8 hours **COOK** 3 minutes per batch

- 3 **lb plum tomatoes**
- 2 **cloves garlic, thinly sliced**
- 1 **can (14.5 oz) reduced-sodium vegetable broth**
- ¼ **cup fresh basil leaves**
- ¼ **tsp salt**
- ¼ **tsp black pepper**
- 12 **slices whole-grain bread**
- 3 **tsp jarred basil pesto**
- 8 **oz fresh mozzarella**
- 1 **large tomato**
- 18 **fresh basil leaves**

■ The night before cooking, core, halve and seed plum tomatoes. Combine garlic in a resealable bag with plum tomatoes. Refrigerate overnight. In the morning, combine plum tomatoes and garlic with broth and ¼ cup basil in a 4-quart slow cooker. Season with salt and pepper, cover and cook on HIGH for 6 hours or LOW for 8 hours.

■ Once soup is almost done, heat panini press. Place 6 slices whole-grain bread on work surface. Spread ½ tsp pesto on each slice. Cut mozzarella and large tomato into 12 thin slices each. Place 2 slices mozzarella on each bread slice. Add 3 basil leaves, then 2 slices tomato, and top each with 1 slice whole-grain bread. Coat both sides of sandwiches with nonstick cooking spray. Cook in panini press for 3 minutes (2 or 3 sandwiches per batch), until browned and cheese is melted.

■ While sandwiches cook, ladle half the tomato mixture into a blender. Blend until smooth. Add remaining tomato mixture to blender if there is space (or do in batches); blend until smooth (or use an immersion blender instead). Divide among 6 bowls.

PER SERVING 385 **CAL**; 17 g **FAT** (8 g **SAT**); 19 g **PRO**; 42 g **CARB**; 12 g **SUGARS**; 9 g **FIBER**; 735 mg **SODIUM**

CAMPANELLE WITH MUSHROOMS AND KALE

Campanelle with Mushrooms and Kale

MAKES 6 servings **PREP** 20 minutes **COOK** 25 minutes

- 1 **lb campanelle pasta**
- 6 **tbsp unsalted butter**
- 1½ **lb mixed mushrooms, sliced**
- 1 **large shallot, diced**
- 12 **cups kale leaves (from one 12 oz bunch), sliced**
- 3 **tbsp all-purpose flour**
- 3 **cups 1% milk**
- 1 **tsp salt**
- ¼ **tsp black pepper**
- ⅛ **tsp nutmeg**

■ Bring a large pot of lightly salted water to a boil. Cook pasta 10 minutes or according to package directions. Drain; set aside. Melt 3 tbsp butter in a large sauté pan over medium-high. Add mushrooms and shallot, stirring occasionally; cook 10 to 12 minutes, until most of the liquid is absorbed. Add kale, stirring until wilted and slightly tender, about 3 minutes.

■ Meanwhile, in pasta pot, melt 3 tbsp butter over medium. Add flour; cook 2 minutes. Pour in milk in a thin stream, whisking constantly. Bring to a simmer and cook 7 minutes, until thickened, whisking occasionally. Stir in salt, pepper and nutmeg. Stir mushroom-kale mixture and pasta into sauce and serve.

PER SERVING 535 **CAL**; 15 g **FAT** (8 g **SAT**); 20 g **PRO**; 81 g **CARB**; 14 g **SUGARS**; 6 g **FIBER**; 504 mg **SODIUM**

Crispy Bean and Cheese Burritos

MAKES 6 servings **PREP** 10 minutes **COOK** 18 minutes

- 1 **bag (3.5 oz) boil-in-bag brown rice (such as Uncle Ben's)**
- 1 **cup jarred salsa**
- ⅓ **cup chopped fresh cilantro**
- 1 **ripe avocado, cut into ½-inch pieces**
- 1 **tbsp fresh lime juice**
- 6 **soft taco-size flour tortillas**
- ¾ **cup shredded pepper Jack cheese**
- 1 **can (15.5 oz) black beans**

■ Cook rice according to package directions, about 10 minutes. Drain and place in a medium bowl. Stir in salsa and cilantro; set aside. Toss avocado with lime juice; set aside.

■ Place tortillas on work surface. Sprinkle 2 tbsp cheese in center of each, from left to right. Drain and rinse beans. Top cheese with heaping ¼ cup beans. Place a heaping ⅓ cup rice mixture over beans, then divide avocado among tortillas. Fold up opposite sides and then bottom and roll to enclose filling; repeat. Heat a large nonstick skillet over medium-high. Coat top and bottom of burritos with nonstick cooking spray. Place 3 burritos in skillet, seam side down; cook 1 to 2 minutes, until lightly browned and crisp. Turn burritos over and cook another 2 minutes. Repeat with remaining burritos, reducing heat if they get too browned.

PER SERVING 415 **CAL**; 15 g **FAT** (4 g **SAT**); 15 g **PRO**; 54 g **CARB**; 2 g **SUGARS**; 7 g **FIBER**; 761 mg **SODIUM**

CRISPY BEAN AND
CHEESE BURRITOS

VEGGIE STIR-FRY

Swap in any vegetables you have on hand or customize with family favorites.

Veggie Stir-Fry

MAKES 4 servings **PREP** 10 minutes
COOK 29 minutes

- **3 tbsp low-sodium soy sauce**
- **2 tbsp packed light brown sugar**
- **1½ tsp sriracha sauce**
- **1 tbsp grated fresh ginger**
- **½ cup cornstarch**
- **1 block (14 oz) firm tofu, cut into 1-inch cubes**
- **2 tbsp vegetable oil**
- **2 large sweet red peppers, seeded and chopped**
- **1 cup baby carrots, diagonally halved**
- **4 oz snow peas, trimmed and halved**
- **6 cups baby spinach**
- **Cooked soba noodles**

■ Stir together soy sauce, brown sugar, sriracha, ginger and 1 tbsp cornstarch. Place 7 tbsp cornstarch in a pie plate; coat tofu on all sides. Heat oil in a large nonstick skillet over medium-high. Add tofu to skillet in 2 batches; cook each 10 minutes or until lightly browned. Remove from skillet. Add peppers, carrots, snow peas and 3 tbsp water to skillet. Cover and cook 6 minutes or until tender. Add spinach; cover and cook 1 minute. Stir in soy sauce mixture; cook 2 minutes or until thickened. Stir in tofu; serve with cooked soba noodles.

PER SERVING 482 **CAL**; 9 g **FAT** (0 g **SAT**); 20 g **PRO**; 62 g **CARB**; 11 g **SUGARS**; 8 g **FIBER**; 795 mg **SODIUM**

EGGPLANT ROLLATINI

Eggplant Rollatini

MAKES 6 servings **PREP** 25 minutes **STAND** 15 minutes **GRILL** 8 minutes
BAKE at 350° for 25 minutes **COOL** 10 minutes

- **2 medium eggplants (2¼ lb total)**
- **½ tsp salt**
- **1½ cups shredded mozzarella**
- **1½ cups part-skim ricotta**
- **1 egg yolk**
- **⅛ tsp dried Italian seasoning**
- **⅛ tsp black pepper**
- **1 jar (12 oz) roasted red pepper pieces, drained**
- **1½ cups jarred marinara sauce**
- **2 tbsp grated Parmesan**
- **Pasta**

■ Trim tops and bottoms from eggplants. Cut each lengthwise into 6 slices about ½ inch thick. Spread onto 2 large cookie sheets lined with paper towels. Sprinkle with ¼ tsp salt, turn over and sprinkle with ¼ tsp more salt. Let stand 15 minutes, flipping slices halfway through.

■ Heat grill or grill pan to medium-high. Rinse eggplant and pat dry. Coat both sides with nonstick cooking spray. Grill until softened and nicely marked, 4 minutes per side. Return slices (do not overlap) to large cookie sheets (without paper towels). Coat a 13 x 9 x 2-inch baking dish with nonstick cooking spray.

■ Heat oven to 350°. In a small bowl, stir ¾ cup mozzarella, the ricotta, egg yolk, Italian seasoning and black pepper until well combined. Divide red pepper pieces evenly among eggplant slices, placing them on the wider end of each slice. Top each pepper with 1 heaping tbsp cheese filling. Place ½ cup marinara sauce on bottom of prepared dish. Roll up eggplant slices, starting at wide end and enclosing filling. Place in dish. Top with 1 cup marinara sauce, ¾ cup mozzarella and Parmesan. Bake 25 minutes. Remove to a wire rack and cool at least 10 minutes before serving. Serve with pasta.

PER SERVING 459 **CAL**; 14 g **FAT** (6 g **SAT**); 18 g **PRO**; 70 g **CARB**; 10 g **SUGARS**; 9 g **FIBER**; 677 mg **SODIUM**

VEGGIE BIBIMBAP

Veggie Bibimbap

MAKES 4 servings **PREP** 15 minutes **COOK** 45 minutes **STAND** 10 minutes

- 1½ **cups brown rice**
- 1 **bag (8 oz) shredded carrots**
- 1 **tsp sesame oil**
- 3 **tsp vegetable oil**
- 11 **oz fresh spinach**
- ⅛ **tsp salt**
- 4 **eggs**
- 1 **can (14 oz) bean sprouts, drained**
  Kimchi (optional)
- 1 **tsp sesame seeds**
- 2 **tsp gochujang (Korean hot chile paste)**

■ In a medium pot, combine rice and 3 cups water. Cover pot and bring to a boil. Reduce heat and cook 45 minutes. Remove from heat and let stand 10 minutes.

■ Meanwhile, bring a separate pot of lightly salted water to a boil. Add carrots and cook 2 minutes, until just tender. Drain and toss in ½ tsp sesame oil. Add 1 tsp vegetable oil and ½ tsp sesame oil to a large skillet over medium-high. Stir in spinach and cook until just wilted, 1 to 2 minutes. Season with salt. Remove to a bowl. Add 2 tsp vegetable oil to skillet. Crack in eggs and fry 2 to 3 minutes each, until whites are set. Divide rice among 4 bowls, followed by spinach and carrots. Divide bean sprouts among bowls and, if desired, add kimchi. Top each serving with 1 egg, sprinkle with sesame seeds and dollop with gochujang.

PER SERVING 460 **CAL**; 13 g **FAT** (3 g **SAT**); 17 g **PRO**; 71 g **CARB**; 5 g **SUGARS**; 9 g **FIBER**; 550 mg **SODIUM**

Squash and Lentil Stew

MAKES 6 servings **PREP** 20 minutes
COOK 56 minutes

- 3 **tbsp olive oil**
- 3 **carrots, peeled and diced**
- 2 **ribs celery, trimmed and sliced**
- 1 **medium onion, diced**
- 5½ **cups butternut squash pieces**
- 2 **tbsp chili powder**
- ½ **tsp ground cumin**
- 1 **can (14.5 oz) low-sodium vegetable broth**
- 1 **can (14.5 oz) diced tomatoes**
- 1½ **cups small brown or green lentils**
- ¾ **tsp salt**
- ⅓ **cup chopped fresh cilantro**

■ Heat olive oil in a large stockpot or Dutch oven over medium. Add carrots, celery and onion, and cook 5 minutes. Add squash pieces, and season with chili powder and cumin. Cook 1 minute. Stir in broth, diced tomatoes and lentils. Cover and simmer over medium-low for 40 minutes, stirring occasionally. Uncover and stir in salt. Simmer, uncovered, for 10 minutes. Stir in cilantro and serve.

PER SERVING 361 **CAL**; 8 g **FAT** (1 g **SAT**); 17 g **PRO**; 81 g **CARB**; 6 g **SUGARS**; 20 g **FIBER**; 504 mg **SODIUM**

VEGGIE
PAELLA

Veggie Paella

MAKES 6 servings **PREP** 20 minutes
REFRIGERATE overnight **BAKE** at 400° for
20 minutes **COOK** 25 minutes

- **1 pkg (14 oz) extra-firm tofu, cut into ¾-inch cubes**
- **4 tbsp olive oil**
- **¼ tsp plus ⅛ tsp seasoned salt**
- **1 head cauliflower, cut into florets**
- **1 green bell pepper, cored and diced**
- **1 medium onion, chopped**
- **1 pkg (10 oz) yellow rice mix**
- **3 plum tomatoes, seeded and diced**
- **1 cup frozen peas, thawed**

■ Spread tofu between layers of paper towels on a plate to drain. Refrigerate overnight.

■ Heat oven to 400°. Toss tofu cubes with 1 tbsp olive oil and ¼ tsp seasoned salt. Spread onto a foil-lined sheet and bake 20 minutes.

■ Meanwhile, heat 3 tbsp olive oil in a large, lidded skillet over medium. Add cauliflower, green pepper and onion. Sauté 5 minutes. Sprinkle with ⅛ tsp seasoned salt. Stir in yellow rice mix, plum tomatoes and 2¼ cups water. Bring to a simmer. Cover and reduce heat to medium-low. Cook 18 to 20 minutes. Uncover and gently stir in baked tofu and peas. Heat through.

PER SERVING 380 **CAL**; 13 g **FAT** (2 g **SAT**); 16 g **PRO**; 53 g **CARB**; 7 g **SUGARS**; 6 g **FIBER**; 792 mg **SODIUM**

SLOW COOKER
3-BEAN CHILI

Slow Cooker 3-Bean Chili

MAKES 8 servings **PREP** 10 minutes **SOAK** overnight **SLOW COOK** on LOW for 7 hours, 30 minutes

- 1 cup (about 6 oz) dried black beans
- 1 cup (about 6 oz) dried pinto beans
- 1 cup (about 6 oz) dried kidney beans
- 1 bay leaf
- 6 tsp ancho chile powder
- 1 tbsp ground cumin
- 1 tsp dried oregano
- 1 medium onion, chopped
- 1 medium green bell pepper, seeded and chopped
- 3 cloves garlic, minced
- 1 can (14.5 oz) diced tomatoes, drained
- 1 pkg (12 oz) soy crumbles (such as Smart Ground)
- ¼ cup ketchup
- ¼ cup cornmeal
- 1 tsp salt
- ½ tsp black pepper
    Shredded Monterey Jack
    Fresh cilantro (optional)

■ Soak beans overnight. Drain beans and place in a slow cooker. Add bay leaf, 2 tsp chile powder and 5 cups water. Cover and cook on LOW for 7 hours or until beans are tender. Stir in 4 tsp chile powder, cumin, oregano, onion, green pepper, garlic, diced tomatoes, soy crumbles, ketchup, cornmeal, salt and pepper; cook 30 minutes. Top with Monterey Jack and fresh cilantro, if desired.

PER SERVING 349 **CAL**; 2 g **FAT** (0 g **SAT**); 26 g **PRO**; 57 g **CARB**; 6 g **SUGARS**; 18 g **FIBER**; 902 mg **SODIUM**

Gemelli with Mint-Pea Pesto

MAKES 6 servings **PREP** 10 minutes
COOK 12 minutes, 30 seconds

- 1 bag (14.4 oz) frozen peas
- 2 cups fresh mint
- 6 tbsp olive oil
- ½ cup sliced almonds
- 1 tbsp fresh lemon juice
- 2 tbsp lemon zest
- 2 tbsp Pecorino-Romano cheese
- ½ tsp salt
- ⅛ tsp black pepper
- 1 lb gemelli pasta

■ Bring a large pot of lightly salted water to a boil. Add frozen peas and blanch for 30 seconds. Immediately remove peas with a slotted spoon and run under cold water until cool; set aside. Reserve water (cover with a lid to keep hot).

■ In a food processor or blender, combine 1½ cups peas, the mint, olive oil, ¼ cup almonds, and lemon juice and zest. Process until well combined. Transfer to a bowl and stir in cheese, salt and pepper. Bring reserved pot of water to a boil; add pasta. Cook 12 minutes or according to package directions.

■ Meanwhile, add pesto to a large sauté pan over medium-low. Drain pasta, reserving 1 cup cooking water; transfer pasta immediately to pan. Stir in cooking water, remaining peas and ¼ cup sliced almonds. Serve immediately.

PER SERVING 533 **CAL**; 20 g **FAT** (4 g **SAT**); 19 g **PRO**; 70 g **CARB**; 6 g **SUGARS**; 9 g **FIBER**; 287 mg **SODIUM**

GEMELLI WITH
MINT-PEA PESTO

THE NEW NORDIC

Wild foods and leafy greens and fatty fish—welcome to the heart-healthy Nordic diet. It's a way of life in Sweden, Denmark, Norway, Finland and Iceland, but these simple recipes will help you eat like a Viking right here at home.

ROASTED SALMON AND ASPARAGUS

Roasted Salmon and Asparagus

MAKES 4 servings **PREP** 15 minutes
COOK 2 minutes **ROAST** at 400° for 12 minutes

- 1 cup skyr or Greek yogurt
- 1½ cups roughly chopped fresh dill, plus more for garnish
- 4 scallions, sliced
- ¼ cup milk
- ¼ cup white wine vinegar
- 1 tsp salt
- 2 bunches asparagus, trimmed
- ¼ cup extra-virgin olive oil
- ¾ tsp black pepper
- 4 fillets (6 oz each) wild-caught salmon (center cut)
- 4 cups baby kale
- 1 cup yellow grape tomatoes, halved

■ Heat oven to 400°. In a food processor, combine skyr, 1 cup dill, 2 scallions, the milk, 1 tbsp vinegar and ¼ tsp salt. Process until well blended. Set aside.

■ Slice asparagus into 2-inch pieces on the bias. Toss on a rimmed baking sheet with 1 tbsp olive oil and ¼ tsp each salt and pepper. Roast at 400° for 12 minutes, until tender and lightly charred.

■ Meanwhile, season salmon with ¼ tsp each salt and pepper. Heat 1 tbsp olive oil in a skillet over medium-high. Add salmon, skin side up, and cook 2 minutes, until browned. Transfer salmon, skin side down, to a foil-lined baking sheet. Roast 5 minutes, until cooked.

■ In a large bowl, whisk 3 tbsp vinegar, 2 tbsp olive oil and ¼ tsp each salt and pepper. Toss with asparagus, kale, tomatoes, 2 scallions and ½ cup dill. Divide among 4 plates and serve salmon on top. Drizzle with yogurt sauce and garnish with more dill. Serve remaining sauce on the side.

PER SERVING 450 **CAL**; 24 g **FAT** (4 g **SAT**); 14 g **PRO**; 14 g **CARB**; 6 g **SUGARS**; 5 g **FIBER**; 690 mg **SODIUM**

CAULIFLOWER AND TART CHERRY SALAD

Cauliflower and Tart Cherry Salad

MAKES 4 servings **PREP** 20 minutes

- 1 medium head cauliflower, cut into large florets
- 3 tbsp tart cherry juice or apple juice
- 2 tbsp extra-virgin olive oil
- 2 tbsp balsamic vinegar
- 1 tsp Dijon mustard
- 1 tsp salt
- ½ tsp black pepper
- 1 small bunch watercress, chopped
- 1 cup dried tart cherries
- ⅓ cup slivered almonds, toasted

■ Using a hand slicer (such as OXO), thinly shave cauliflower.

■ Whisk next 6 ingredients (through pepper). Gently toss with cauliflower, watercress, cherries and almonds.

PER SERVING 270 **CAL**; 12 g **FAT** (2 g **SAT**); 6 g **PRO**; 37 g **CARB**; 19 g **SUGARS**; 12 g **FIBER**; 660 mg **SODIUM**

WILD MUSHROOM AND
EGG TOAST

*Bison is naturally leaner
than beef. Watch it carefully
while cooking to avoid
drying it out.*

Bison Steak Salad

MAKES 4 servings **PREP** 15 minutes
ROAST at 400° for 35 minutes
COOK 12 minutes **STAND** 5 minutes

- 1 **lb red and yellow beets, trimmed and cut into 2-inch wedges**
- ¼ **cup extra-virgin olive oil**
- 1 **tsp salt**
- ¾ **tsp black pepper**
- 3 **tsp balsamic vinegar**
- 2 **tsp Dijon mustard**
- 1¼ **lb bison steak or sirloin**
- 1 **package (5 oz) baby spinach**
- ⅓ **cup thinly sliced red onion**
- ⅓ **cup hazelnuts, toasted and chopped**

■ Heat oven to 400°. Toss beets with 1 tbsp oil and ¼ tsp each salt and pepper. Wrap tightly in foil and place on a baking sheet. Roast 35 minutes, until fork-tender. Cool slightly, then peel. Cut wedges in half.

■ Whisk 2 tbsp oil, the vinegar, mustard and ¼ tsp each salt and pepper. Set aside.

■ In a cast-iron or stainless pan, heat 1 tbsp oil over medium-high. Season steak with ½ tsp salt and ¼ tsp pepper. Sear on high for 5 minutes, until a crust starts to form. Flip and sear another 5 to 7 minutes, until medium-rare. Let rest 5 minutes, then thinly slice against the grain.

■ Toss steak with beets, spinach, onion, hazelnuts and dressing.

PER SERVING 380 CAL; 24 g **FAT** (15 g **SAT**); 26 g **PRO**; 16 g **CARB**; 8 g **SUGARS**; 5 g **FIBER**; 800 mg **SODIUM**

Wild Mushroom and Egg Toast

MAKES 4 servings **PREP** 15 minutes **COOK** 23 minutes

- 3 **tbsp unsalted butter**
- 2 **lb wild mushrooms, quartered or sliced**
- 2 **cloves garlic, sliced**
- ¼ **cup chopped fresh parsley, plus more for serving (optional)**
- ½ **tsp salt**
- ¼ **tsp black pepper**
- 8 **eggs**
- 8 **square slices or 4 rectangular slices whole rye bread (such as Mestemacher), toasted**

■ In a large skillet, heat butter over medium-high. Add mushrooms and garlic. Cook 15 minutes, stirring occasionally, until mushrooms soften. Stir in parsley, ½ tsp salt, and ¼ tsp black pepper.

■ Fill a large, deep-sided skillet three-fourths full with water. Bring water to barely simmering and cover. Crack 4 eggs into separate cups. Pour into simmering water one by one. Poach eggs 3 to 4 minutes, until whites are set. Remove with a slotted spoon and set aside. Repeat with remaining eggs.

■ Divide mushrooms evenly over toast and place 1 egg on each square slice (or 2 eggs on each rectangular one). Season with salt and pepper to taste. Add more parsley, if desired.

PER SERVING 390 CAL; 19 g **FAT** (9 g **SAT**); 22 g **PRO**; 36 g **CARB**; 6 g **SUGARS**; 7 g **FIBER**; 806 mg **SODIUM**

BISON STEAK
SALAD

NORDIC-STYLE
BREAKFAST

Rødgrød—a Danish mixed-berry compote similar to the topping in our Nordic-Style Breakfast—is practically a national dish. It's often served as a dessert with milk or ice cream.

Nordic-Style Breakfast

MAKES 4 servings **PREP** 10 minutes
COOK 12 minutes **STAND** 5 minutes

- 1 **cup diced fresh strawberries**
- 1 **cup blackberries**
- 1 **tbsp plus 2⅓ cups water**
- ¼ **cup packed light brown sugar**
- 1 **cup raspberries**
- ¼ **tsp salt**
- 1⅓ **cups quick-cook barley**
- ¼ **cup heavy cream, plus more for serving**

■ In a medium pot, combine strawberries, blackberries, 1 tbsp water and 1 tbsp brown sugar. Bring to a simmer and cook 5 minutes, until berries begin to burst. Stir in raspberries and cook 2 minutes. Set aside.

■ Meanwhile, combine 2⅓ cups water and the salt; bring to a boil. Add barley, reduce heat and cover. Cook 10 to 12 minutes, until tender. Let stand, covered, 5 minutes. Stir in 3 tbsp brown sugar and ¼ cup heavy cream.

■ Serve with a spoonful of berries and more cream drizzled on top.

PER SERVING 280 **CAL**; 6 g **FAT** (4 g **SAT**);
6 g **PRO**; 54 g **CARB**; 15 g **SUGARS**; 7 g **FIBER**;
150 mg **SODIUM**

POTATOES, FENNEL AND DILL

Potatoes, Fennel and Dill

MAKES 6 servings **PREP** 15 minutes **ROAST** at 400° for 25 minutes

- 2 **lb mixed baby potatoes, halved**
- 5 **tbsp canola oil**
- 1 **tsp salt**
- ½ **tsp black pepper**
- 3 **tbsp cider vinegar**
- 2 **tsp whole-grain mustard**
- 2 **tbsp drained capers**
- 1 **small fennel bulb, cored and thinly sliced**
- ½ **cup chopped fresh dill**

■ Heat oven to 400°. Toss potatoes with 2 tbsp oil and ½ tsp each salt and pepper. Place on a rimmed baking sheet and roast 25 minutes, stirring once halfway.

■ Whisk 3 tbsp oil, the vinegar, mustard, capers and ½ tsp salt. Toss with potatoes, fennel and dill. Serve warm or at room temperature.

PER SERVING 230 **CAL**; 12 g **FAT** (1 g **SAT**);
3 g **PRO**; 29 g **CARB**; 2 g **SUGARS**; 4 g **FIBER**;
530 mg **SODIUM**

FROZEN-FRUIT DESSERTS

Enjoy fresh-picked flavor from your freezer.

CHERRY-APPLE COBBLER

Cherry-Apple Cobbler

MAKES 10 servings **PREP** 15 minutes
BAKE at 350° for 55 minutes

- **2** bags (12 oz each) pitted dark sweet cherries
- **1** cup plus 3 tbsp all-purpose flour
- **¾** cup whole wheat flour
- **3** tbsp plus ⅓ cup granulated sugar
- **1** tbsp baking powder
- **¼** tsp salt
- **½** cup milk
- **⅓** cup olive oil
- **2** Granny Smith apples, peeled, cored and diced
- **½** tsp ground cinnamon
   Pinch of salt
- **1** tbsp confectioners' sugar

■ Thaw cherries. Meanwhile, make dough: Whisk 1 cup all-purpose flour and the whole wheat flour with 3 tbsp granulated sugar, the baking powder and salt. Create a well in center of dry ingredients, and pour in milk and oil. Stir until dough comes together.

■ On a floured surface, roll dough to ¼-inch thickness. Cut out 2½-inch circles with a cookie cutter, re-rolling scraps as needed. You should get about 18 rounds. Toss thawed cherries with apples, ⅓ cup granulated sugar, 3 tbsp all-purpose flour, the cinnamon and a pinch of salt.

■ Heat oven to 350°. Coat a 2-quart baking dish with nonstick cooking spray and add cherry mixture. Top with dough rounds, overlapping slightly. Bake 55 minutes. Dust with confectioners' sugar before serving.

PER SERVING 270 **CAL**; 8 g **FAT** (1 g **SAT**); 4 g **PRO**; 48 g **CARB**; 30 g **SUGARS**; 3 g **FIBER**; 144 mg **SODIUM**

BLUEBERRY BLINTZES

Blueberry Blintzes

MAKES 6 servings **PREP** 10 minutes **COOK** 3 minutes **BAKE** at 350° for 20 minutes

- **3¼** cups frozen Maine blueberries, thawed
- **1** tbsp plus ¼ cup honey
- **1** tsp cornstarch
   Pinch of salt
- **2¼** cups ricotta
- **2** tbsp lemon juice
- **1** tsp grated lemon peel
- **12** (12-inch) crepes (recipe follows)

■ Mix 1½ cups berries in a saucepan with 1 tbsp honey, the cornstarch, 2 tbsp water and a pinch of salt. Bring to a simmer and cook 3 minutes, until thickened. Set aside.

■ Heat oven to 350°. In a small bowl, beat ricotta, ¼ cup honey, and lemon juice and peel. Place 1 prepared crepe on a cutting board. Spread 2 heaping tbsp ricotta mixture onto center of each crepe, and top with 1 tbsp blueberries. Fold opposite sides of

crepe over filling, then fold up bottom edge. Roll up like a burrito and place on a foil-lined cookie sheet. Repeat with 11 more crepes, remaining ricotta mixture and blueberries. Bake 20 minutes. Serve 2 per person, topped with blueberry sauce.

PER SERVING 325 **CAL**; 13 g **FAT** (8 g **SAT**); 13 g **PRO**; 39 g **CARB**; 25 g **SUGARS**; 4 g **FIBER**; 181 mg **SODIUM**

Easy Homemade Crepes In a blender, combine 2¼ cups milk, 1½ cups all-purpose flour, 6 large eggs, 4½ tbsp melted unsalted butter, 1½ tbsp sugar and ¼ tsp salt. Blend until smooth and bubbly, about 30 seconds. Let stand 15 minutes. Pour ⅓ cup batter into a buttered 12-inch nonstick skillet over medium, swirling so batter coats pan. Cook until underside is browned, 2 minutes. Carefully flip; cook 1 minute. Slide from pan and repeat.

Pineapple-Mango Crisp

MAKES 8 servings PREP 10 minutes
BAKE at 350° for 55 minutes COOL 15 minutes

- ½ cup almond flour
- 5 tbsp packed brown sugar
- 4 tbsp cold butter, cut into cubes
- ½ cup sliced almonds
- ½ cup sweetened flake coconut
- ½ cup old-fashioned oats
- 1 bag (16 oz) pineapple chunks, thawed
- 1 bag (10 oz) mango chunks, thawed
- 2 tbsp fresh lime juice
- 2 tbsp cornstarch
- 2 tsp grated fresh ginger
-    Ice cream (optional)

■ Heat oven to 350°. Combine flour and 3 tbsp brown sugar until blended. With your hands, work in butter until evenly distributed. Stir in almonds, coconut and oats. Set aside.

■ Toss thawed fruit with 2 tbsp brown sugar, lime juice, cornstarch and ginger. Pour fruit mixture into an 8-inch baking dish and top with almond crumb mixture. Bake 55 minutes, until bubbly and browned. Cool 15 minutes. Serve with a scoop of ice cream, if desired.

PER SERVING 346 **CAL**; 19 g **FAT** (7 g **SAT**); 6 g **PRO**; 43 g **CARB**; 27 g **SUGARS**; 5 g **FIBER**; 28 mg **SODIUM**

MIXED-BERRY MINI PIES

PINEAPPLE-MANGO CRISP

Mixed-Berry Mini Pies

MAKES 12 servings PREP 25 minutes BAKE at 350° for 30 minutes

- 2 cups frozen mixed berries, thawed
- ¼ cup sugar
- 2 tbsp minute tapioca
- 1 pkg (15 oz) refrigerated piecrusts

■ Heat oven to 350°. Coarsely chop any large pieces of thawed berries. Toss with sugar and tapioca. Let stand while cutting out crust.

■ Unroll piecrusts. Cut out twelve 3½-inch circles and twelve 3-inch circles, re-rolling scraps. Fit larger circles into a nonstick standard-size muffin pan, pressing into bottom and sides of each cup. Divide fruit evenly among muffin cups, about 2 tbsp per cup. With a drinking straw or small cutter, cut vent holes out of smaller dough circles. Place on top of filling, crimping together with bottom crusts. (Alternately, cut slits in tops.) Bake 30 minutes. Remove with a spatula to a wire rack to cool.

PER SERVING 177 **CAL**; 9 g **FAT** (4 g **SAT**); 1 g **PRO**; 24 g **CARB**; 6 g **SUGARS**; 1 g **FIBER**; 184 mg **SODIUM**

Peach Danish

MAKES 6 servings   **PREP** 20 minutes
BAKE at 400° for 25 minutes

- 2   **cups frozen sliced peaches**
- 1   **sheet puff pastry (from a 17.3 oz pkg)**
- 4   **oz cream cheese**
- 2   **tbsp plus ½ tsp sugar**
- 1   **tbsp flour**
- ¼   **tsp ground cinnamon**

■ Thaw peaches and puff pastry. Beat cream cheese, 2 tbsp sugar, flour and cinnamon. Unfold pastry and roll to an 11-inch square. Transfer to a large parchment-lined baking sheet. Spread cream cheese mixture down center of pastry. Dry peaches on paper towels and stack onto cream cheese filling. Make diagonal cuts in dough, just up to filling. Fold alternating pastry strips over filling to resemble a braid (one from left side, then one from right)

■ Heat oven to 400°. Brush dough with water and sprinkle with ½ tsp sugar. Bake 25 minutes, until puffed and golden brown.

PER SERVING 273 **CAL**; 17 g **FAT** (7 g **SAT**); 5 g **PRO**; 25 g **CARB**; 10 g **SUGARS**; 2 g **FIBER**; 268 mg **SODIUM**

Folding the Danish

Step 1: cutting the dough

Step 2: folding the dough

PEACH DANISH

FOUR WAYS WITH VEGGIE NOODLES

Cut carbs and enjoy the flavor and nutrition of spiralized vegetables as stand-ins for regular pasta and noodles.

BEETS WITH CHICKEN, GOAT CHEESE AND PISTACHIOS

Beets with Chicken, Goat Cheese and Pistachios

MAKES 4 servings **PREP** 30 minutes
MARINATE 15 minutes **GRILL** 12 minutes

- 3 large beets (1½ lb total)
- ¼ cup fresh lemon juice
- 2 tsp honey mustard
- 1 tsp sugar
- ½ tsp salt
- ½ tsp black pepper
- ¼ cup extra-virgin olive oil
- 2 small boneless, skinless chicken breasts (6 oz each)
- ¼ cup salted pistachios, coarsely chopped
- 4 oz soft goat cheese

■ Peel beets and spiral-cut with the smallest spiralizer blade. Then using kitchen scissors, snip through strands every 6 inches.

■ In a medium bowl, whisk lemon juice, honey mustard, sugar, salt and pepper. While whisking, drizzle in olive oil; whisk until blended. Toss beet noodles with ⅓ cup dressing and set aside. Combine chicken with remaining dressing in a resealable plastic bag and marinate 15 to 20 minutes.

■ Heat a stovetop grill pan to medium-high. Grill chicken 12 minutes, turning once, or until cooked through. Add pistachios to beet noodles and toss. Crumble goat cheese and scatter over beets. Dice chicken; toss with or sprinkle over noodles.

PER SERVING 344 **CAL**; 20 g **FAT** (6 g **SAT**); 27 g **PRO**; 18 g **CARB**; 12 g **SUGARS**; 5 g **FIBER**; 569 mg **SODIUM**

Spring Veggie Pasta with Basil Pesto

MAKES 6 servings **PREP** 20 minutes
COOK 12 minutes

- 1 head garlic
- Olive oil
- 12 oz thin linguine
- 8 oz sugar snap peas, trimmed and halved
- ½ bunch pencil-thin asparagus, trimmed and cut into 3-inch pieces
- 1 large carrot (8 oz), peeled and spiral-cut with smallest spiralizer blade
- 1 cup red grape tomatoes, halved
- 1 cup loosely packed fresh basil leaves
- ¼ cup lemon juice
- 3 tbsp grated Parmesan
- 1 tsp salt
- 1 tsp pepper

■ Bring a large pot of salted water to a boil. Slice top off head of garlic; place in a small glass bowl. Add 3 tbsp water and drizzle with olive oil. Cover and microwave at 50% power for 3 minutes. Test tenderness with a fork; if not soft, re-cover and microwave at 50% for 3 minutes. Let stand 5 minutes. Squeeze cloves into a mini chopper.

■ Add linguine to boiling water and cook 6 minutes (1 minute less than al dente). Add peas, asparagus, carrot and tomatoes. Cook 1 minute. Drain, reserving ½ cup pasta water.

■ Meanwhile, add 5 tbsp olive oil, basil leaves, lemon juice, Parmesan and ½ tsp each salt and pepper to mini chopper. Process until smooth. Toss pasta and veggies with pesto and ½ tsp each salt and pepper, adding some pasta water to loosen sauce. Sprinkle with additional grated Parmesan and basil leaves.

PER SERVING 382 **CAL**; 14 g **FAT** (2 g **SAT**); 12 g **PRO**; 50 g **CARB**; 8 g **SUGARS**; 6 g **FIBER**; 449 mg **SODIUM**

Cucumber and Shrimp Salad

MAKES 4 servings **PREP** 20 minutes

- 2 seedless cucumbers
- ½ cup plain Greek yogurt
- ¼ cup white vinegar
- 2 tbsp chopped fresh dill
- 2 tsp sugar
- ½ tsp salt
- ½ tsp black pepper
- ¾ lb cooked shrimp
- 1 cup cherry tomatoes, halved
- ½ cup crumbled feta

■ Spiral-slice cucumbers through the thickest spiralizer blade. Then using kitchen scissors, snip through strands every 6 inches. Place between paper towels to remove excess liquid.

■ Meanwhile, whisk yogurt, vinegar, dill, sugar, salt and pepper. In a large bowl, combine cucumbers, shrimp, tomatoes and feta. Gently toss salad with ½ cup dressing. Serve extra dressing on the side.

PER SERVING 202 **CAL**; 7 g **FAT** (5 g **SAT**); 26 g **PRO**; 8 g **CARB**; 6 g **SUGARS**; 2 g **FIBER**; 591 mg **SODIUM**

SPRING VEGGIE
PASTA
WITH BASIL
PESTO

CUCUMBER AND
SHRIMP SALAD

Curried Zucchini and Beef

MAKES 4 servings   **PREP** 20 minutes
COOK 15 minutes

- 3   **medium zucchini**
- 1   **tbsp vegetable oil**
- ½   **lb skirt steak**
- ¾   **tsp salt**
- ½   **tsp black pepper**
- 1   **tbsp madras curry powder**
- 1   **can (13 oz) coconut milk**
- 2   **plum tomatoes, diced**
- 1   **tbsp grated fresh ginger**
- 2   **cups packed baby spinach**

■ Spiral cut zucchini with the medium spiralizer blade (you'll need 9 cups). Heat oil in a large stainless skillet over medium-high. Slice steak across the grain into thick 2-inch strips. Cook 2 minutes, stirring, seasoning with ¼ tsp each salt and pepper. Remove to a bowl. Reduce heat to medium and add curry powder. Cook 1 minute, then add coconut milk, tomatoes and ginger. Simmer 5 minutes, scraping bottom of pan, then add spinach, zucchini noodles, ½ tsp salt and ¼ tsp pepper. Cook 3 minutes, then stir beef back into skillet.

PER SERVING 213 **CAL**; 14 g **FAT** (5 g **SAT**); 15 g **PRO**; 10 g **CARB**; 4 g **SUGARS**; 3 g **FIBER**; 506 mg **SODIUM**

CURRIED ZUCCHINI
AND BEEF

ASIAN PEANUT NOODLE
SLAW WITH SHREDDED
CHICKEN, PAGE 97

APRIL →

93

103

105

LET THE GOOD TIMES ROLL!

Entertaining is all about Big and Easy with these New Orleans-style dishes.

TROUT
ALMONDINE

SHRIMP RÉMOULADE

Trout is typical for this dish, but you can also try flounder.

Trout Almondine

MAKES 6 servings **PREP** 5 minutes
COOK 11 minutes

- **6 skinless trout fillets (4 oz each)**
- **¼ tsp black pepper**
- **1 cup all-purpose flour**
- **1 tsp Creole Spice (recipe follows)**
- **8 tbsp unsalted butter**
- **½ cup sliced almonds**
   Juice of 1 lemon
- **2 tbsp minced fresh parsley**
- **⅛ tsp salt**

■ Season fish with pepper. Mix flour with Creole Spice in a shallow bowl, and dredge fillets in seasoned flour.

■ In a large skillet, melt 4 tbsp butter over medium-high. Add fish and cook until golden brown, about 3 minutes per side. Transfer to a serving platter.

■ Add 4 tbsp butter to skillet, swirling over medium-high so that it melts evenly and takes on a brownish hue, 3 minutes. Reduce heat to medium-low, add almonds and cook, stirring gently, until toasty brown, about 2 minutes. Add lemon juice, parsley and salt. To serve, spoon browned butter and almonds over fish.

Creole Spice Combine 2 tbsp celery salt, 1 tbsp sweet paprika, 1 tbsp coarse sea salt, 1 tbsp black pepper, 1 tbsp garlic powder, 1 tbsp onion powder, 2 tsp cayenne pepper and ½ tsp ground allspice. Mix well.

PER SERVING 419 **CAL**; 26 g **FAT** (11 g **SAT**); 27 g **PRO**; 18 g **CARB** 1 g **SUGARS**; 2 g **FIBER**; 60 mg **SODIUM**

Shrimp Rémoulade

MAKES 12 servings **PREP** 10 minutes **STAND** 10 minutes **MARINATE** 2 hours

- **1 cup mayonnaise**
- **½ cup Dijon mustard**
- **2 tbsp prepared horseradish**
- **½ rib celery, minced**
- **2 tbsp chopped fresh parsley**
- **1 clove garlic, minced**
- **1 tbsp white wine vinegar**
   Juice of 1 lemon
- **1 tsp hot sauce (such as Tabasco)**
- **¼ tsp cayenne pepper**
- **24 cooked jumbo wild American shrimp (see Shrimp Boil, recipe follows)**

■ Combine all ingredients except shrimp in a medium bowl and mix well.

■ At least 2 hours before serving, stir cooked shrimp into rémoulade sauce and marinate in the refrigerator. Serve with a slotted spoon.

Shrimp Boil Fill a large stockpot with water and mix in ¼ cup kosher salt, ¼ cup sweet paprika, 1 tsp cayenne pepper, 1 tsp garlic powder, 1 quartered lemon, 4 bay leaves, 1 small onion sliced ¼ inch thick, 1 head garlic halved crosswise, and 1 tbsp whole coriander seeds. Bring to a boil. Add shrimp and remove from heat. Cover and let stand 10 minutes. Drain.

PER 2 SHRIMP 61 **CAL**; 4 g **FAT** (1 g **SAT**); 5 g **PRO**; 1 g **CARB**; 0 g **SUGARS**; 0 g **FIBER**; 500 mg **SODIUM**

BAKED CHEESY
GRITS

Baked Cheesy Grits

MAKES 6 servings **PREP** 5 minutes
COOK 20 minutes **BROIL** 4 minutes

- 1 **quart water**
- 4 **tbsp unsalted butter**
- 1 **tsp salt**
- 1 **cup stone-ground grits**
- 1 **cup grated provolone or mozzarella**
- ½ **cup cream cheese**
   Pinch of red pepper flakes

■ In a large saucepan, bring water, butter and salt to a boil, then slowly whisk in grits. Lower heat and cook, stirring often, until grits become soft and creamy, about 20 minutes.

■ Set aside 3 tbsp grated cheese. Remove grits from heat, and fold in remaining cheeses and the red pepper. Heat broiler. Transfer grits to a medium skillet and top with

reserved cheese. Broil 3 to 4 minutes, until browned.

PER SERVING 291 **CAL**; 19 g **FAT** (11 g **SAT**); 9 g **PRO**; 24 g **CARB**; 1 g **SUGARS**; 1 g **FIBER**; 563 mg **SODIUM**

Fried Eggplant Salad

MAKES 8 servings **PREP** 15 minutes
FRY 5 minutes per batch

- 4½ **cups olive oil**
- 4 **eggs**
- 1 **large Italian eggplant, peeled and cut into ½-inch cubes**
- 2 **cups Italian bread crumbs**
   Salt
- ¼ **cup sherry vinegar**
- 1 **tsp sugar**
   Black pepper
- 2 **cups mixed greens**
- 4 **mini peppers, cored, seeded and sliced**

- 2 **cups cherry tomatoes, halved**
- 2 **tbsp chopped fresh parsley**
   Shaved Parmesan

■ In a medium pot, heat 4 cups oil over medium to 350° on a deep-fry thermometer. Meanwhile, whisk eggs in a shallow bowl. Dip eggplant in eggs, then in bread crumbs, coating well.

■ Working in batches, carefully fry eggplant until golden brown on all sides, about 5 minutes. Drain on paper towels and season with salt. Repeat, returning oil to 350° between batches.

■ Whisk ½ cup oil, the vinegar, sugar, ¼ tsp salt and ⅛ tsp pepper until well blended. Spoon vinaigrette onto a serving platter. Top with eggplant, greens, peppers and tomatoes. Season with salt and black pepper to taste. Sprinkle parsley and Parmesan over top and serve.

PER SERVING 210 **CAL**; 20 g **FAT** (3 g **SAT**); 2 g **PRO**; 7 g **CARB**; 3 g **SUGARS**; 2 g **FIBER**; 240 mg **SODIUM**

Roasted Beet Salad

MAKES 6 servings **PREP** 25 minutes
ROAST at 425° for 40 minutes

- 2 **lb small red and yellow beets**
- ½ **cup olive oil**
   Salt
- 1 **medium red onion, thinly sliced**
- ½ **cup rice wine vinegar**
- 2 **tbsp sugar**
   Black pepper

■ Heat oven to 425°. Rub beets all over with ¼ cup oil, then salt generously. Place on a baking sheet and roast until soft all the way through, about 30 to 40 minutes.

■ When beets are cool enough to handle, peel and quarter them. Transfer to a bowl with ¼ cup oil, the red onion, vinegar and sugar. Season with salt and pepper, then toss.

PER SERVING 280 **CAL**; 18 g **FAT** (3 g **SAT**); 3 g **PRO**; 28 g **CARB**; 22 g **SUGARS**; 5 g **FIBER**; 440 mg **SODIUM**

**FRIED EGGPLANT
SALAD**

**ROASTED BEET
SALAD**

CAJUN STUFFED
PORK CHOPS

The key to making this recipe is to find thick, luscious chops that will allow deep cuts to make roomy pockets to stuff.

Cajun Stuffed Pork Chops

MAKES 6 servings **PREP** 15 minutes
COOK 21 minutes **BAKE** at 350° for 30 minutes

- 2 **tsp plus 2 tbsp canola oil**
- ½ **lb pork sausage, casings removed**
- 1 **onion, finely chopped**
- 1 **rib celery, finely chopped**
- 3 **cloves garlic, minced**
- ¼ **cup unsalted chicken stock**
- 1 **egg, beaten**
- ½ **cup Italian bread crumbs**
- 1 **tsp crushed red pepper flakes**
- 6 **bone-in center-cut pork chops (about 1½ inches thick)**
- **Salt and black pepper**

■ Heat oven to 350°. In a large skillet, heat 2 tsp oil over medium-high and add sausage. Cook, stirring, for 5 minutes or until sausage is browned. Remove with a slotted spoon to a large bowl. Add onion to skillet; cook 5 minutes. Add celery and garlic; cook 3 to 5 minutes. Add to bowl with sausage and mix in stock, egg, bread crumbs and red pepper.

■ Create a large pocket in each pork chop with a small knife, cutting meat in half just to the bone. Fill each chop with sausage stuffing, and season outside with plenty of salt and pepper.

■ In a large ovenproof skillet, sear chops in 2 tbsp oil over medium-high for 3 minutes per side (turning once) until golden brown on both sides; work in batches if necessary. Place skillet in oven for 25 to 30 minutes, until chops are cooked through.

PER SERVING 590 **CAL**; 34 g **FAT** (9 g **SAT**); 56 g **PRO**; 12 g **CARB**; 4 g **SUGARS**; 1 g **FIBER**; 450 mg **SODIUM**

BANANAS FOSTER

Bananas Foster

MAKES 6 servings **PREP** 5 minutes **COOK** 9 minutes

- 1 **stick (8 tbsp) unsalted butter**
- ½ **cup packed light brown sugar**
- 1 **tsp cinnamon**
- **Pinch of ground nutmeg**
- 3 **tbsp orange juice**
- 6 **bananas, peeled and halved lengthwise, then crosswise**
- ½ **cup dark rum**
- **Vanilla or your favorite flavor ice cream**

■ In a large skillet, heat butter and brown sugar over high, stirring until they melt into a caramel. Cook 3 minutes, stirring constantly. Stir in cinnamon, nutmeg and orange juice, then add bananas. Cook 3 minutes, stirring gently to coat bananas, spooning sauce over them.

■ Remove pan from heat and, holding skillet away from you, carefully add rum. Return skillet to heat and cook 3 minutes, but be aware that alcohol may ignite if you're cooking over an open flame (you can also carefully use a lit match to flambé the sauce and burn off alcohol). Serve immediately on individual plates and top with a scoop of ice cream.

PER SERVING WITHOUT ICE CREAM 346 **CAL**; 16 g **FAT** (10 g **SAT**); 2 g **PRO**; 44 g **CARB**; 31 g **SUGARS**; 3 g **FIBER**; 3 mg **SODIUM**

HEALTHY FAMILY DINNERS

Try these 10 easy recipes on crazy-busy nights.

SHEET PAN CHICKEN DINNER

GREEK CHICKEN SALAD

Sheet Pan Chicken Dinner

MAKES 6 servings **PREP** 20 minutes
BAKE at 400° for 70 minutes

- 1½ **lb small red potatoes, quartered**
- 3 **large carrots, sliced**
- 1 **large onion, cut into thin wedges**
- 3 **tbsp olive oil**
- ¾ **tsp kosher salt**
- ½ **tsp black pepper**
- ¼ **cup lemon juice**
- 1 **tbsp dried oregano**
- 5 **cloves garlic, chopped**
- 1 **whole chicken (4 to 4½ lb), cut into 8 pieces**

■ Set rack in upper third of oven. Heat oven to 400°. Place potatoes, carrots and onion on a large baking sheet. Toss with 1 tbsp oil and ¼ tsp each salt and pepper. Bake 30 minutes.

■ Meanwhile, in a large bowl, whisk lemon juice, 2 tbsp olive oil, ½ tsp salt, ¼ tsp pepper, the oregano and garlic. Add chicken to marinade.

■ Remove vegetables from oven. Stir with a spatula and arrange chicken among vegetables. Drizzle any remaining marinade over chicken. Bake 35 to 40 minutes, until vegetables are tender and chicken reaches 165°.

PER SERVING 530 **CAL**; 24 g **FAT** (5 g **SAT**); 48 g **PRO**; 30 g **CARB**; 6 g **SUGARS**; 5 g **FIBER**; 316 mg **SODIUM**

Greek Chicken Salad

MAKES 4 servings **PREP** 15 minutes **MARINATE** 5 minutes **BROIL** 4 minutes

- 1⅓ **lb boneless, skinless chicken breasts, cut into 1-inch cubes**
- 1 **large clove garlic, minced**
- 1¼ **cups plain nonfat yogurt***
- 3 **tbsp finely chopped fresh mint**
- 1 **tbsp olive oil**
- ½ **heaping tsp cumin**
- ½ **tsp kosher salt**
- ¼ **tsp black pepper**
- 1 **cup sliced English cucumber**
- 16 **cherry tomatoes, halved**
- 4 **cups torn romaine**
  Pita bread, cut into wedges

■ Set rack at top of oven. Place chicken in a medium bowl and rub garlic into chicken.

■ In a small bowl, whisk yogurt, mint, olive oil, cumin, salt and pepper. Pour one-third of dressing over chicken; stir and marinate 5 minutes. Place chicken on a greased baking sheet in a single layer. Broil until no longer pink in center, 4 minutes.

■ In a large bowl, toss chicken with cucumber, tomatoes and romaine. Divide among 4 bowls and drizzle with some of the remaining dressing. Serve with warmed pita bread wedges.

*Note If you have Greek yogurt on hand, use it for this dressing but thin it with a little skim milk or water.

PER SERVING 431 **CAL**; 8 g **FAT** (1 g **SAT**); 44 g **PRO**; 43 g **CARB**; 8 g **SUGARS**; 3 g **FIBER**; 582 mg **SODIUM**

FISHWICHES WITH SPECIAL SAUCE AND PICKLED ONION SLAW

To coax sausage from its casing, run a knife lengthwise down the link and turn inside out.

Oven Farro Risotto with Sausage, Mushrooms and Kale

MAKES 4 servings **PREP** 15 minutes **COOK** 10 minutes **BAKE** at 400° for 30 minutes

2	tsp olive oil
1	red onion, sliced
8	oz sweet or spicy Italian sausage (casings removed)
8	oz sliced mushrooms
1	cup pearled farro
2½	cups low-sodium chicken broth
2	tbsp lemon juice
½	tsp salt
4	packed cups stemmed and chopped kale
	Parmesan

■ Heat oven to 400°. In a large Dutch oven with an ovenproof lid, heat olive oil over medium-high. Add onion and saute 1 minute. Add sausage and cook 1 minute, breaking up meat with a spoon. Add mushrooms and cook until they are softened and tender, 8 minutes. Add farro, broth, lemon juice and salt. Stir and bring to a boil over high.

■ Cover and bake 20 minutes. Remove from oven and add kale. Cover and bake until farro is just tender, 10 minutes. Stir well. Serve in shallow bowls with Parmesan to grate over top.

PER SERVING 375 **CAL**; 10 g **FAT** (3 g **SAT**); 24 g **PRO**; 53 g **CARB**; 6 g **SUGARS**; 9 g **FIBER**; 757 mg **SODIUM**

Fishwiches with Special Sauce and Pickled Onion Slaw

MAKES 4 servings **PREP** 15 minutes **BAKE** at 425° for 24 minutes

½	medium red onion, thinly sliced
¼	cup apple cider vinegar
2	tsp sugar
8	frozen breaded fish fillets
2	cups finely shredded cabbage
⅛	tsp black pepper
½	cup plain nonfat Greek yogurt
1	tbsp light mayonnaise
1	tsp Dijon mustard
2	tsp ketchup
1	tbsp sweet pickle relish
4	hamburger buns

■ Heat oven to 425°. In a medium bowl, combine onion, vinegar and sugar. Toss and let stand, stirring occasionally.

■ Bake fish per package directions, about 24 minutes. Stir cabbage and pepper into pickled onions and toss. In a small bowl, whisk yogurt, mayonnaise, mustard, ketchup and relish.

■ Lightly toast buns. Place 2 fish fillets on bottom of each bun, followed by slaw. Spread sauce on cut side of each bun top; cover and serve.

PER SERVING 435 **CAL**; 17 g **FAT** (6 g **SAT**); 17 g **PRO**; 50 g **CARB**; 11 g **SUGARS**; 2 g **FIBER**; 855 mg **SODIUM**

OVEN FARRO RISOTTO WITH SAUSAGE, MUSHROOMS AND KALE

ROAST PORK TENDERLOIN
WITH WARM GINGER APPLES

Pink Lady apples, with their sweet-tart flavor, can stand up to the spicy notes of the pork tenderloin.

Roast Pork Tenderloin with Warm Ginger Apples

MAKES 4 servings **PREP** 15 minutes
COOK 5 minutes **BAKE** at 400° for 25 minutes

- 1 **tbsp whole-grain Dijon mustard**
- 2 **tsp plus 1½ tbsp maple syrup**
- 2 **cloves garlic, chopped**
- ½ **tsp dried rosemary**
- ¼ **tsp plus ⅛ tsp kosher salt**
- ¼ **tsp black pepper**
- 1¼ **lb pork tenderloin**
- 2 **tsp olive oil**
- 3 **Pink Lady apples, cut into ½-inch wedges**
- 1 **tbsp butter, cut into pieces**
- 1 **tsp grated fresh ginger**

■ Set rack in center of oven. Heat oven to 400°. In a large bowl combine mustard, 2 tsp maple syrup, the garlic, rosemary, ¼ tsp salt and pepper. Add pork to bowl and coat with mustard mixture. In a large, heavy ovenproof skillet, heat olive oil over medium-high. Brown pork on all sides, 5 minutes.

■ Meanwhile, in an 8-inch square baking pan, place apples, 2 tbsp water, 1½ tbsp maple syrup, the butter, ginger and ⅛ tsp salt. Put skillet with pork and pan with apples into oven. Bake apples 25 minutes, until tender, and pork 20 minutes, until it reaches 140°. Let pork rest 5 minutes. Slice and serve with apples on the side.

PER SERVING 269 **CAL**; 8 g **FAT** (3 g **SAT**); 29 g **PRO**; 20 g **CARB**; 15 g **SUGARS**; 2 g **FIBER**; 236 mg **SODIUM**

ASIAN PEANUT NOODLE SLAW WITH SHREDDED CHICKEN

Asian Peanut Noodle Slaw with Shredded Chicken

MAKES 4 servings **PREP** 15 minutes **COOK** 10 minutes

- 4 **oz spaghetti**
- ⅓ **cup creamy peanut butter**
- 3 **tbsp seasoned rice vinegar**
- 3 **tbsp lime juice**
- 1 **tbsp packed brown sugar**
- 1 **tbsp low-sodium soy sauce**
- 1 **tsp sriracha sauce (or to taste)**
- 2½ **cups shredded rotisserie chicken**
- 6 **packed cups shredded cabbage**
- 2 **cups shredded carrots**
- 3 **scallions, thinly sliced**
- ½ **cup roughly chopped fresh cilantro**
- ¼ **cup chopped roasted peanuts**

■ Cook spaghetti according to package directions, about 10 minutes. Drain and rinse to cool. In a large bowl, whisk peanut butter, ¼ cup water, the rice vinegar, lime juice, brown sugar, soy sauce and sriracha until smooth. Add spaghetti, chicken, cabbage, carrots, scallions and cilantro. Toss well. Scatter peanuts over top.

PER SERVING 453 **CAL**; 19 g **FAT** (4 g **SAT**); 36 g **PRO**; 39 g **CARB**; 10 g **SUGARS**; 6 g **FIBER**; 657 mg **SODIUM**

SPRING VEGETABLE
PASTA WITH LEMON
AND PARMESAN

Spring Vegetable Pasta with Lemon and Parmesan

MAKES 6 servings **PREP** 15 minutes **COOK** 15 minutes

- **1 lb rotini pasta**
- **3 tbsp olive oil**
- **2 large shallots, thinly sliced (1 cup)**
- **1 large clove garlic, chopped**
- **1 heaping cup fresh or frozen peas**
- **1 large bunch asparagus, cut into 1-inch pieces**
- **1¼ tsp kosher salt**
- **½ cup chopped fresh mint**
- **⅓ cup grated Parmesan**
- **¼ cup lemon juice**

■ Cook pasta in lightly salted water according to package directions, about 8 minutes. Drain, reserving ½ cup pasta cooking water.

■ In a large skillet heat 1 tbsp olive oil over medium-high. Add shallots and saute 3 minutes. Add garlic and saute 1 minute. Add peas, asparagus and ¾ tsp salt. Saute until asparagus is tender, 3 minutes. Reduce heat to low and add pasta, reserved pasta water, mint, Parmesan, lemon juice, 2 tbsp olive oil and ½ tsp salt. Stir well.

PER SERVING 370 **CAL**; 5 g **FAT** (1 g **SAT**); 14 g **PRO**; 68 g **CARB**; 6 g **SUGARS**; 6 g **FIBER**; 232 mg **SODIUM**

Slow Cooker Italian Lamb Stew

MAKES 5 servings **PREP** 15 minutes
COOK 8 minutes **SLOW COOK** on HIGH for 4 hours or LOW for 7 hours

- **1¼ lb lamb stew meat**
- **¼ tsp salt**
- **¼ tsp black pepper**
- **1 tbsp olive oil**
- **1 large yellow onion, chopped**
- **2 cloves garlic, sliced**
- **2 large carrots, cut into 1-inch pieces**
- **1 can (14.5 oz) fire-roasted tomatoes**
- **½ cup red wine**
- **1 bay leaf**
- **1 can (15 oz) cannellini beans**
- **2 big handfuls baby spinach**
- **Jarred basil pesto**

■ Season lamb with salt and pepper. In a large skillet, heat olive oil over high. Brown lamb on all sides, turning, 5 minutes; transfer to a slow cooker. Add onion to skillet and saute 3 minutes. Transfer onion to slow cooker along with garlic, carrots, tomatoes, wine, bay leaf and ¼ cup water. Cover and cook on HIGH for 4 hours or LOW for 7 hours.

■ When lamb is tender enough to cut with a fork, stir in beans and spinach. Cover and let stand 5 minutes. Remove bay leaf. Ladle into bowls and top each serving with 1 tsp pesto.

PER SERVING 292 **CAL**; 9 g **FAT** (2 g **SAT**); 22 g **PRO**; 27 g **CARB**; 7 g **SUGARS**; 7 g **FIBER**; 626 mg **SODIUM**

**SLOW COOKER
ITALIAN LAMB STEW**

THAI-STYLE
SHRIMP CURRY

LAYERED SLOW COOKER ENCHILADAS

Create a custom variation: Swap in thinly sliced chicken breast for the shrimp—just cook a few minutes longer.

Thai-Style Shrimp Curry

MAKES 4 servings **PREP** 10 minutes
COOK 40 minutes

- 1 **cup brown basmati rice**
- 2 **tsp canola oil**
- 1 **medium yellow onion, chopped**
- 1 **can (13.5 oz) light coconut milk**
- 1 **tbsp Thai green curry paste**
- 1½ **tbsp brown sugar**
- 2 **tsp fish sauce**
- 2 **medium zucchini, sliced**
- 1 **lb medium shrimp, peeled and deveined**
- ½ **cup roughly chopped cilantro**

■ Cook rice according to package directions, about 40 minutes.

■ Meanwhile, in a large, deep skillet, heat oil over medium. Add onion and saute until tender, 5 minutes. Add coconut milk, curry paste, brown sugar and fish sauce. Stir to blend and dissolve sugar. Adjust heat so that liquid simmers. Add zucchini and cook, stirring occasionally, 1 minute. Add shrimp and cook until opaque, 3 minutes. Scatter cilantro over top. Serve curry over rice.

PER SERVING 376 **CAL**; 10 g **FAT** (5 g **SAT**); 25 g **PRO**; 50 g **CARB**; 8 g **SUGARS**; 5 g **FIBER**; 662 mg **SODIUM**

Layered Slow Cooker Enchiladas

MAKES 4 servings **PREP** 10 minutes **COOK** 7 minutes **SLOW COOK** on HIGH for 2 hours or LOW for 3½ hours

- 2 **tsp olive oil**
- 1 **large onion, diced**
- 1 **cup fresh or frozen corn**
- 2 **medium zucchini, diced**
- 1 **can (15.5 oz) low-sodium black beans, drained and rinsed**
- 2 **tbsp lime juice**
- ¾ **cup shredded sharp cheddar**
- 1 **can (15 oz) green enchilada sauce**
- 6 **corn tortillas**
- ¾ **cup shredded cheddar**
  Sour cream

■ In a large skillet, heat olive oil over medium-high. Add onion and saute until tender, 5 minutes. Add corn and zucchini. Saute 2 minutes. Add beans, lime juice and sharp cheddar. Stir and remove from heat.

■ Coat a slow cooker with nonstick cooking spray and pour in one-third of the enchilada sauce. Top with 2 corn tortillas (okay to overlap). Spread half the vegetables over tortillas. Top with 2 tortillas and one-third more enchilada sauce. Add remaining vegetables, 2 more tortillas and remaining enchilada sauce. Sprinkle with shredded cheddar. Cover; cook on HIGH for 2 hours or LOW for 3½ hours. Serve with sour cream.

PER SERVING 293 **CAL**; 13 g **FAT** (6 g **SAT**); 12 g **PRO**; 35 g **CARB**; 6 g **SUGARS**; 7 g **FIBER**; 596 mg **SODIUM**

SPRING TO IT

Here are some sweet ideas for celebrating Easter and Passover.

EASTER
CARROT CAKE

Easter Carrot Cake

MAKES 12 servings **PREP** 25 minutes
BAKE at 350° for 35 minutes

- 2½ **cups all-purpose flour**
- 2 **tsp baking powder**
- 1½ **tsp baking soda**
- 2 **tsp pumpkin pie spice**
- ½ **tsp salt**
- 2 **sticks (1 cup) unsalted butter, melted and cooled**
- 4 **large eggs**
- 1⅓ **cups packed dark brown sugar**
- 2½ **tsp vanilla extract**
- 3 **large carrots, peeled and finely shredded (about 1⅓ cups)**
- 1 **can (8 oz) crushed pineapple**
- ¾ **cup chopped walnuts (optional)**
- ½ **cup golden raisins, chopped**
- 1 **pkg (8 oz) cream cheese, softened**
- 1 **stick (½ cup) unsalted butter, softened**
- 2¾ **cups confectioners' sugar**
- ¼ **cup heavy cream**
     Orange and green gel food coloring

■ Heat oven to 350°. Coat two 9-inch round cake pans with nonstick cooking spray. Line bottoms of pans with parchment paper. Coat paper with spray.

■ In a medium bowl, whisk first 5 ingredients (through salt). Set aside. In a large bowl, beat melted butter, eggs, brown sugar and 1½ tsp vanilla. On low speed, beat in flour mixture. Fold in carrots, pineapple, walnuts (if using) and raisins. Divide batter between prepared pans. Bake 35 minutes.

■ Cool layers in pans on racks for 10 minutes, then invert onto racks, remove pans and parchment, and cool completely.

■ While cakes cool, make frosting: Beat cream cheese, softened butter, confectioners' sugar and 1 tsp vanilla on medium speed until smooth. Add heavy cream and beat until spreadable. Spoon ¼ cup frosting into a small bowl and tint orange. Spoon 2 tbsp frosting into

CHOCOLATE-FILLED MACAROONS

another bowl and tint green. Transfer to separate small resealable bags. Snip a small corner from each bag.

■ Place 1 cake layer on a pedestal. Spread top with ¾ cup frosting. Add second layer, and frost top and sides with remaining frosting. Pipe carrots on top of cake.

PER SERVING 648 **CAL**; 33 g **FAT** (20 g **SAT**); 7 g **PRO**; 82 g **CARB**; 60 g **SUGARS**; 2 g **FIBER**; 360 mg **SODIUM**

Chocolate-Filled Macaroons

MAKES 30 macaroons **PREP** 7 minutes
MICROWAVE 2 minutes
REFRIGERATE 30 minutes
BAKE at 325° for 30 minutes

- 1⅓ **cups sugar**
- 2 **tsp potato starch**
- 4 **egg whites**
- 3 **cups unsweetened finely shredded coconut**
- ⅓ **cup almond flour**
- ⅛ **tsp salt**
- 1 **tsp orange zest**
- ½ **tsp vanilla extract**
- ⅓ **cup semisweet chocolate chips**
     Chocolate Drizzle (recipe follows)

■ In a large glass bowl, combine sugar with potato starch. Whisk in egg whites until well incorporated and

slightly foamy. Mix in coconut, 3 tbsp water, the almond flour and salt until combined.

■ Microwave mixture for 30 seconds. Mix well with a silicone spatula, making sure to scrape sides of bowl. Repeat 3 times. Stir in orange zest and vanilla. Refrigerate 30 minutes.

■ Heat oven to 325°. Stir mixture. Spoon 30 rounded teaspoonfuls of mixture onto 2 parchment-lined baking sheets. Press 2 or 3 chocolate chips inside center of each cookie. Gently spoon 1 level tsp coconut mixture on top of each cookie. With moistened hands, bring up bottom layer to top layer and enclose chocolate. Round each mound to resemble a ball.

■ Bake 25 to 30 minutes, until golden brown. Remove from oven and cool 10 minutes, then transfer to a wire rack to cool completely.

■ With a spoon, dribble a stream of Chocolate Drizzle over macaroons.

PER MACAROON 114 **CAL**; 7 g **FAT** (5 g **SAT**); 1 g **PRO**; 13 g **CARB**; 11 g **SUGARS**; 2 g **FIBER**; 21 mg **SODIUM**

Chocolate Drizzle Combine ¼ cup semisweet chocolate chips and ½ tsp coconut oil or light olive oil in a small glass bowl. Microwave for 30 seconds. Stir. Microwave for an additional 30 seconds, then stir until chocolate is completely melted.

FOUR WAYS WITH HARD-BOILED EGGS

Inexpensive and infinitely versatile, they aren't just for breakfast anymore.

Egg and Avocado Toasts

MAKES 4 servings **PREP** 10 minutes

- **2 ripe avocados**
- **¼ cup plus 2 tbsp crumbled goat cheese**
- **1 tbsp lime juice**
- **½ tsp salt**
- **¼ tsp plus ⅛ tsp black pepper**
- **4 slices seeded whole-grain bread, toasted**
- **3 hard-boiled eggs**

■ Peel and pit avocados; smash with a fork in a bowl. Fold in ¼ cup goat cheese, the lime juice, ¼ tsp salt and ¼ tsp pepper. Spread onto bread. Slice eggs into 4 wedges each. Arrange over avocado spread. Scatter 2 tbsp goat cheese over toasts, then season with ¼ tsp salt and ⅛ tsp pepper.

PER SERVING 270 **CAL**; 18 g **FAT** (5 g **SAT**); 10 g **PRO**; 19 g **CARB**; 3 g **SUGARS**; 5 g **FIBER**; 520 mg **SODIUM**

Veggie Ramen

MAKES 4 servings **PREP** 5 minutes **COOK** 10 minutes

- **1 box (32 oz) ramen broth (such as Imagine)**
- **2 pkg (3 oz each) oriental flavor ramen (such as Nissin Top Ramen)**
- **4 oz extra-firm tofu, sliced**
- **4 hard-boiled eggs, halved**
- **1⅓ cups thinly sliced shiitake mushrooms**
- **1 cup fresh cilantro leaves**
- **½ cup sliced scallions**
- **Chili oil**

■ In a small pot, heat broth until simmering; cover and turn off heat.

■ Bring a medium pot of water to a boil. Add noodles and cook until tender, 3 minutes. (Do not add flavor packets.) Distribute noodles and broth among 4 bowls. To each bowl, add 1 oz sliced tofu, 1 egg, ⅓ cup mushrooms, ¼ cup cilantro and 2 tbsp scallions. Drizzle with chili oil.

PER SERVING 220 **CAL**; 10 g **FAT** (4 g **SAT**); 13 g **PRO**; 19 g **CARB**; 4 g **SUGARS**; 0 g **FIBER**; 950 mg **SODIUM**

VEGGIE RAMEN

EGG AND AVOCADO TOASTS

SABICHES
(ISRAELI PITA
SANDWICHES)

Sabiches (Israeli Pita Sandwiches)

MAKES 4 servings **PREP** 20 minutes
COOK 15 minutes

- 1 medium eggplant
- 2 tbsp extra-virgin olive oil
- ¼ tsp plus ⅛ tsp salt
- 2 vine tomatoes
- ½ English cucumber
- ½ cup chopped fresh parsley
- 2 tsp lemon juice
- 4 pitas
- 4 tsp harissa (North African hot sauce)
- ½ cup plain hummus
- 4 hard-boiled eggs
- 8 tsp tahini

■ Slice eggplant into ¼-inch-thick rounds. In a large skillet, heat 1 tbsp olive oil over medium-high. Add half the eggplant slices and cook until browned, 3 minutes. Flip and cook 3 more minutes. Repeat with remaining oil and eggplant. Season with ¼ tsp salt. Dice tomatoes and cucumber; toss with parsley, lemon juice and ⅛ tsp salt. Slice pitas halfway open. Spread 1 tsp harissa and 2 tbsp hummus inside each pita. Add 2 or 3 eggplant slices, 1 sliced hard-boiled egg and ¼ cup tomato-cucumber salad. Drizzle with 2 tsp tahini. Repeat with remaining pitas.

PER SERVING 410 **CAL**; 15 g **FAT** (3 g **SAT**); 18 g **PRO**; 51 g **CARB**; 7 g **SUGARS**; 5 g **FIBER**; 770 mg **SODIUM**

Italian Cobb Salad

MAKES 4 servings **PREP** 20 minutes

- 4 tbsp balsamic vinegar
- 3 tbsp extra-virgin olive oil
- 1 tbsp honey
- ½ tsp salt
- ¼ tsp black pepper
- 8 cups baby arugula
- 2 oz crumbled Gorgonzola
- ½ cup thinly sliced red onion
- 8 oz cooked chicken, diced
- 4 hard-boiled eggs, chopped
- 2 oz prosciutto or ½ cup chopped cooked bacon
- 2 cups sliced heirloom cherry tomatoes

■ Whisk first 5 ingredients (through pepper) until blended; set aside. Place arugula on a large platter. Arrange Gorgonzola, onion, chicken, eggs, prosciutto and tomatoes in rows. Drizzle with dressing.

PER SERVING 410 **CAL**; 24 g **FAT** (7 g **SAT**); 34 g **PRO**; 16 g **CARB**; 12 g **SUGARS**; 2 g **FIBER**; 1,000 mg **SODIUM**

ITALIAN COBB SALAD

BLUEBERRY ICEBOX PIE,
PAGE 113

110

121

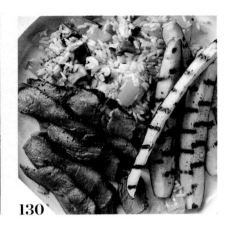

130

FRUIT LOOP

Kick off berry season with these cakes and pies.

LEMON-BERRY LAYERED CAKE

Lemon-Berry Layered Cake

MAKES 18 servings **PREP** 45 minutes
BAKE at 350° for 30 minutes

- 3½ **cups all-purpose flour**
- 2 **tsp baking soda**
- ½ **tsp salt**
- 4 **sticks (2 cups) unsalted butter, softened**
- 1¾ **cups granulated sugar**
- 4 **whole eggs plus 4 egg whites**
- ¾ **cup plus 2 tbsp milk**
- ½ **cup lemon juice**
- 2 **tbsp lemon zest, plus more for decorating**
- 2 **tsp vanilla extract**
- 1 **lb confectioners' sugar**
- ¾ **cup jarred lemon curd**
- ¾ **cup each blueberries, raspberries, quartered strawberries and halved blackberries, mixed**

■ Heat oven to 350°. Line two 9-inch square baking pans with foil and coat with nonstick cooking spray. In a medium bowl, whisk flour, baking soda and salt. In a large bowl, beat 2 sticks butter with the sugar for 2 minutes, until fluffy. Mix in eggs one at a time, followed by egg whites. Beat in ¾ cup milk, the lemon juice, lemon zest and 1 tsp vanilla. Add flour mixture and beat until just combined. Divide evenly between baking pans. Bake 30 minutes, until lightly browned and a toothpick inserted in center comes out clean. Cool slightly, lift from pan with foil and cool completely on a rack.

■ With a mixer, beat 2 sticks butter, confectioners' sugar, 2 tbsp milk and 1 tsp vanilla on low speed until combined, then on high for 5 minutes. Set aside.

■ Remove foil from cakes and trim tops to make them flat. Place one layer on a stand and spread lemon curd on top. Scatter 2 cups berries over curd and press second cake on top. Ice cake, starting at top and spreading frosting around sides. Top cake in center with remaining berries and garnish with lemon zest.

■ Cut cake in half, then slice each half crosswise into 9 pieces.

PER SERVING 550 **CAL**; 24 g **FAT** (14 g **SAT**); 6 g **PRO**; 79 g **CARB**; 59 g **SUGARS**; 1 g **FIBER**; 250 mg **SODIUM**

RASPBERRY
ANGEL FOOD CAKE

Raspberry Angel Food Cake

MAKES 12 servings **PREP** 15 minutes **COOK** 5 minutes **BAKE** at 350° for 45 minutes

- 1½ **cups raspberries, plus more for serving**
- 1⅓ **cups plus 2 tbsp superfine sugar**
- 1 **tbsp lemon juice**
- 1 **tsp cornstarch**
- 12 **egg whites, at room temperature**
- 1 **tsp cream of tartar**
- 1 **tsp vanilla extract**
- ¼ **tsp salt**
- 1 **cup cake flour (not self-rising)**
-   **Whipped cream (optional)**

■ Heat oven to 350°. In a small pot, combine raspberries, 2 tbsp sugar, the lemon juice and cornstarch. Bring to a simmer; cook 5 minutes. Pour through a fine-mesh strainer into a bowl, pressing to release liquid; discard solids. Cool completely.

■ In a large bowl, beat egg whites, cream of tartar, vanilla and salt to soft peaks. Gradually add 1⅓ cups sugar (a couple tablespoons at a time) until stiff peaks form.

■ Sift ⅓ cup flour over egg whites. Gently fold in with a large whisk until combined. Repeat twice with remaining flour.

■ Spoon a third of the batter into an ungreased tube pan. Spoon a third of the raspberry sauce over batter (don't allow any to touch pan's edges); swirl with a knife. Gently even out layer with an offset spatula. Repeat layering and swirling twice with remaining batter and sauce. Bake 40 to 45 minutes, until golden.

■ Immediately invert cake but leave in pan; cool completely. Loosen cake from edges with a long, sharp knife. Serve with raspberries and, if using, whipped cream.

PER SERVING 120 **CAL**; 0 g **FAT** (0 g **SAT**); 4 g **PRO**; 26 g **CARB**; 24 g **SUGARS**; 1 g **FIBER**; 105 mg **SODIUM**

Creamy, crunchy, tart and sweet—a cool ice cream cake with everything you want on a steamy summer night.

Frozen Raspberry-Chocolate Cake

MAKES 8 servings **PREP** 10 minutes **STAND** 30 minutes **FREEZE** 4 hours, 45 minutes **COOK** 3 minutes

- **1 pint raspberry sorbet**
- **½ box (4.5 oz) chocolate wafers (such as Nabisco Famous)**
- **3 tbsp unsalted butter, melted**
- **½ cup mini semisweet chocolate chips**
- **2 cups raspberries**
- **1 pint vanilla bean ice cream**

■ Let sorbet stand at room temperature for 15 minutes. Meanwhile, combine wafers and butter in a food processor. Pulse until mixture looks like wet sand. Line a standard loaf pan with plastic wrap. Using a measuring cup, press wafer crust firmly into bottom of pan. Spread softened sorbet on top. Scatter chocolate chips over sorbet, then 1 cup raspberries. Cover with plastic wrap and freeze for 45 minutes.

■ Meanwhile, combine 1 cup raspberries and 1 tbsp water in a small pot. Bring to a simmer and cook 3 minutes. Remove from heat; cool 15 minutes. Meanwhile, let ice cream stand at room temperature for 15 minutes. Transfer to a bowl and add cooked raspberries. Combine with a hand mixer until just blended.

■ Remove cake from freezer. Spread ice cream over cake, smoothing out top. Cover with plastic wrap and freeze completely, at least 4 hours.

■ Remove cake from freezer. Wrap loaf pan in a clean kitchen towel warmed with tap water. Invert pan onto a cutting board, and remove pan and plastic wrap; slice.

PER SERVING 350 **CAL**; 18 g **FAT** (10 g **SAT**); 4 g **PRO**; 44 g **CARB**; 35 g **SUGARS**; 2 g **FIBER**; 95 mg **SODIUM**

FROZEN RASPBERRY-
CHOCOLATE CAKE

BLACKBERRY SKILLET
CUSTARD PIE

Blackberry Skillet Custard Pie

MAKES 8 servings **PREP** 10 minutes
BAKE at 350° for 40 minutes

- 1 **tbsp unsalted butter**
- 1½ **cups milk**
- ⅔ **cup all-purpose flour**
- ⅓ **cup plus 2 tbsp granulated sugar**
- 4 **eggs**
- 1 **tsp vanilla extract**
- ¼ **tsp salt**
- 3 **cups blackberries**
  Confectioners' sugar, for dusting

■ Heat oven to 350°. Butter a 12-inch cast-iron skillet.

■ In a blender, combine milk, flour, ⅓ cup sugar, the eggs, vanilla and salt. Pour batter into skillet. Scatter berries on top, then sprinkle with 2 tbsp sugar.

■ Bake 40 minutes, until puffed and a knife inserted in center comes out clean. Serve warm, dusted with confectioners' sugar.

PER SERVING 180 **CAL**; 5 g **FAT** (3 g **SAT**); 6 g **PRO**; 27 g **CARB**; 16 g **SUGARS**; 3 g **FIBER**; 130 mg **SODIUM**

BLUEBERRY
ICEBOX PIE

Blueberry Icebox Pie

MAKES 12 servings **PREP** 10 minutes **BAKE** at 375° for 15 minutes **COOK** 5 minutes
REFRIGERATE overnight

- 16 **graham cracker boards**
- ½ **cup plus 3 tbsp sugar**
- 8 **tbsp unsalted butter, melted**
- 2½ **cups blueberries**
- 1 **envelope (¼ oz) powdered gelatin**
- ¼ **cup fresh lemon juice**
- 1 **can (14 oz) sweetened condensed milk**
- 4 **oz (½ pkg) cream cheese, softened**
- 2 **cups heavy cream, chilled**

■ Heat oven to 375°. Combine graham crackers and 2 tbsp sugar in a food processor until small crumbs form. Add butter and pulse until combined. Using a measuring cup, press into bottom and up sides of a deep 9-inch pie dish. Bake 15 minutes. Cool completely.

■ Meanwhile, clean and dry food processor, then add 1½ cups blueberries and ½ cup sugar. Pulse several times until finely chopped. Transfer to a saucepan with gelatin and lemon juice. Bring to a simmer and cook 5 minutes, stirring occasionally, until gelatin dissolves.

■ Beat condensed milk and cream cheese until smooth. Beat in blueberry mixture until combined, then fold in ½ cup blueberries. In a separate bowl, beat 1 cup heavy cream. Gently fold into mixture until no white streaks remain. Spread into crust. Loosely cover with plastic wrap and refrigerate overnight.

■ Beat 1 cup heavy cream with 1 tbsp sugar. Spread over chilled pie, leaving a 1½-inch border. Scatter ½ cup blueberries on top. Slice into wedges and serve.

PER SERVING 490 **CAL**; 30 g **FAT** (18 g **SAT**); 7 g **PRO**; 52 g **CARB**; 39 g **SUGARS**; 1 g **FIBER**; 180 mg **SODIUM**

STRAWBERRY-COCONUT CHEESECAKE

Strawberry-Coconut Cheesecake

MAKES 16 servings **PREP** 25 minutes **BAKE** at 325° for 1 hour, 10 minutes
REFRIGERATE overnight, plus 1 hour

- **2** boxes (5.3 oz each) shortbread rounds (such as Walkers)
- **¾** cup sweetened flake coconut, toasted
- **5** tbsp unsalted butter, melted
- **½** cup sugar
- **2** tbsp cornstarch
- **¼** tsp salt
- **3** pkg (8 oz each) cream cheese, at room temperature
- **3** eggs, at room temperature
- **1** can (15 oz) cream of coconut
- **½** cup heavy cream, at room temperature
- **1** tsp vanilla extract
- **½** cup strawberry jam
- **2** cups sliced strawberries

■ Heat oven to 325°. Combine shortbread rounds and ½ cup coconut in a food processor until small crumbs form. Add butter and pulse until combined. Using a measuring cup, press into bottom and halfway up sides of a 9-inch springform pan. Place on a rimmed baking sheet.

■ In a large bowl, whisk sugar, cornstarch and salt until blended.

With a hand mixer, beat in cream cheese for 2 minutes. Beat in eggs one at a time on low speed, then beat in cream of coconut, heavy cream and vanilla just until smooth. Pour into pan over crust.

■ Fill a 13 x 9-inch baking dish halfway with warm water; place on bottom oven rack. Place cake on middle rack and bake 1 hour and 10 minutes, until set (cake will still be a bit jiggly in center). Turn off oven and keep cake inside for 30 minutes, with the oven door slightly ajar. Transfer to a rack on the counter to cool completely. Refrigerate overnight.

■ Bring jam to a simmer in a small saucepan. Stir in strawberries. Remove from heat and cool 15 minutes. Remove cheesecake from refrigerator. Carefully run a knife along edges of cake to loosen, then release from springform pan. Pour strawberry glaze on top, allowing some to drip down sides. Refrigerate 1 hour. Sprinkle with ¼ cup coconut just before serving.

PER SERVING 500 **CAL**; 34 g **FAT** (22 g **SAT**); 5 g **PRO**; 44 g **CARB**; 33 g **SUGARS**; 1 g **FIBER**; 280 mg **SODIUM**

Strawberry Pie

MAKES 12 servings **PREP** 25 minutes
REFRIGERATE 2 hours, 15 minutes
BAKE at 375° for 1 hour

- **2½** cups plus 3 tbsp all-purpose flour
- **2** sticks (1 cup) unsalted butter, cut into pieces and chilled
- **1** tsp salt
- **½** cup ice water
- **6** cups hulled and halved strawberries
- **¼** cup plus 1 tbsp sugar
- **1** tbsp lemon juice
- **1** egg, beaten

■ Combine 2½ cups flour, the butter and salt in a food processor. Pulse until mixture is the size of peas. With processor running, slowly pour in ¼ to ½ cup ice water, until dough just comes together. Form into 2 equal rounds, wrap in plastic wrap and refrigerate 2 hours.

■ Heat oven to 375°. On a lightly floured surface, roll one round of dough to fit inside a 9-inch pie dish. Repeat with second round but slice into 10 strips. Place both on baking sheets and refrigerate 15 minutes.

■ Combine strawberries, ¼ cup sugar, 3 tbsp flour and the lemon juice. Remove dough from refrigerator and fit whole round into pie dish. Pour in strawberry mixture. Create a lattice pattern with strips of dough. Crimp edges. Brush top and edges with egg, then sprinkle on 1 tbsp sugar.

■ Bake 30 minutes. Carefully wrap foil around edges of crust to prevent burning, then bake another 30 minutes, until golden. Cool completely before slicing.

PER SERVING 280 **CAL**; 16 g **FAT** (10 g **SAT**); 4 g **PRO**; 33 g **CARB**; 9 g **SUGARS**; 2 g **FIBER**; 200 mg **SODIUM**

STRAWBERRY
PIE

SPRING CHICKEN

Your family will flock to the table when one of these super-simple dinners is on deck.

PARMESAN-PANKO
DRUMSTICKS

DRUMSTICKS

These hand-held favorites are budget-conscious and fun to eat. Dress them up with a crisp bread-crumb coating, BBQ sauce, or a sticky Asian-style glaze.

Parmesan-Panko Drumsticks

MAKES 4 servings **PREP** 10 minutes
BAKE at 425° for 35 minutes

- ⅓ **cup all-purpose flour**
- ¼ **tsp salt**
- ¼ **tsp black pepper**
- 2 **large eggs**
- ⅔ **cup grated Parmesan**
- ⅔ **cup plain panko bread crumbs**
- 8 **chicken drumsticks (about 2 lb)**

■ Heat oven to 425°. In a shallow dish, combine flour, salt and pepper. Lightly beat eggs in a second dish. Combine Parmesan and bread crumbs in a third dish.

■ Dip drumsticks in flour mixture, then eggs and finally bread crumb mixture. Place on a rack fitted into a rimmed baking sheet. Bake 35 minutes, until coating is crisp and drumsticks are cooked through.

PER DRUMSTICK 206 **CAL**; 10 g **FAT** (4 g **SAT**); 19 g **PRO**; 6 g **CARB**; 0 g **SUGARS**; 0 g **FIBER**; 299 mg **SODIUM**

BBQ Drumsticks

MAKES 4 servings
PREP 15 minutes **COOK** 5 minutes
BAKE at 400° for 35 minutes

- ½ **cup ketchup**
- 3 **tbsp packed dark brown sugar**
- 3 **tbsp cider vinegar**
- 2 **tbsp molasses**
- 1 **tbsp dried minced onion**
- ¾ **tsp ground black pepper**
- 2 **tbsp unsalted butter**
- 8 **chicken drumsticks (about 2 lb)**
- ¼ **tsp salt**

■ Heat oven to 400°. In a small saucepan, whisk first 5 ingredients (through onion) plus ½ tsp pepper. Bring to a simmer over medium and cook 5 minutes. Remove from heat and whisk in butter until smooth.

■ Season drumsticks with salt and ¼ tsp pepper. Bake 20 minutes. Brush with sauce; bake 15 minutes.

PER DRUMSTICK 188 **CAL**; 8 g **FAT** (3 g **SAT**) 14 g **PRO**; 14 g **CARB**; 13 g **SUGARS**; 0 g **FIBER**; 347 mg **SODIUM**

Honey-Sesame Soy Drumsticks

MAKES 4 servings **PREP** 15 minutes
BAKE at 400° for 40 minutes

- ⅓ **cup honey**
- 2 **tbsp low-sodium soy sauce**
- 1 **tsp cornstarch**
- 1 **tsp sesame oil**
- ½ **tsp ground ginger**
- ½ **tsp garlic powder**
- 8 **chicken drumsticks (about 2 lb)**
- ½ **tsp toasted sesame seeds**

■ Heat oven to 400°. In a small pot, whisk first 6 ingredients (through garlic powder). Bring to a simmer; cook 3 minutes. Place drumsticks on a nonstick-foil-lined baking sheet and bake 20 minutes.

■ Brush with 3 tbsp honey mixture, cover with foil and bake 20 minutes more. Drizzle with remaining honey mixture and sprinkle with sesame seeds.

PER DRUMSTICK 173 **CAL**; 8 g **FAT** (2 g **SAT**); 14 g **PRO**; 12 g **CARB**; 11 g **SUGARS**; 0 g **FIBER**; 225 mg **SODIUM**

ROTISSERIE CHICKEN

Cooked chicken from your supermarket's delicatessen is a lifesaver when time is short, and there are so many more interesting ways to enjoy it than simply carved up and plated.

Orange and Arugula Chicken Salad

MAKES 4 servings **PREP** 15 minutes

- 3 navel oranges
- 1 pkg (5 oz) arugula or 50/50 arugula and spinach blend
- 2 cups shredded rotisserie chicken
- ½ cup crumbled goat cheese
- ¼ cup sliced almonds
- ⅓ cup bottled poppy seed dressing
- 1 tbsp white wine vinegar

■ Peel oranges and cut into ¼-inch-thick slices. Fan onto a serving platter.

■ In a very large bowl, combine arugula, chicken, goat cheese and almonds. In a small bowl, whisk dressing and vinegar. Pour over arugula mixture and gently toss to combine. Pile over orange slices and serve.

PER SERVING 345 **CAL**; 20 g **FAT** (6 g **SAT**); 23 g **PRO**; 22 g **CARB**; 15 g **SUGARS**; 3 g **FIBER**; 572 mg **SODIUM**

Buffalo Chicken Baked Potatoes

MAKES 6 servings **PREP** 15 minutes
BAKE at 400° for 1 hour, 15 minutes
COOK 5 minutes

- 6 potatoes (8 oz each), scrubbed and pierced with a fork
- 2 cups shredded rotisserie chicken, chopped into small pieces
- 4 oz (½ pkg) cream cheese, cut up
- ¼ cup Buffalo-style hot sauce (such as Frank's RedHot)
- ¼ cup bottled blue cheese or ranch dressing
- 2 scallions, sliced

■ Heat oven to 400°. Place potatoes directly on oven rack and bake 1 hour. Test doneness; bake 15 minutes longer if not tender.

■ Remove potatoes from oven and let cool slightly.

■ In a medium saucepan, combine chicken, cream cheese, hot sauce, dressing and half the scallions. Cook, stirring, over medium until cheese is melted and mixture is steaming, about 5 minutes.

■ Cut a notch in top of potatoes and remove about ¼ of the flesh (save for another use). Fluff inside of potatoes with a fork, then spoon a scant ½ cup chicken mixture into each potato, mounding slightly. Sprinkle with remaining scallions and serve.

PER POTATO 386 **CAL**; 16 g **FAT** (6 g **SAT**); 18 g **PRO**; 43 g **CARB**; 4 g **SUGARS**; 5 g **FIBER**; 681 mg **SODIUM**

Chicken and Apple Tartine

MAKES 6 servings **PREP** 20 minutes
BROIL 3 minutes

- 4 cups shredded rotisserie chicken, chopped
- 1 Gala or Pink Lady apple, cored and cut into ¼-inch pieces
- 2 ribs celery, finely diced
- ½ cup light mayonnaise
- 2 tbsp Dijon mustard
- 2 tbsp cider vinegar
- ¼ tsp salt
- ¼ tsp ground black pepper
- 6 large slices whole wheat (or your favorite) bread
- 6 slices Swiss cheese

■ Heat broiler. In a large bowl, toss chicken, apple and celery.

■ In a small bowl, whisk mayonnaise and next 4 ingredients (through pepper). Fold into chicken mixture, then divide among bread slices, spreading to edges. Top each with a slice of cheese and broil, 4 inches from heat, 3 minutes, until melted and bubbly. Slice diagonally in half.

PER TARTINE 384 **CAL**; 20 g **FAT** (7 g **SAT**); 32 g **PRO**; 17 g **CARB**; 5 g **SUGARS**; 1 g **FIBER**; 951 mg **SODIUM**

ORANGE AND ARUGULA
CHICKEN SALAD

ASIAN
LETTUCE
WRAPS

GROUND CHICKEN

*Quick-cooking ground chicken adapts easily to both
Asian and Latin American flavors in these recipes.*

Asian Lettuce Wraps

MAKES 4 servings **PREP** 20 minutes
COOK 20 minutes **STAND** 10 minutes

- 1 **cup sushi rice**
- 1¾ **cups water**
- 3 **tbsp canola oil**
- 1 **lb ground chicken**
- ¼ **tsp each salt and black pepper**
- 1 **pkg (8 oz) sliced fresh mushrooms**
- 2 **cups shredded red cabbage**
- 3 **scallions, sliced**
- ⅔ **cup hoisin sauce**
- 2 **heads Boston or Bibb lettuce**
  Fresh cilantro leaves (optional)

■ Rinse rice in a mesh strainer under running water for 1 minute. Combine in a pot with 1½ cups water and bring to a boil. Cover, reduce heat to medium-low and simmer 20 minutes. Remove from heat and let stand 10 minutes.

■ Meanwhile, heat 2 tbsp oil in a large nonstick skillet over medium-high. Crumble in chicken and cook, breaking apart, 5 minutes. Sprinkle with salt and pepper, and remove to a plate.

■ Add mushrooms to skillet and cook 3 minutes. Stir in cabbage, scallions and 1 tbsp oil. Saute 3 minutes, then whisk hoisin and ¼ cup water; stir in along with chicken. Remove from heat.

■ Separate lettuce leaves, rinse and pat dry. On each lettuce leaf, layer a spoonful of rice and some chicken mixture. Finish with cilantro, if using.

PER SERVING 512 **CAL**; 22 g **FAT** (4 g **SAT**); 26 g **PRO**; 54 g **CARB**; 15 g **SUGARS**; 3 g **FIBER**; 914 mg **SODIUM**

Chicken Empanadas

MAKES 20 empanadas **PREP** 10 minutes
COOK 13 minutes **BAKE** at 400° for 20 minutes

- 2 **tbsp canola oil**
- 1 **small onion, diced**
- 1 **lb ground chicken**
- ½ **tsp ground cumin**
- ¼ **tsp each salt and black pepper**
- 2 **cups baby spinach, coarsely chopped**
- ¾ **cup frozen corn, thawed**
- ¼ **cup tomatillo salsa, plus more for dipping**
- 1 **cup crumbled Cotija cheese or grated Parmesan**
- 2 **pkg (14 oz each) frozen Goya discos dough for turnover pastries, thawed**

■ Heat oven to 400°. In a large nonstick skillet, heat oil over medium. Add onion and saute 4 minutes. Crumble in chicken and season with cumin, salt and pepper. Cook, breaking apart, 5 minutes.

■ Stir in spinach, corn and ¼ cup salsa; cook 4 minutes, until spinach is wilted. Remove from heat and stir in cheese.

■ Place 1 disco on a cutting board and roll out slightly. Place 2 tbsp filling in center of disco and fold in half to enclose filling. Pinch edge to seal and place on a large nonstick baking sheet. Repeat with remaining discos and filling.

■ Bake 18 to 20 minutes, until golden. Serve with tomatillo salsa on the side for dipping.

PER EMPANADA 207 **CAL**; 9 g **FAT** (3 g **SAT**); 9 g **PRO**; 25 g **CARB**; 2 g **SUGARS**; 1 g **FIBER**; 259 mg **SODIUM**

Golden Chicken Chili

MAKES 6 servings **PREP** 20 minutes
COOK 24 minutes

- 3 **tbsp olive oil**
- 1 **large sweet onion, diced**
- 1 **sweet yellow pepper, cored and diced**
- 3 **tbsp chili powder**
- ½ **tsp ground turmeric**
- 1 **tsp salt**
- ¼ **tsp black pepper**
- 1 **lb ground chicken**
- 2 **cups yellow cherry tomatoes, halved**
- ½ **cup water**
- 1 **can (15.5 oz) small white beans, drained and rinsed**
  Sour cream
  Fresh cilantro

■ In a large stockpot, heat oil over medium. Add onion and pepper and saute 5 minutes.

■ Increase heat to medium-high and stir in chili powder, turmeric, salt and black pepper. Cook 1 minute, then crumble in chicken. Brown 3 minutes and stir in cherry tomatoes and water.

■ Reduce heat to medium-low, partially cover pot and simmer 15 minutes, stirring occasionally.

■ Add beans and heat through. Serve chili topped with sour cream and cilantro.

PER SERVING 264 **CAL**; 13 g **FAT** (3 g **SAT**); 18 g **PRO**; 20 g **CARB**; 3 g **SUGARS**; 5 g **FIBER**; 839 mg **SODIUM**

BONELESS BREAST

Lean, low-calorie, and incredibly versatile, this cut is like a blank canvas for a world of flavors.

Lemony Cutlets

MAKES 4 servings **PREP** 20 minutes
COOK 10 minutes

- 2 large zucchini (8 oz each)
- 1 large yellow squash (12 oz)
- 3 tbsp lemon juice
- 2 tsp Dijon mustard
- 1 tsp honey
- ¼ tsp each salt and black pepper
- 8 tbsp extra-virgin olive oil
- 2 large egg whites
- 4 small boneless, skinless chicken breast halves (5 oz each)
- ¾ cup seasoned bread crumbs

■ Rinse and trim zucchini and squash. Shave them into long ribbons with a vegetable peeler (or use the ribbon blade on a spiral vegetable cutter). Place in a large bowl.

■ In a medium bowl, whisk lemon juice, mustard, honey, salt and pepper. While whisking, gradually add 2 tbsp olive oil. Remove 1 tbsp dressing to a shallow dish and toss the rest with squash. Set aside.

■ Whisk egg whites into reserved 1 tbsp dressing. Pound chicken to ¼-inch thickness and dip in egg white mixture, then bread crumbs.

■ In a large stainless skillet, heat 3 tbsp oil over medium-high. Add 2 cutlets and cook 4 to 5 minutes, turning once. Repeat with 3 more tbsp oil and remaining chicken. Serve cutlets topped with shaved squash salad.

PER SERVING 170 **CAL**; 12 g **FAT** (5 g **SAT**); 3 g **PRO**; 14 g **CARB**; 5 g **SUGARS**; 1 g **FIBER**; 60 mg **SODIUM**

One-Pot Tuscan Chicken

MAKES 6 servings **PREP** 15 minutes
COOK 23 minutes

- 3 tbsp unsalted butter or olive oil
- 1 lb boneless, skinless chicken breasts
- ¾ tsp salt
- ½ tsp black pepper
- 3 cloves garlic, sliced
- 2 cups water
- 1 cup chicken broth
- 1 box (12 oz) no-drain penne pasta (such as Barilla Pronto)
- 1 box (9 oz) frozen artichoke hearts, thawed
- ⅓ cup soft sun-dried tomatoes, sliced
- ½ cup heavy cream
- ¼ cup sliced fresh basil leaves

■ In a 12-inch stainless skillet, heat butter or oil over medium-high. Season chicken with ¼ tsp each salt and pepper. Add to pan and cook 10 to 12 minutes, turning once, until cooked through. Remove from pan and reduce heat to medium.

■ Add garlic to skillet; cook 1 minute. Stir in water and broth, scraping browned bits from bottom of pan. Add pasta and increase heat to high. Cook 5 minutes, stirring frequently.

■ Add artichoke hearts and sun-dried tomatoes. Cook 5 more minutes.

■ Meanwhile, slice chicken into bite-size pieces. Add to skillet with cream, ½ tsp salt and ¼ tsp pepper. Sprinkle with basil.

PER SERVING 456 **CAL**; 16 g **FAT** (9 g **SAT**); 26 g **PRO**; 49 g **CARB**; 4 g **SUGARS**; 3 g **FIBER**; 532 mg **SODIUM**

Grilled Chicken Club Pasta Salad

MAKES 6 servings **PREP** 25 minutes
GRILL 12 minutes **COOK** 9 minutes

- 1 lb boneless, skinless chicken breast halves
- 1 large red onion, cut into ½-inch-thick rounds
- 1 tbsp plus ¼ cup olive oil
- ¾ tsp salt
- ½ tsp black pepper
- 1 lb medium pasta shells
- 1 pkg (2 cups) mixed cherry tomatoes, halved
- 4 slices cooked bacon, diced
- 4 oz thinly sliced ham, cut into strips (¾ cup)
- ¾ cup diced cheddar
- ⅓ cup white wine vinegar
- 1 tbsp coarse-grain mustard

■ Heat grill or grill pan to medium-high. Coat chicken and onion with 1 tbsp oil; season with ¼ tsp each salt and pepper. Grill both 12 minutes, turning once, or until onion is tender and chicken is cooked through. Cool slightly and cut both into ½-inch pieces.

■ Meanwhile, cook pasta per package directions, about 9 minutes; drain.

■ In a large serving bowl, combine pasta, chicken, onion, tomatoes, bacon, ham and cheddar. In a small bowl, whisk vinegar, mustard, ½ tsp salt and ¼ tsp pepper. While whisking, add ¼ cup olive oil in a thin stream. Gently stir into pasta mixture and serve.

PER SERVING 609 **CAL**; 23 g **FAT** (6 g **SAT**); 36 g **PRO**; 63 g **CARB**; 7 g **SUGARS**; 1 g **FIBER**; 791 mg **SODIUM**

LEMONY
CUTLETS

PEANUT CHICKEN SKEWERS

BONELESS THIGHS

Flavorful thighs stay juicy no matter how they're cooked—grilled, braised or stir-fried.

Peanut Chicken Skewers

MAKES 4 servings **PREP** 25 minutes
COOK 15 minutes **GRILL** 14 minutes

- 2¼ cups water
- 1 cup quinoa (any color)
- ¾ tsp salt
- ⅓ cup creamy peanut butter
- 4 tbsp lime juice
- 2 tbsp low-sodium soy sauce
- 2 tsp sugar
- ½ tsp chili oil (optional)
- 1½ lb boneless, skinless chicken thighs, cut into 1-inch pieces
- 1 sweet onion, cut into 1-inch pieces
- 2 tbsp canola oil
- ¼ tsp black pepper
- 2 tbsp chopped fresh parsley
  Steamed green beans (optional)

■ In a medium lidded saucepan, bring 2 cups water, the quinoa and ½ tsp salt to a boil over high. Cover, reduce heat to medium-low and cook 15 minutes.

■ Meanwhile, whisk peanut butter, ¼ cup water, 2 tbsp lime juice, the soy sauce and sugar until blended. Add chili oil, if using.

■ Heat grill or grill pan to medium-high. Thread skewers with chicken, alternating with onion. Whisk oil with 2 tbsp lime juice, ¼ tsp salt and the pepper. Brush onto skewers. Grill skewers 12 to 14 minutes, turning often. Spoon quinoa onto a platter with steamed green beans, if desired, and sprinkle with parsley. Add skewers and drizzle with some sauce. Serve remaining sauce on the side.

PER SERVING 585 **CAL**; 29 g **FAT** (5 g **SAT**); 41 g **PRO**; 42 g **CARB**; 8 g **SUGARS**; 5 g **FIBER**; 950 mg **SODIUM**

Quick-Braised Thighs

MAKES 6 servings **PREP** 10 minutes
COOK 6 minutes **BAKE** at 350° for 35 minutes

- 6 boneless, skinless chicken thighs
- ½ tsp each salt and black pepper
- 2 tbsp extra-virgin olive oil
- 1 can (28 oz) fire-roasted crushed tomatoes
- ½ cup fresh basil leaves, coarsely chopped, plus more for serving
- ½ cup red wine
- 3 cups cooked orzo
  Grated Parmesan

■ Heat oven to 350°. Season chicken with salt and pepper. Heat oil in a large stainless skillet over high. Add chicken and brown 4 minutes, turning once. Transfer to a medium (11 x 7-inch) baking dish.

■ Reduce heat to medium and carefully add tomatoes, basil and wine (they will spatter). Cook, stirring, 2 minutes. Pour over chicken and transfer to oven. Bake 35 minutes or until chicken reaches 165°. Serve chicken and sauce over orzo, topped with Parmesan and additional basil.

PER SERVING 541 **CAL**; 17 g **FAT** (5 g **SAT**); 39 g **PRO**; 51 g **CARB**; 6 g **SUGARS**; 2 g **FIBER**; 726 mg **SODIUM**

Chicken Thigh Stir-Fry

MAKES 6 servings **PREP** 15 minutes
COOK 10 minutes

- 1 cup chicken broth
- ¼ cup rice vinegar
- 2 tbsp sugar
- 1 tbsp low-sodium soy sauce
- 1 tbsp cornstarch
- ¼ to ½ tsp red pepper flakes
- 1 lb boneless, skinless chicken thighs
- 2 tbsp vegetable oil
- ¼ tsp each salt and pepper
- ½ head savoy cabbage, diced
- 1 cup shredded carrots
- 1 sweet red pepper, cored and sliced
- 1 small onion, sliced
- 2 garlic cloves, sliced
- 1 can (8 oz) sliced water chestnuts, drained
  Cooked soba noodles or rice

■ In a medium bowl, whisk first 6 ingredients (through red pepper flakes). Set aside.

■ Slice chicken into thin strips. In a large stainless skillet, heat oil over high. Add chicken, season with salt and pepper and cook 4 minutes. Remove chicken to a plate; add next 5 ingredients (through garlic) to skillet. Stir-fry 4 minutes, until crisp-tender.

■ Whisk broth mixture and add to skillet along with chicken and water chestnuts. Cook 2 minutes, until thickened. Serve over noodles or rice.

PER SERVING 390 **CAL**; 12 g **FAT** (2 g **SAT**); 23 g **PRO**; 49 g **CARB**; 11 g **SUGARS**; 3 g **FIBER**; 594 mg **SODIUM**

HEALTHY FAMILY DINNERS

Try these 7 easy meals on crazy-busy nights.

VEGETARIAN FRIED RICE

Vegetarian Fried Rice

MAKES 6 servings **PREP** 10 minutes
COOK 20 minutes

- 1½ **cups brown rice**
- 1 **lb extra-firm tofu, cut into 1-inch cubes**
- 2 **tbsp cornstarch**
- ¼ **tsp salt**
- 4 **tbsp vegetable oil**
- 3 **eggs, beaten**
- 2 **sweet red or yellow peppers, diced**
- 1 **medium onion, diced**
- 3 **cloves garlic, sliced**
- 1 **pkg (5 oz) baby spinach**
- ⅓ **cup low-sodium soy sauce**
- **Sriracha sauce (optional)**
- **Chopped scallions (optional)**

■ Add 3 cups water and rice to a medium pot and bring to a boil. Reduce heat to medium-low. Cover and cook 20 minutes, until water is absorbed. Set aside.

■ Meanwhile, toss tofu with cornstarch and salt. Heat 1 tbsp oil in a large skillet over medium-high. Add eggs and scramble 1 minute. Remove to a plate with a slotted spoon. Pour in 2 tbsp oil. Add tofu and cook 4 minutes, carefully stirring every minute. Remove to plate with eggs. Add 1 tbsp oil and stir in peppers, onion and garlic. Saute 5 minutes. Stir in spinach until wilted, 1 minute. Add rice to pan. Saute 1 minute. Stir in soy sauce, then carefully fold in eggs and tofu. If desired, serve with sriracha, scallions and more soy sauce.

PER SERVING 380 **CAL**; 15 g **FAT** (2 g **SAT**); 16 g **PRO**; 46 g **CARB**; 4 g **SUGARS**; 4 g **FIBER**; 620 mg **SODIUM**

CITRUSY SALMON SALAD

Citrusy Salmon Salad

MAKES 4 servings **PREP** 15 minutes **COOK** 6 minutes

- 4 **skin-on salmon fillets (5 oz each)**
- ¾ **tsp salt**
- ⅛ **tsp black pepper**
- 3 **tbsp extra-virgin olive oil**
- 2 **tbsp lemon juice**
- 2 **tsp lemon zest**
- 1 **tsp Dijon mustard**
- 10 **oz frozen peas, thawed**
- 6 **cups watercress**
- 1 **pkg (5 oz) mesclun**
- ½ **cup roasted and salted sunflower seeds (optional)**

■ Pat dry salmon fillets. Season with ¼ tsp salt and the pepper. In a saute pan heat 1 tbsp oil over medium-high. Place salmon skin side up in pan; cook 3 minutes. Flip and cook 3 more minutes for medium. Cool slightly on a plate, then cover with plastic wrap and refrigerate until cold.

■ In a large bowl whisk 2 tbsp oil, the lemon juice, lemon zest, mustard and ½ tsp salt. Remove salmon from fridge and flake into large pieces with a fork, discarding skin.

■ In a bowl, gently toss salmon with peas, watercress, mesclun and, if desired, sunflower seeds.

PER SERVING 385 **CAL**; 21 g **FAT** (3 g **SAT**); 37 g **PRO**; 10 g **CARB**; 3 g **SUGARS**; 3 g **FIBER**; 610 mg **SODIUM**

TURKEY SAUSAGE AND SPINACH ORECCHIETTE

Turkey Sausage and Spinach Orecchiette

MAKES 6 servings **PREP** 10 minutes **COOK** 12 minutes

- 4 **sweet Italian turkey sausages, casings removed**
- 1 **cup chopped onion**
- 2 **tbsp chopped garlic**
- 2 **cups sliced sweet red and yellow peppers**
- ½ **tsp dried Italian seasoning**
- 1 **can (8 oz) no-salt-added tomato sauce**
- 1 **lb orecchiette pasta**
- 1 **bag (6 oz) baby spinach**
- ⅓ **cup shredded Asiago cheese**

■ Heat a large nonstick skillet over medium-high. Add sausages, onion and garlic; cook 5 minutes, stirring occasionally. Stir in peppers and Italian seasoning; cook 5 more minutes, stirring occasionally. Add tomato sauce and simmer 2 minutes.

■ Meanwhile, cook orecchiette per package directions (about 10 minutes). Drain, reserving 1 cup cooking water. Gradually stir spinach into skillet. In pasta pot, combine pasta and sausage sauce, adding some reserved cooking water if needed to loosen sauce. Spoon pasta into a large serving bowl. Top with Asiago cheese.

PER SERVING 430 **CAL**; 10 g **FAT** (2 g **SAT**); 22 g **PRO**; 64 g **CARB**; 7 g **SUGARS**; 2 g **FIBER**; 460 mg **SODIUM**

Broccoli Shrimp Scampi

MAKES 8 servings **PREP** 10 minutes **COOK** 19 minutes

- 3 **cups broccoli florets**
- 3 **tbsp olive oil**
- 1 **lb rotini or radiatore pasta**
- 2 **tbsp unsalted butter**
- ¼ **cup lemon juice**
- ¼ **tsp garlic salt**
- 4 **cloves garlic, minced**
- 1½ **lb medium shrimp, cleaned**
- ½ **tsp salt**
- ⅛ **tsp black pepper**
- 3 **tbsp Italian seasoned bread crumbs**

■ Bring a large pot of lightly salted water to a boil. Add broccoli and cook 3 minutes. Scoop broccoli from water and transfer to a 12-inch skillet along with olive oil. Return water to a boil and cook pasta per package directions (about 12 minutes). Drain and transfer to a serving bowl. Toss with butter, 2 tbsp lemon juice and the garlic salt. Keep warm.

■ Meanwhile, heat broccoli and oil over medium-high until sizzling. Add garlic and shrimp. Cook 3 to 4 minutes, until shrimp are opaque. Add 2 tbsp lemon juice and the salt and pepper. Stir in bread crumbs and serve over pasta.

PER SERVING 371 **CAL**; 10 g **FAT** (3 g **SAT**); 21 g **PRO**; 48 g **CARB**; 2 g **SUGARS**; 1 g **FIBER**; 748 mg **SODIUM**

BROCCOLI SHRIMP
SCAMPI

Coffee-Rubbed Steak with Charred Zucchini

MAKES 6 servings **PREP** 15 minutes
GRILL 8 minutes **MICROWAVE** 1½ minutes
REST 5 minutes

2	**tbsp espresso ground coffee**
1	**tsp chili powder**
1	**tsp garlic powder**
1	**tsp sugar**
1¼	**tsp salt**
½	**tsp smoked paprika**
¼	**tsp plus ⅛ tsp black pepper**
1½	**lb boneless sirloin steak (at least 1 inch thick)**
4	**small zucchini, trimmed and quartered lengthwise**
1	**pkg (10 oz) trimmed button mushrooms**
1	**yellow pepper, cut into 4 pieces**
2	**tbsp light balsamic salad dressing**
2	**cups heat-and-serve white or brown rice**

■ Heat grill to medium-high. In a small bowl combine coffee, chili powder, garlic powder, sugar, ¾ tsp salt, the paprika and ¼ tsp black pepper. Sprinkle 1 tbsp of the rub over one side of steak and press in with your hands. Turn over steak and repeat. Reserve remaining rub for another use. Season zucchini with ¼ tsp salt and ⅛ tsp pepper.

■ Thread mushrooms onto 2 skewers. Brush mushrooms and yellow pepper with salad dressing. Grill vegetables 6 minutes, turning once. Grill steak 6 to 8 minutes, depending on thickness, turning once.

■ Meanwhile, microwave rice 1½ minutes. Remove steak from grill and let rest 5 minutes. Quarter mushrooms and dice yellow pepper. Toss in a bowl with rice and ¼ tsp salt. Slice steak and serve with zucchini and grilled veggie rice.

PER SERVING 408 **CAL**; 19 g **FAT** (7 g **SAT**); 34 g **PRO**; 26 g **CARB**; 4 g **SUGARS**; 2 g **FIBER**; 550 mg **SODIUM**

COFFEE-RUBBED STEAK WITH CHARRED ZUCCHINI

QUICK BEEF
STIR-FRY

Turkey Pizza Burgers

MAKES 6 servings **PREP** 10 minutes
GRILL 8 minutes

1⅓	**lb lean ground turkey**
½	**cup plus 1 tbsp jarred marinara sauce**
1	**tsp Italian seasoning**
½	**tsp garlic salt**
½	**tsp onion salt**
¼	**cup plus 2 tbsp reduced-fat mozzarella**
12	**basil leaves**
	Hamburger buns or hard rolls

■ Heat gas grill to medium-high, or prepare charcoal grill with medium-hot coals and set up one side for indirect grilling. Lightly coat grill rack with oil or nonstick cooking spray.

■ In a large bowl, mix turkey, 3 tbsp marinara sauce, the Italian seasoning, garlic salt and onion salt. Form into 6 equal patties. Grill 4 minutes per side or until temperature reaches 160°. Turn off grill.

■ Top each burger with 1 tbsp marinara sauce, 1 tbsp reduced-fat mozzarella and 2 basil leaves. Close grill and wait 5 minutes, until cheese melts. If using charcoal, place burgers over indirect heat. Serve on hamburger buns or hard rolls.

PER SERVING 500 **CAL**; 18 g **FAT** (8 g **SAT**); 27 g **PRO**; 58 g **CARB**; 7 g **SUGARS**; 2 g **FIBER**; 770 mg **SODIUM**

Quick Beef Stir-Fry

MAKES 6 servings **PREP** 5 minutes **COOK** 20 minutes

1½	**cups white rice**
1	**flank steak (about 1¼ lb)**
2	**tbsp oil**
1	**pkg (¾ lb) pepper strips**
1	**pkg (¾ lb) broccoli**
¾	**cup stir-fry sauce**

■ Bring 3 cups water to a boil; stir in rice. Reduce heat; cover and cook 20 minutes. Meanwhile, slice steak across the grain into thin strips, about 3 inches long.

■ In a large skillet, heat oil over medium-high. Add beef and stir-fry 3 minutes. Remove to a platter with a slotted spoon. Stir pepper strips, broccoli and ⅓ cup water into pan. Cover and cook 4 minutes. Uncover and add beef and stir-fry sauce. Cook 1 minute. Serve with rice on the side.

PER SERVING 480 **CAL**; 21 g **FAT** (7 g **SAT**); 32 g **PRO**; 41 g **CARB**; 7 g **SUGARS**; 3 g **FIBER**; 770 mg **SODIUM**

TURKEY PIZZA
BURGERS

FOUR WAYS WITH AVOCADOS

Rich-tasting and creamy, this beautiful green fruit tastes like an indulgence but is loaded with healthful fats.

Gently press the stem end of the avocado— if it gives, the fruit is ready to eat.

Salmon-Avocado Sushi Burrito

MAKES 4 snack servings or 2 lunch servings
PREP 15 minutes

- **2 standard-size nori sheets**
- **1½ cups cooked rice**
- **4 oz smoked salmon**
- **2 oz cold cream cheese (cut into planks from an 8 oz block)**
- **1 avocado, pitted, peeled, and sliced**
- **½ cup English cucumber, cut into matchsticks**

■ Place 1 nori sheet on a piece of plastic wrap. Spread ¾ cup rice to within 1 inch of edges of nori. Place 2 oz salmon slightly to center right, followed by 1 oz cream cheese, ½ of the avocado and ¼ cup cucumber. Roll tightly, using plastic wrap. Slice in half on the bias. Repeat with a second nori sheet and the remaining ingredients. Serve with soy sauce.

PER SERVING 250 **CAL**; 11 g **FAT** (4 g **SAT**); 10 g **PRO**; 27 g **CARB**; 1 g **SUGARS**; 3 g **FIBER**; 240 mg **SODIUM**

Crab, Avocado and Tomato Salad

MAKES 6 servings **PREP** 15 minutes

- **⅓ cup plain Greek yogurt**
- **⅓ cup mayonnaise**
- **3 tbsp fresh lemon juice**
- **1 tsp Old Bay seasoning**
- **2 cans (6 oz each) crabmeat, drained**
- **2 avocados, pitted, peeled and diced**
- **2 ribs celery, chopped**
- **1 cup halved heirloom grape tomatoes**
- **⅓ cup sliced scallions**
- **Butter lettuce**

■ Whisk yogurt, mayonnaise, lemon juice and seasoning until blended. Fold in crabmeat, avocados, celery, tomatoes and scallions. Serve chilled over butter lettuce.

PER SERVING 230 **CAL**; 17 g **FAT** (3 g **SAT**); 13 g **PRO**; 7 g **CARB**; 2 g **SUGARS**; 4 g **FIBER**; 530 mg **SODIUM**

SALMON-AVOCADO SUSHI BURRITO

CRAB, AVOCADO AND TOMATO SALAD

Coconut-Avocado Shake

MAKES 6 servings **PREP** 5 minutes

- **2 avocados, pitted and peeled**
- **4 cups ice**
- **2 cups unsweetened vanilla coconut milk**
- **1½ cups whisked coconut milk**
- **½ cup agave nectar**
- **Toasted coconut**

■ In a blender, combine avocados, ice, vanilla coconut milk, coconut milk and nectar. Serve cold in a tall glass topped with toasted coconut.

PER SERVING 300 **CAL**; 21 g **FAT** (14 g **SAT**); 2 g **PRO**; 28 g **CARB**; 22 g **SUGARS**; 3 g **FIBER**; 60 mg **SODIUM**

Taco-Stuffed Avocados

MAKES 8 servings **PREP** 10 minutes
COOK 5 minutes

- **1 tbsp extra-virgin olive oil**
- **½ lb ground beef**
- **¼ cup finely chopped red onion**
- **2 cloves garlic, chopped**
- **2 tsp chili powder**
- **½ tsp ground cumin**
- **¼ tsp salt**
- **1 vine tomato, diced**
- **½ cup chopped fresh cilantro**
- **4 avocados, halved, pitted and peeled**
- **Sour cream, shredded Mexican cheese and cilantro for topping**

■ In a skillet, heat olive oil over medium-high. Stir in ground beef, onion, garlic, chili powder, cumin and salt. Cook 5 minutes. Stir in tomato and cilantro. Scoop into avocado halves. Top with sour cream, cheese and additional cilantro.

PER SERVING 210 **CAL**; 17 g **FAT** (4 g **SAT**); 8 g **PRO**; 8 g **CARB**; 1 g **SUGARS**; 5 g **FIBER**; 140 mg **SODIUM**

TACO-STUFFED AVOCADOS

COCONUT-AVOCADO SHAKE

Speed up ripening by placing avocados in a closed paper bag at room temp. Slow it down in the fridge, where they'll last for several days.

MEXICAN ELOTE
SALAD WITH SHRIMP,
PAGE 144

JUNE

137

143

151

CHEF'S TABLE

Aussie celebrity chef Curtis Stone lays out a big, bold backyard bash with shrimp, rib eyes, grilled veggies and more.

BYRON BAY SALAD

Byron Bay Salad

MAKES 8 servings **PREP** 30 minutes

- ⅔ **cup olive oil**
- ½ **cup lime juice**
- 2½ **tbsp minced shallots**
- 1 **tbsp lime zest**
- ⅛ **tsp plus ¼ tsp fine sea salt**
- 3 **cups cooked medium-grain brown rice, at room temperature**
- 3 **cups baby arugula**
- 4 **radishes, thinly sliced**
- 2 **ribs celery, thinly sliced diagonally**
- 2 **small zucchini (about 8 oz), julienned**
- 2 **small avocados, pitted and sliced**
- 1 **yellow tomato, cut into thin wedges**
- ½ **cup thinly sliced scallions**
- ½ **cup sprouts (optional)**
- ½ **cup fresh cilantro leaves**
- ½ **cup whole almonds, toasted and coarsely chopped**
- ¼ **cup shelled roasted pumpkin seeds**
- ¼ **cup shelled roasted sunflower seeds**

■ In a small bowl, whisk first 4 ingredients. Season with ⅛ tsp salt.

■ Divide rice between 2 platters. Top with next 7 ingredients and sprouts, if using, distributing evenly between platters. Drizzle vinaigrette over salad. Sprinkle with cilantro, almonds and seeds. Season each platter with ¼ tsp salt and serve immediately.

PER SERVING 395 **CAL**; 30 g **FAT** (4 g **SAT**); 6 g **PRO**; 30 g **CARB**; 2 g **SUGARS**; 6 g **FIBER**; 36 mg **SODIUM**

SHRIMP WITH GAZPACHO COCKTAIL SAUCE

Shrimp with Gazpacho Cocktail Sauce

MAKES 8 servings **PREP** 15 minutes **COOK** 6 minutes **REFRIGERATE** 1 hour

- 1 **slice ciabatta bread (about 2 oz)**
- 1¼ **lb small vine-ripened tomatoes, coarsely chopped**
- 2 **garlic cloves**
- 1 **jalapeño, seeded and coarsely chopped**
- 1 **large shallot, coarsely chopped**
- ½ **sweet red pepper, coarsely chopped**
- ⅓ **cup extra-virgin olive oil, plus more for serving**
- ⅓ **cup lemon juice, plus more to taste**
- 2 **pieces lemon peel, removed with a vegetable peeler**
- 2 **pale inner celery ribs with leaves, ribs finely chopped, leaves reserved for garnish**
- **Salt**
- 24 **cooked large shrimp (about 1¼ lb), peeled**
- **Sea salt flakes**
- **Freshly ground black pepper**

■ Heat a medium frying pan over medium-high. Add bread, cut side down, and toast 6 minutes, until charred. Tear into pieces.

■ In a blender, combine bread pieces and next 8 ingredients (through lemon peel) and half the chopped celery until smooth and thick. Season with salt and more lemon juice to taste. Strain through a fine-mesh sieve. Cover and refrigerate 1 hour.

■ Spoon about ⅓ cup sauce into each of 8 shallow bowls. Place 3 shrimp in each. Drizzle with oil and sprinkle with remaining chopped celery, the celery leaves, sea salt and black pepper.

PER SERVING 153 **CAL**; 10 g **FAT** (1 g **SAT**); 6 g **PRO**; 13 g **CARB**; 5 g **SUGARS**; 2 g **FIBER**; 352 mg **SODIUM**

STRAWBERRY-HIBISCUS PUNCH

PICKLED ONIONS AND MUSTARD SEEDS

Not only does hibiscus produce a beautiful red, nicely tart tea, but it's loaded with antioxidant vitamins A and C. Here, it's sweetened with sugar and flavored with strawberries and ginger.

Strawberry-Hibiscus Punch

MAKES 6 to 8 servings **PREP** 5 minutes
COOK 2 minutes **STEEP** 2 hours

- **1 cup sugar**
- **6 hibiscus tea bags**
- **8 oz fresh strawberries, hulled and sliced, plus more for garnish**
- **1 2-inch piece ginger, thinly sliced**

■ In a large saucepan, combine sugar with 4 cups water. Bring to a simmer over medium-high, stirring until sugar is dissolved, about 2 minutes.

■ Remove pan from heat and add tea bags, strawberries and ginger. Steep about 2 hours.

■ Strain liquid into a bowl and add 2 to 4 cups filtered water for desired level of sweetness. Serve over ice and garnish with strawberries.

PER SERVING 133 **CAL**; 0 g **FAT** (0 g **SAT**); 1 g **PRO**; 33 g **CARB**; 27 g **SUGARS**; 1 g **FIBER**; 3 mg **SODIUM**

Pickled Onions and Mustard Seeds

MAKES 2 cups **PREP** 10 minutes
COOK 30 minutes **REFRIGERATE** 12 hours

- **1 cup Champagne vinegar or white wine vinegar**
- **½ cup water**
- **2 tbsp granulated sugar**
- **1 tsp kosher salt**
- **2 sprigs fresh tarragon**
- **2 sprigs fresh thyme**
- **¼ cup yellow mustard seeds**
- **10 oz red or white pearl onions, peeled**

■ In a heavy saucepan, combine first 6 ingredients (through thyme) and bring to a boil over high. Add mustard seeds, reduce heat to medium and simmer about 30 minutes, until mustard seeds are plump. Transfer to a bowl.

■ Meanwhile, in a large pot of salted boiling water, add onions and cook about 5 minutes, until just tender. Transfer onions to an ice bath. Drain well and cut in half, separating each layer into petals. Transfer onions to mustard seed mixture. Cover loosely and refrigerate at least 12 hours before using.

PER ¼ CUP 56 **CAL**; 1 g **FAT** (0 g **SAT**); 1 g **PRO**; 11 g **CARB**; 5 g **SUGARS**; 0 g **FIBER**; 247 mg **SODIUM**

Charcoal Grilled
Rib-Eye Steaks

MAKES 6 servings **PREP** 2 minutes
COOK 35 minutes **REST** 10 minutes

- **2 bone-in rib-eye steaks (1½ lb each, about 2 inches thick, cap attached)**
  Olive oil
  Kosher salt
  Freshly ground black pepper
  Pickled Onions and Mustard Seeds (recipe, page 139)

■ Prepare grill for indirect high heat. For charcoal: Fill chimney starter with hardwood lump charcoal and ignite. When coals are covered with white ash, dump them in an even layer on one half of grill, leaving other half empty. Place grill grate in position and preheat for 5 minutes. For gas: Preheat all burners to high. Before grilling, turn off half the burners.

■ Pat steaks dry with paper towels. Lightly coat each steak with oil and season liberally with salt (about 1½ tsp) and pepper (about 1 tsp). Place steaks on unlit side of grill and cover. Cook, turning halfway through, 30 to 35 minutes, or until steaks reach 130° in center. Let rest 10 minutes. Internal temp will increase to 135°.

■ Cut meat from bone and separate eye (center) from outer piece of meat by cutting through the fat that separates them. Carve each piece against the grain. Serve with any resting juices and Pickled Onions and Mustard Seeds.

PER SERVING 482 **CAL**; 38 g **FAT** (15 g **SAT**); 33 g **PRO**; 0 g **CARB**; 0 g **SUGARS**; 0 g **FIBER**; 673 mg **SODIUM**

Grilled Flatbreads with
Garlic-Rosemary Oil

MAKES 8 servings **PREP** 15 minutes
COOK 10 minutes **RISE** 45 minutes
GRILL 4 minutes per batch

GARLIC-ROSEMARY OIL

- ⅔ **cup extra-virgin olive oil**
- 1 **garlic clove, finely chopped**
- 1 **shallot, finely chopped**
- 1 **fresh rosemary sprig**
  Kosher salt

Freshly ground black pepper

FLATBREADS

- 1 **cup warm water (110° to 115°)**
- 2¼ **tsp active dry yeast**
- 2 **tsp sugar**
- 2⅔ **cups all-purpose flour, plus more for dusting**
- 2 **tsp kosher salt**

■ **Garlic-Rosemary Oil.** In a small saucepan, combine first 4 ingredients and heat over low about 10 minutes, until fragrant. Remove pan from heat, and season with salt and pepper to taste.

■ **Flatbreads.** In a small bowl, stir first 3 ingredients to blend. Let stand 5 minutes, until foamy.

■ In a food processor, combine flour and salt, and process to blend. With machine running, add yeast mixture and 1 tbsp garlic-rosemary oil, and process just until dough comes together. Transfer dough to a work surface, and knead until smooth and elastic.

■ Divide dough into 8 pieces (about 3 oz each) and shape into balls. Place on an oiled baking sheet, and rub lightly with some garlic-rosemary oil. Cover with a piece of oiled plastic wrap, and let rise in a warm, draft-free spot for about 45 minutes, until doubled in size.

■ Prepare a grill for medium-high heat. Lightly oil grill grates.

■ Using a rolling pin, roll each dough ball out on a floured work surface into a thin 11 x 5-inch oval (the shape does not have to be perfect). Set flatbreads aside on oiled baking sheets.

■ Working in batches, brush flatbreads with garlic-rosemary oil and lay them on grill grate. Grill 1½ to 2 minutes per side, until grill marks form and flatbreads are cooked through. Wrap in a clean kitchen towel to keep warm.

■ To serve, brush flatbreads with more garlic-rosemary oil, if desired. Serve with any remaining oil for dipping.

PER SERVING 238 **CAL**; 9 g **FAT** (1 g **SAT**); 5 g **PRO**; 33 g **CARB**; 1 g **SUGARS**; 1 g **FIBER**; 482 mg **SODIUM**

Grilled Eggplant with
Mint Vinaigrette

MAKES 4 servings **PREP** 20 minutes
STAND 30 minutes **COOK** 20 minutes

- 2 **eggplants (1 lb each), cut crosswise into ½-inch-thick slices**
  Kosher salt
- 8 **tbsp extra-virgin olive oil**
  Freshly ground black pepper
- 1 **lemon, zested and juiced**
- 2 **tbsp white wine vinegar**
- ¼ **cup finely chopped shallots**
- 1 **tbsp finely chopped fresh mint, plus small leaves for garnish**
- 1 **small square feta cheese**

■ Lay eggplant slices in a single layer on 2 baking sheets and sprinkle both sides with salt. Let stand 30 minutes, until moisture beads on top of eggplant. Prepare grill for medium-high heat.

■ Rinse eggplant to remove excess salt and pat dry. Brush slices with 3 tbsp oil, coating both sides. Season with salt and pepper. Working in batches, grill eggplant for about 5 minutes per side, or until char marks form and eggplant is very tender. Transfer to a platter as you finish each batch.

■ Meanwhile, in a bowl, combine lemon zest and 2 tbsp lemon juice. Whisk in vinegar, shallots, mint and 5 tbsp oil. Season to taste. Spoon vinaigrette over eggplant and sprinkle with mint leaves. Shave thin slices of feta over eggplant.

PER SERVING 333 **CAL**; 30 g **FAT** (5 g **SAT**); 5 g **PRO**; 16 g **CARB**; 8 g **SUGARS**; 7 g **FIBER**; 182 mg **SODIUM**

GRILLED EGGPLANT WITH MINT VINAIGRETTE

GRILLED FLATBREADS WITH GARLIC-ROSEMARY OIL

CHARCOAL GRILLED RIB-EYE STEAKS

CHARRED AND CHOPPED

Grilling takes salads to the next level.

MOROCCAN
CHOPPED SALAD

Moroccan Chopped Salad

MAKES 4 servings PREP 20 minutes
GRILL 10 minutes

- 5 tbsp extra-virgin olive oil
- 3 tbsp lemon juice
- 1 tsp lemon zest
- 2 tbsp honey
- 1 tbsp ras el hanout (Moroccan spice blend)
- 1 tsp salt
- ¼ to ½ tsp red pepper flakes
- 2 small Italian eggplants, cut into ¾-inch planks
- 2 medium zucchini, cut into ¾-inch planks
- 2 sweet red peppers
- ½ cup chopped parsley
- ½ cup golden raisins
- ⅓ cup sliced almonds, toasted
- Pita slices

■ Heat grill to medium-high. In a bowl, whisk 3 tbsp oil, the lemon juice and zest, honey, 1 tsp ras el hanout, ¼ tsp salt and the red pepper flakes.

■ Toss eggplant, zucchini and sweet peppers with 2 tbsp oil, 2 tsp ras el hanout and ½ tsp salt. Grill eggplant 4 to 5 minutes per side and zucchini 3 minutes per side. Grill peppers 2 minutes per side, rotating 3 times, for a total of 8 minutes. Chop eggplant and zucchini into 1-inch pieces. Stem and core peppers, then slice into 1-inch pieces.

■ Toss veggies with parsley, raisins, almonds, dressing and ¼ tsp salt. Serve with pita slices.

PER SERVING 260 CAL; 22 g FAT (3 g SAT); 6 g PRO; 41 g CARB; 32 g SUGARS; 8 g FIBER; 610 mg SODIUM

GRILLED TUSCAN SALAD

Grilled Tuscan Salad

MAKES 4 servings PREP 20 minutes GRILL 6 minutes

- 2 tbsp white wine vinegar
- 2 tbsp lemon juice
- ¼ cup plus 2 tbsp extra-virgin olive oil
- 1 tbsp honey
- ¾ tsp salt
- ½ tsp black pepper
- 2 small heads radicchio, quartered
- 1 large bunch (12 oz) Tuscan kale
- 3 cups halved cherry tomatoes
- 1 can (15 oz) cannellini beans, rinsed and drained
- 1 cup torn fresh basil
- 4 oz truffle or plain burrata (such as BelGioioso; from an 8 oz pkg)

■ Heat grill to medium-high. In a bowl, whisk vinegar, lemon juice, ¼ cup oil, the honey, ½ tsp salt and ¼ tsp pepper.

■ Toss quartered radicchio and kale leaves in 2 tbsp oil. Grill radicchio 2 minutes, turning twice, for a total of 6 minutes. Grill kale 1 to 2 minutes per side. Core and chop radicchio. Remove and discard stems from kale; chop.

■ Toss radicchio and kale with tomatoes, beans, basil, dressing and ¼ tsp each salt and pepper. Serve topped with burrata.

PER SERVING 430 CAL; 27 g FAT (7 g SAT); 15 g PRO; 34 g CARB; 9 g SUGARS; 8 g FIBER; 830 mg SODIUM

GRILLED ROMAINE STEAKHOUSE CAESAR

Mexican Elote Salad with Shrimp

Pictured on page 134.

MAKES 4 servings **PREP** 15 minutes
GRILL 12 minutes

⅓	**cup sour cream**
2	**tbsp lime juice**
1	**tsp lime zest**
¼	**tsp plus ⅛ tsp salt**
¼	**tsp cayenne pepper**
6	**ears corn, husked**
2	**poblano peppers**
2	**tbsp extra-virgin olive oil**
1	**lb peeled and deveined shrimp**
4	**scallions, chopped**
⅔	**cup chopped fresh cilantro, plus more for serving**
¼	**cup crumbled Cotija cheese, plus more for serving**

■ Heat grill to medium-high. In a bowl, whisk sour cream, lime juice and zest, ⅛ tsp salt and ⅛ tsp cayenne.

■ Rub corn and peppers with 1 tbsp oil. Grill 2 minutes and rotate, repeating 3 times, for a total of 8 minutes. Remove peppers and place in a bowl covered with plastic wrap for 5 minutes. Remove skin from peppers, core, seed and dice. Let corn cool slightly, then remove kernels with a knife.

■ Toss shrimp in 1 tbsp oil and ⅛ tsp cayenne. Thread onto 4 skewers. Grill 2 minutes per side.

■ In a large bowl, toss corn kernels, diced peppers, scallions, cilantro, Cotija and ¼ tsp salt. Serve with shrimp skewers, drizzle with dressing and scatter more cilantro and Cotija on top.

PER SERVING 270 **CAL**; 14 g **FAT** (5 g **SAT**);
23 g **PRO**; 11 g **CARB**; 4 g **SUGARS**; 2 g **FIBER**;
1,000 mg **SODIUM**

Grilled Romaine Steakhouse Caesar

MAKES 6 servings **PREP** 15 minutes **GRILL** 20 minutes **REST** 5 minutes

5	**tbsp extra-virgin olive oil**
1	**pasteurized egg yolk**
2	**tbsp lemon juice**
¼	**cup grated Parmesan**
2	**anchovy fillets, minced***
1	**clove garlic, grated**
½	**tsp Dijon mustard**
¾	**tsp salt**
½	**tsp black pepper**
8	**oz ciabatta bread, sliced lengthwise**
2	**strip steaks (10 to 12 oz each)***
6	**romaine hearts**

■ Heat grill to medium-high. Whisk 4 tbsp oil, egg yolk, lemon juice, 2 tbsp Parmesan, anchovies, garlic, mustard, ¼ tsp salt and ¼ tsp pepper until well blended.

■ Brush 1 tbsp oil on ciabatta and grill 2 minutes per side; cut into cubes. Season steaks with ½ tsp salt and ¼ tsp pepper. Grill 5 to 6 minutes per side or until steaks are medium-rare. Let rest 5 minutes.

■ While steak is resting, grill romaine 1 minute per side, turning 3 times, for a total of 4 minutes.

■ Scatter ciabatta croutons over romaine and drizzle with dressing. Serve with sliced steak.

*Tip Don't want to open an entire tin of anchovies? Use the paste—it lasts in the fridge for months.

PER SERVING 420 **CAL**; 28 g **FAT** (9 g **SAT**);
23 g **PRO**; 17 g **CARB**; 0 g **SUGARS**; 0 g **FIBER**;
640 mg **SODIUM**

Tataki is a Japanese cooking style in which fish or meat is quickly seared.

Tuna Tataki Bowl

MAKES 4 servings **PREP** 10 minutes
COOK 15 minutes **GRILL** 4 minutes

- 1 **cup uncooked red quinoa**
- ¼ **cup dried seaweed (wakame)**
- ½ **cup light mayonnaise**
- 2 **tbsp sriracha sauce**
- 1 **tbsp toasted sesame oil**
- 1 **tsp rice vinegar**
- 1 **lb tuna steaks**
- ½ **tsp salt**
- 1 **avocado, peeled, pitted and halved**
- 1 **cup shredded carrots**
- ½ **small cucumber, cut into matchsticks**
- 4 **tsp toasted sesame seeds**

■ Heat grill to medium-high. In a small pot, combine quinoa with 2 cups water. Bring to a boil. Reduce heat and simmer 15 minutes, until cooked. Remove from heat.

■ Place seaweed in a bowl and cover with 2 inches water. Let stand at least 5 minutes, until using.

■ In another bowl, whisk mayonnaise, sriracha, 1 tbsp water, 1 tsp sesame oil and the vinegar until smooth.

■ Rub tuna with 2 tsp sesame oil and season with ¼ tsp salt. Grill 1 to 2 minutes per side, just to sear. Grill avocado 2 minutes per side. Slice tuna and avocado.

■ Fluff quinoa with a fork and season with ¼ tsp salt. Divide evenly among 4 bowls, followed by tuna, avocado, seaweed, carrots, cucumber and sesame seeds. Drizzle with dressing.

PER SERVING 530 **CAL**; 26 g **FAT** (4 g **SAT**); 35 g **PRO**; 40 g **CARB**; 8 g **SUGARS**; 8 g **FIBER**; 930 mg **SODIUM**

TUNA TATAKI BOWL

HEALTHY FAMILY DINNERS

Try these 6 easy recipes on crazy-busy nights.

**MEGA OMEGA
FARFALLE**

Fatty fish—such as salmon—is one of the most concentrated sources of heart-healthy omega-3s.

Mega Omega Farfalle

MAKES 6 servings **PREP** 20 minutes
COOK 11 minutes **GRILL** 9 minutes

- 1 **lb salmon fillet**
- 1 **tsp salt**
- ½ **tsp black pepper**
- 1 **cup fresh basil leaves**
- ½ **cup pumpkin seeds (pepitas)**
- ¼ **cup grated Parmesan**
- 1 **clove garlic**
- 3 **tbsp olive oil**
- 2 **tbsp warm water**
- 1 **lb farfalle pasta**
- 1 **bunch asparagus, trimmed**

■ Heat grill or grill pan to medium-high. Bring a large pot of salted water to a boil. Season salmon with ¼ tsp each salt and pepper.

■ Combine ½ tsp salt, ¼ tsp pepper, the basil and next 3 ingredients in a food processor; process until finely chopped. With machine running, gradually add oil and water. Continue to blend until smooth.

■ Add pasta to boiling water; cook 11 minutes and drain, reserving 1 cup cooking water. Meanwhile, grill salmon 9 minutes, turning once, and asparagus 5 minutes, turning often.

■ Place pasta in a large bowl. Cut asparagus into 2-inch pieces and add to pasta. Flake salmon with a fork (discard skin) and toss with pasta along with pesto, ¼ tsp salt and reserved pasta water. Serve warm.

PER SERVING 568 **CAL**; 20 g **FAT** (4 g **SAT**); 34 g **PRO**; 60 g **CARB**; 2 g **SUGARS**; 5 g **FIBER**; 510 mg **SODIUM**

CRISPY KOREAN TOFU

Crispy Korean Tofu

MAKES 4 servings **PREP** 20 minutes **COOK** 15 minutes

- 1 **pkg (5 oz) baby arugula or mixed greens**
- 1 **cup shredded carrots**
- ½ **seedless cucumber, thinly sliced into half-moons**
- 1 **pkg (14 oz) extra-firm tofu**
- ¾ **tsp salt**
- ½ **cup cornstarch**
- 4 **tbsp canola oil**
- 2 **portobello mushroom caps, cut in half and sliced**
- 3 **cups cooked brown rice**
- ¼ **cup rice vinegar**
- 2 **tbsp gochujang (such as Annie Chun's Korean Sweet & Spicy Sauce)**
- ½ **cup mung bean sprouts**

■ On a large platter or in a large salad bowl, combine first 3 ingredients.

■ Drain tofu and pat dry. Cut into 1-inch cubes, toss with ½ tsp salt and coat with cornstarch.

■ Heat 2 tbsp oil in a large stainless skillet over high. Add half the tofu and stir-fry, turning frequently, 5 minutes. Transfer to paper towels and add 2 tbsp oil to pan. Add remaining tofu and stir-fry 5 minutes. Remove to paper towels and reduce heat in pan to medium.

■ Add mushrooms to pan and cook, stirring, 3 minutes. Stir in rice. In a small bowl, whisk vinegar and gochujang. Add to pan; cook 2 minutes. Toss mushroom mixture with salad and ¼ tsp salt. Top with tofu and bean sprouts.

PER SERVING 530 **CAL**; 21 g **FAT** (2 g **SAT**); 18 g **PRO**; 67 g **CARB**; 7 g **SUGARS**; 7 g **FIBER**; 799 mg **SODIUM**

BBQ PORK AND APPLE SLAW

Gyro, My Hero

MAKES 6 servings **PREP** 25 minutes
BROIL 8 minutes

6	whole wheat pitas or soft round flatbreads
1	summer squash (6 oz)
½	English cucumber
1	lb ground lamb or beef
¾	cup crumbled feta cheese
3	tbsp chopped fresh mint
1	tsp onion powder
1½	tsp garlic powder
½	tsp each salt and black pepper
1	container (7 oz) 2% Greek yogurt
2	tbsp fresh lemon juice
2	cups shredded lettuce
	Cooked rice (optional)

■ Heat broiler. Wrap pitas in foil and place in oven to warm while making meatballs.

■ Using the large-hole side of a box grater, shred squash into a large bowl. Rinse grater and shred cucumber into a medium bowl. To squash, add ground meat, ¼ cup plus 2 tbsp feta, 2 tbsp mint, the onion powder, 1 tsp garlic powder and ¼ tsp each salt and pepper. Shape into 36 meatballs, (about 1 level tbsp mixture for each), and place on a broiler rack or on a rack fitted into a large rimmed sheet pan.

■ Broil meatballs 3 inches from heat for 8 minutes or until cooked through. Meanwhile, blend yogurt, 1 tbsp mint, the lemon juice, ½ tsp garlic powder and ¼ tsp each salt and pepper into grated cucumber.

■ To assemble gyros, layer ⅓ cup lettuce, 6 meatballs, some sauce and 1 tbsp crumbled feta onto each piece of bread. Serve with rice, if desired.

PER SERVING 367 **CAL**; 16 g **FAT** (7 g **SAT**); 26 g **PRO**; 31 g **CARB**; 5 g **SUGARS**; 5 g **FIBER**; 649 mg **SODIUM**

BBQ Pork and Apple Slaw

MAKES 4 servings **PREP** 15 minutes **BAKE** at 450° for 25 minutes

1	pork tenderloin (1¼ lb)
½	cup bottled barbecue sauce
1	large Granny Smith apple, cored and cut into matchsticks
2	ribs celery, cut into matchsticks
¾	cup grated carrots
⅓	cup light mayonnaise
2	tbsp cider vinegar
2	tsp Dijon mustard
¼	tsp salt
¼	tsp black pepper
	Small pieces of Quick Cornbread (recipe follows) or rolls

■ Heat oven to 450°. Place pork on a small foil-lined rimmed baking sheet and spoon 3 tbsp barbecue sauce on top. Bake 15 minutes.

■ In a medium bowl, toss apple, celery and carrots. In a small bowl, whisk mayo and next 4 ingredients. Add to apple mixture and toss to combine.

■ Spoon remaining barbecue sauce over pork and bake 5 to 10 more minutes, until temperature reaches 145°. Slice pork and serve with apple slaw and cornbread or rolls.

Quick Cornbread Combine 1 box (8½ oz) cornbread mix, ⅓ cup milk and 1 large egg in a bowl. If desired, stir in 3 slices chopped cooked bacon. Spread into an 8-inch square pan and bake at 400° for 15 to 20 minutes.

PER SERVING 449 **CAL**; 15 g **FAT** (3 g **SAT**); 32 g **PRO**; 45 g **CARB**; 24 g **SUGARS**; 5 g **FIBER**; 786 mg **SODIUM**

GYRO, MY
HERO

STREET CART
TACOS

Street Cart Tacos

MAKES 4 servings **PREP** 20 minutes
GRILL 15 minutes

- 3 cups diced fresh pineapple
- ½ cup minced red onion
- 1 tbsp minced jalapeño
- 2 tbsp fresh lime juice
- 1 tsp olive oil
- ¼ tsp each salt and pepper
- 2 tsp ancho chile powder
- ½ tsp ground cumin
- 1 lb boneless, skinless chicken breasts
- ¾ lb skirt steak
- 2 sweet red peppers, cut into planks
- 12 flour tortillas
- 1 avocado, pitted and sliced
- 4 radishes, thinly sliced
- Crumbled queso fresco, fresh cilantro leaves, lime wedges and hot sauce, for serving

■ Heat grill or grill pan to medium-high. In a medium bowl, combine first 3 ingredients. Drizzle with 1 tbsp lime juice and the olive oil. Season with ⅛ tsp each salt and pepper.

■ Mix ⅛ tsp each salt and pepper with the chile powder and cumin. Rub on chicken and steak. Drizzle with 1 tbsp lime juice.

■ Grill pepper planks and chicken for 12 to 15 minutes and steak for 8 to 10 minutes, turning halfway through. Remove from grill and let rest 5 minutes. Meanwhile, lightly char tortillas on grill. Slice pepper, chicken and steak into strips and arrange on a platter. Serve with warm tortillas, pineapple salsa, avocado, radishes, queso fresco, cilantro, lime wedges and hot sauce for make-your-own tacos.

PER SERVING 535 **CAL**; 20 g **FAT** (6 g **SAT**); 39 g **PRO**; 49 g **CARB**; 9 g **SUGARS**; 5 g **FIBER**; 817 mg **SODIUM**

CHARRED CITRUS CHICKEN

Charred Citrus Chicken

MAKES 4 servings **PREP** 15 minutes **MARINATE** 20 minutes **COOK** 15 minutes **GRILL** 25 minutes

- 4 whole chicken legs (2 lb)
- 2 navel oranges
- ¾ tsp salt
- ½ tsp black pepper
- 2 red grapefruit
- 4 scallions, sliced
- 2 cups water
- 1 cup quick-cook wheat berries
- 2 tbsp olive oil
- 3 tbsp chopped fresh parsley or cilantro

■ Place chicken in a resealable bag. Add juice of 1 orange and ¼ tsp each salt and pepper. Marinate 20 minutes in the fridge.

■ Heat grill to medium-high for indirect grilling. (For charcoal, stack coals to one side, leaving other side empty. For gas, leave one burner off.)

■ Peel and cut sections from 1 orange and 1 grapefruit; dice. Cut second grapefruit in half and juice one half. Save second half for another use. Toss fruit with ¼ tsp salt and half the scallions.

■ Place chicken on hot side of grill. Cover and grill 5 minutes. Flip over and grill 5 minutes, then move to cooler side of grill and cook 10 to 15 more minutes, until chicken reaches 165°.

■ Meanwhile, combine water and wheat berries in a lidded pot. Bring to a boil. Reduce heat, cover and simmer 15 minutes, until tender. Drain and toss with reserved grapefruit juice, the olive oil, ¼ tsp each salt and pepper, remaining scallions and the parsley. Top chicken with fruit and serve wheat berries alongside.

PER SERVING 556 **CAL**; 20 g **FAT** (4 g **SAT**); 34 g **PRO**; 65 g **CARB**; 20 g **SUGARS**; 16 g **FIBER**; 649 mg **SODIUM**

PINEAPPLE
UPSIDE-DOWN CAKE,
PAGE 165

JULY

156

164

169

BURGER KINGS

We're taking the summer staple up a notch.

Half-and-Half Burger

MAKES 4 servings **PREP** 10 minutes
GRILL 10 minutes

- 1 **lb ground beef**
- 1 **clove garlic, grated**
- 1 **jar pesto**
- ½ **tsp salt**
- ¼ **tsp black pepper**
- 4 **medium portobello mushrooms**
- 1 **tbsp extra-virgin olive oil**
- 4 **slices (1 oz each) smoked mozzarella**
- 4 **seeded buns**
- 1 **tomato, sliced**

■ Heat grill to medium-high. Combine ground beef, garlic, 2 tbsp pesto, ¼ tsp salt and pepper. Form into 4 patties.

■ Remove and discard gills from portobello mushrooms. Brush with oil and season with ¼ tsp salt.

■ Grill burgers and mushrooms 4 to 5 minutes, flip and add 1 cheese slice to each burger. Grill another 4 to 5 minutes for medium-rare (135°). Stack mushrooms on top of cheeseburgers and place on bottom halves of buns. Add 1 slice tomato, 1 tbsp pesto and a bun top to each burger.

PER SERVING 570 **CAL**; 31 g **FAT** (10 g **SAT**); 31 g **PRO**; 35 g **CARB**; 8 g **SUGARS**; 2 g **FIBER**; 970 mg **SODIUM**

HALF-AND-HALF BURGER

MILLION-DOLLAR BURGER

Million-Dollar Burger

MAKES 4 servings **PREP** 15 minutes **REFRIGERATE** 30 minutes **GRILL** 12 minutes

- ¼ cup mayonnaise
- 1 small clove garlic, grated
- ¾ tsp truffle oil
- ⅛ tsp black pepper
- 4 oz truffle goat cheese
- 2 tsp heavy cream
- 1 lb ground chicken breast
- 1 egg
- 1 tsp grated shallot
- 1 tsp truffle oil
- ½ tsp salt
- ¼ tsp black pepper
- 4 brioche buns
- 1 cup arugula
- ¾ tsp extra-virgin olive oil
- ¼ tsp truffle oil

■ In a small bowl, combine mayonnaise, garlic, ¾ tsp. truffle oil and ⅛ tsp pepper.

■ In a separate bowl, beat truffle goat cheese and heavy cream until spreadable.

■ In a large bowl, combine ground chicken, egg, shallot, 1 tsp truffle oil, the salt and ¼ tsp pepper until well blended. Form into 4 patties and place on a baking sheet lined with plastic wrap. Refrigerate 30 minutes.

■ Heat grill to medium. Grill burgers 6 minutes per side, until cooked through (165°). Meanwhile, split buns and, during last minute, grill cut sides down. Place burgers on bottom bun halves, then add truffle mayo.

■ Toss arugula with extra-virgin olive oil and ¼ tsp truffle oil; add to burger. Spread goat cheese on cut sides of bun tops, then add to burgers.

PER SERVING 480 **CAL**; 19 g **FAT** (8 g **SAT**); 35 g **PRO**; 45 g **CARB**; 6 g **SUGARS**; 0 g **FIBER**; 880 mg **SODIUM**

Angry Bison Burger

MAKES 4 servings **PREP** 10 minutes
COOK 20 minutes **GRILL** 8 minutes

- 2 tbsp unsalted butter
- 1 large yellow onion, sliced
- ¼ tsp salt
- 1 lb ground bison or grass-fed beef
- 1 can (4 oz) diced hot Hatch chiles
- ⅓ cup chopped fresh cilantro
- 2 tbsp sliced scallions
- ½ tsp salt
- 4 slices (1 oz each) pepper Jack cheese
- 4 whole wheat buns
  Tomatillo salsa

■ Add butter to a skillet over medium-low. Add onion and cook 20 minutes, stirring frequently, until onions begin to caramelize. Season with ¼ tsp salt and cover.

■ Heat grill to medium-high. In a bowl, combine ground bison, Hatch chiles, cilantro, scallions and the ½ tsp salt. Form into 4 patties. Grill 4 minutes, flip and add 1 cheese slice to each burger. Grill another 4 minutes for medium-rare (135°).

■ Serve on buns with caramelized onions and tomatillo salsa.

PER SERVING 470 **CAL**; 21 g **FAT** (11 g **SAT**); 40 g **PRO**; 31 g **CARB**; 6 g **SUGARS**; 1 g **FIBER**; 970 mg **SODIUM**

ANGRY BISON BURGER

THAI SHRIMP BURGER

Thai Shrimp Burger

MAKES 4 servings **PREP** 15 minutes
REFRIGERATE 1 hour **GRILL** 12 minutes

- 1 **lb raw shrimp, peeled and deveined**
- ½ **cup panko bread crumbs**
- ½ **cup fresh basil leaves**
- ½ **cup fresh cilantro leaves**
- ½ **cup grated carrot**
- 2 **tbsp brown sugar**
- 1 **tbsp fish sauce**
- 1 **tbsp lime juice**
- ¼ **cup mayonnaise**
- 1 **tbsp sriracha sauce**
- 4 **split rolls**
  Carrot cut into ribbons, basil, cilantro

■ In a food processor, combine shrimp, panko, basil, cilantro, grated carrot, brown sugar, fish sauce and lime juice. Process until blended and form into 4 patties. Place on a baking sheet lined with plastic wrap. Refrigerate at least 1 hour.

■ Heat grill to medium. In a small bowl, whisk mayonnaise and sriracha. (Or serve with jarred sriracha mayo.) Grill burgers 6 minutes per side, until cooked through. Serve on rolls with sriracha mayo, carrots (cut into ribbons with a vegetable peeler), basil and cilantro.

PER SERVING 400 **CAL**; 13 g **FAT** (2 g **SAT**); 19 g **PRO**; 49 g **CARB**; 10 g **SUGARS**; 1 g **FIBER**; 1,230 mg **SODIUM**

Breakfast Burger

MAKES 4 servings **PREP** 10 minutes **GRILL** 10 minutes **COOK** 2 minutes

- ¾ **lb ground pork**
- 4 **oz diced smoked bacon**
- ¼ **tsp salt**
- ½ **tsp black pepper**
- 4 **slices American cheese**
- 4 **English muffins**
- 4 **eggs**
- 1 **tbsp extra-virgin olive oil**
- ⅛ **tsp salt**
- ⅛ **tsp black pepper**

■ Heat grill to medium. Combine pork, bacon, ¼ tsp salt and ½ tsp pepper until well blended. Form into 4 patties.

■ Grill 5 minutes, flip, add a slice of cheese to each burger and grill 5 more minutes, until cooked (145°).

■ Meanwhile, slice English muffins in half and, during last minute, grill cut sides down. Remove burgers and muffins from grill and cover loosely with foil.

■ Fry eggs in extra-virgin olive oil over medium-high for 2 minutes. Season with ⅛ tsp each salt and pepper. Place each burger on a muffin half, then add egg and top muffin half.

PER SERVING 520 **CAL**; 31 g **FAT** (11 g **SAT**); 36 g **PRO**; 27 g **CARB**; 2 g **SUGARS**; 0 g **FIBER**; 1,040 mg **SODIUM**

BREAKFAST BURGER

LAMB AND HUMMUS BURGER

Lamb and Hummus Burger

MAKES 4 servings **PREP** 15 minutes
GRILL 10 minutes

- ½ **cup plain Greek yogurt**
- ½ **cup crumbled feta**
- 2 **tbsp milk**
- 2 **tbsp grated cucumber**
- 4 **tbsp chopped fresh parsley**
- ⅛ **tsp salt**
- ⅛ **tsp black pepper**
- 1 **lb ground lamb**
- 2 **tbsp grated red onion**
- 1½ **tsp ras el hanout (Moroccan spice blend)**
- ½ **tsp salt**
- 4 **medium pitas**
- 2 **tbsp hummus**
    Sliced cucumber, red onion, parsley

■ Heat grill to medium-high. In a small bowl, combine yogurt, feta, milk, and grated cucumber, 1 tbsp chopped parsley, ⅛ tsp salt and the black pepper.

■ In a large bowl, combine ground lamb, 3 tbsp chopped parsley, the grated red onion, ras el hanout and ½ tsp salt. Form into 4 patties.

■ Grill 4 to 5 minutes per side for medium-rare (135°). During last minute, grill pitas, flipping once. Spread hummus on pitas, then layer

with sliced cucumber and red onion, a burger, yogurt sauce and parsley.

PER SERVING 430 **CAL**; 23 g **FAT** (10 g **SAT**); 31 g **PRO**; 25 g **CARB**; 4 g **SUGARS**; 1 g **FIBER**; 880 mg **SODIUM**

The Ultimate Veggie Burger

MAKES 4 servings **PREP** 15 minutes
REFRIGERATE 1 hour **GRILL** 10 minutes

- 1 **cup cooked brown rice**
- 1 **cup cooked lentils**
- 1 **cup pinto beans, rinsed and drained**
- 1 **cup cooked beets, finely diced**
- ½ **cup rolled oats**
- 2 **tbsp low-sodium soy sauce**
- 1 **tbsp molasses**
- ½ **tsp onion powder**
- ¼ **tsp salt**
- ¼ **tsp black pepper**
- ¼ **cup mayonnaise**
- 2 **tbsp chopped pickles**
- 1 **tbsp minced white onion**
- 1 **tbsp ketchup**
- 1 **tbsp extra-virgin olive oil**
- 4 **potato buns**
    Sliced pickles, white onion, tomato, butter lettuce

■ In a large bowl, combine rice, lentils, beans, beets, oats, soy sauce, molasses, onion powder, salt and pepper. Transfer two-thirds of the mixture to a food processor. Pulse until it reaches the consistency of cooked oatmeal. Return to bowl and combine with remaining mixture. Form into 4 patties.

■ Place on a baking sheet lined with plastic wrap. Refrigerate at least 1 hour.

■ Meanwhile, in a small bowl, combine mayonnaise, chopped pickles, minced white onion and ketchup.

■ Heat grill to medium. Add oil to a large cast-iron skillet and place on grill. Add burgers and cook 4 to 5 minutes per side. During last minute, grill buns cut sides down. Layer burgers on buns with sauce; sliced pickles, white onion and tomato; and butter lettuce.

PER SERVING 480 **CAL**; 15 g **FAT** (3 g **SAT**); 15 g **PRO**; 73 g **CARB**; 13 g **SUGARS**; 8 g **FIBER**; 1,050 mg **SODIUM**

THE ULTIMATE VEGGIE BURGER

FISH TALE

Try these 5 techniques for cooking fish on the grill.

GREEK-STYLE
WHOLE FISH,
PAGE 163

SWORDFISH
KABOBS,
PAGE 163

SESAME TUNA AND BROCCOLI

Sesame Tuna and Broccoli

MAKES 4 servings **PREP** 10 minutes **GRILL** 17 minutes

- **3** tbsp low-sodium soy sauce
- **2** tbsp lemon juice
- **1** tbsp dark sesame oil
- **¾** tsp plus ⅛ tsp salt
- **¾** tsp black pepper
- **1** bunch (1¼ lb) broccoli, cut into large spears
- **4** tuna steaks (about 1¼ lb total)
- **2** tbsp tahini
- **2** tsp sesame seeds

■ Heat grill to medium-high. Lightly coat grates with oil.

■ In a small bowl, whisk soy sauce, lemon juice, sesame oil, ¾ tsp salt and the pepper.

■ In a large bowl, toss broccoli with 2 tbsp soy mixture. Grill 12 minutes, turning 3 times.

■ Toss tuna steaks with remaining soy mixture and grill 5 minutes for medium, turning once.

■ Place broccoli on a platter and drizzle with tahini. Add tuna; sprinkle sesame seeds over all and season tuna with ⅛ tsp salt.

PER SERVING 327 **CAL**; 15 g **FAT** (3 g **SAT**); 40 g **PRO**; 10 g **CARB**; 2 g **SUGARS**; 4 g **FIBER**; 894 mg **SODIUM**

Cedar-Planked Cod

MAKES 4 servings **PREP** 15 minutes
SOAK 2 hours **GRILL** 20 minutes

- **1** to 2 large cedar grilling planks

AIOLI
- **½** cup mayonnaise
- **2** tsp white wine vinegar
- **1** clove garlic, grated
- **¾** tsp smoked paprika

FISH
- **1** tbsp chopped parsley
- **2** tsp olive oil
- **1** tsp chopped garlic
- **½** tsp salt
- **¼** tsp coarsely ground black pepper
- **2** lb cod or haddock (1 large or 2 small pieces)

■ Soak cedar planks in warm water for 1 to 2 hours.

■ **Aioli.** In a small bowl, whisk all aioli ingredients. Cover with plastic.

■ **Fish.** In a small bowl, combine first 5 ingredients. Spread on fish.

■ Heat grill to medium-high. Remove planks from water and pat dry. Char one side of plank for 2 minutes. Flip and add fish. Cover grill and cook 15 to 20 minutes, until fish is opaque and flakes easily with a fork. Serve with aioli on the side.

PER SERVING 377 **CAL**; 24 g **FAT** (4 g **SAT**); 36 g **PRO**; 1 g **CARB**; 0 g **SUGARS**; 0 g **FIBER**; 589 mg **SODIUM**

CEDAR-PLANKED COD

FOIL PACKET
FLOUNDER

Take a look at the calorie counts and amounts of healthy vs. saturated fats in these recipes, and you can see that fish is a terrific taste and nutritional bargain.

Foil Packet Flounder

MAKES 4 servings **PREP** 10 minutes
GRILL 13 minutes

- **8** cups (1 lb) zucchini "noodles"
- **9** tbsp sun-dried tomato tapenade
- **2** tbsp chopped fresh parsley
- **¼** tsp plus ⅛ tsp salt
- **¼** tsp freshly cracked black pepper
- **4** flounder fillets (4 oz each)

■ Heat grill to medium-high.

■ Tear off four 12-inch pieces extra-wide heavy-duty foil. In a large bowl, toss zucchini, 3 tbsp tapenade, 1 tbsp parsley, ¼ tsp salt and the pepper, and divide among foil pieces.

■ Spread 6 tbsp tapenade over flounder fillets and season with ⅛ tsp salt. Place fillets on top of zucchini.

■ Fold long sides of foil together and fold over twice. Roll up ends tightly to seal. Transfer to grill and cook 10 to 13 minutes, until fish flakes easily with a fork (be careful when testing doneness as steam will escape from bag).

PER SERVING 138 **CAL**; 5 g **FAT** (1 g **SAT**); 15 g **PRO**; 8 g **CARB**; 5 g **SUGARS**; 2 g **FIBER**; 867 mg **SODIUM**

Greek-Style Whole Fish

Pictured on page 158.

MAKES 4 servings **PREP** 15 minutes
GRILL 25 minutes

- **2** cleaned red snappers, branzinos or small striped bass (cleaned weight 1½ to 1¾ lb each)
- **2** tbsp olive oil
- **½** tsp salt
- **½** tsp freshly ground black pepper
- **1** lemon, cut into 8 slices
- **4** sprigs fresh thyme
- **4** sprigs fresh oregano
- **4** cloves garlic, smashed

■ Prepare outdoor grill with medium-low to medium coals, or heat gas grill to medium (about 325°).

■ Rinse fish and pat dry. Cut 3 slashes on each side and rub all over with oil. Season with salt and pepper.

■ Stuff 3 lemon slices into cavity of each fish. Divide thyme, oregano and garlic between cavities.

■ Oil grill grate. Grill fish 4 to 5 inches from heat, covered, for 10 to 12 minutes, until just beginning to char. Turn over carefully. Cover each eye with a lemon slice. Grill 11 to 13 minutes, until flesh flakes easily with a fork.

PER SERVING 286 **CAL**; 12 g **FAT** (2 g **SAT**); 41 g **PRO**; 1 g **CARB**; 0 g **SUGARS**; 0 g **FIBER**; 447 mg **SODIUM**

Swordfish Kabobs

Pictured on page 159.

MAKES 4 servings **PREP** 20 minutes
COOK 8 minutes **GRILL** 8 minutes

FISH AND POTATOES

- **16** small tricolor new potatoes, larger ones halved
- **1** lb center-cut swordfish, trimmed and cut into 1-inch pieces

VINAIGRETTE

- **2** tbsp lemon juice
- **2** tsp honey
- **½** tsp chopped fresh rosemary
- **½** tsp salt
- **¼** tsp black pepper
- **⅓** cup olive oil

■ Heat grill to medium-high. Lightly coat grates with oil.

■ **Fish and Potatoes.** Bring a medium pot of lightly salted water to a boil. Add potatoes and cook 8 minutes. Drain and rinse until cool. Place in a large bowl with fish.

■ **Vinaigrette.** In a small bowl, whisk first 5 ingredients. While whisking, add oil in a thin stream.

■ Add ¼ cup vinaigrette to potatoes and fish. Thread fish and potatoes onto 4 metal skewers, alternating pieces.

■ Grill over medium-high for 8 minutes, turning frequently. Drizzle with some of the remaining vinaigrette and serve.

PER SERVING 400 **CAL**; 24 g **FAT** (4 g **SAT**); 22 g **PRO**; 23 g **CARB**; 4 g **SUGARS**; 2 g **FIBER**; 378 mg **SODIUM**

CAST IRON MOVES OUTDOORS

Cast-iron is an amazing material. It can go on the stovetop, in the oven—even on the grill.

GRILLED SHRIMP FAJITAS

Grilled Shrimp Fajitas

MAKES 6 servings **PREP** 15 minutes
GRILL 18 minutes

1	avocado, pitted and peeled
¼	cup sour cream
1	tbsp lime juice
	Pinch of salt
2	sweet red peppers
1	green bell pepper
1	large sweet onion
1	lb peeled tail-on shrimp
½	tsp dried oregano
½	tsp garlic powder
½	tsp chili powder
½	tsp salt
¼	tsp black pepper
1	tbsp oil
¼	cup salsa, plus more for garnish
1	dash hot sauce
12	flour tortillas

■ Heat grill to medium-high. In a mini chopper or small blender, combine avocado, sour cream, lime juice and pinch of salt. Puree until smooth.

■ Cut sweet red peppers and green bell pepper into planks. Cut sweet onion into ½-inch-thick wedges. Grill veggies for 10 minutes, turning often, until crisp-tender. Transfer to a cutting board and cut into strips.

■ Toss shrimp with dried oregano, garlic powder, chili powder, ½ tsp salt and the black pepper. Heat an 11-inch cast-iron skillet on grill. Add oil and shrimp. Cook 2 minutes. Add veggies and salsa. Cook 2 minutes. Add hot sauce and remove from heat.

■ Add 6 flour tortillas to grill; cook 2 minutes, turning once. Repeat with 6 more flour tortillas. Serve shrimp mixture with tortillas, avocado cream and more salsa.

PER SERVING 390 **CAL**; 13 g **FAT** (4 g **SAT**); 18 g **PRO**; 48 g **CARB**; 8 g **SUGARS**; 5 g **FIBER**; 1,169 mg **SODIUM**

GREEN EGGS
AND HAM

Green Eggs and Ham

MAKES 4 servings **PREP** 10 minutes **GRILL** 15 minutes

- 1 lb asparagus
- 1 tsp olive oil
- ½ tsp salt
  Freshly ground black pepper
- 1 bunch scallions, trimmed
- 8 large eggs
- 2 tbsp fresh dill, chopped
- 2 tsp oil
- 4 slices sourdough bread
- 8 slices breakfast ham or Canadian bacon
- ¾ cup shredded white cheddar

■ Heat grill to medium-high. Trim asparagus; toss with 1 tsp olive oil and sprinkle with ¼ tsp salt and some freshly ground black pepper. Add asparagus to grill, along with scallions. Grill 10 minutes, turning frequently, until just tender. Remove to a cutting board and chop.

■ Place an 11-inch cast-iron skillet on one side of grill grate. Whisk eggs, dill, ¼ tsp salt and some pepper in a bowl. Add 2 tsp oil to skillet and stir in egg mixture and chopped grilled veggies. Grill, stirring, 5 minutes.

■ Meanwhile, grill sourdough and breakfast ham until well marked, about 1 to 2 minutes per side. Sprinkle white cheddar over eggs and fold in to combine. Place bread on plates; top with ham and eggs.

PER SERVING 407 **CAL**; 22 g **FAT** (8 g **SAT**); 21 g **PRO**; 22 g **CARB**; 2 g **SUGARS**; 3 g **FIBER**; 1,129 mg **SODIUM**

Pineapple Upside-Down Cake

MAKES 12 servings **PREP** 15 minutes
GRILL 35 minutes

- 1 18.25 oz box pineapple upside-down or French vanilla cake mix
- 1 cup water
- ⅓ cup oil
- 3 large eggs
- 1 pineapple, cored
- 2 tbsp melted butter
- ¼ cup unsalted butter
- ½ cup dark brown sugar
  Fresh raspberries

■ Heat grill to medium-high indirect heat. Prepare cake mix per package directions, adding water, oil and eggs.

■ Cut seven ½-inch slices from pineapple. Brush with 2 tbsp melted butter and grill over hot side of grill for 4 minutes, turning once.

■ Place an 11-inch cast-iron skillet directly on hot side of grill. Melt ¼ cup unsalted butter in skillet. Top with dark brown sugar and grill 1 minute, until melted. Move skillet to cooler side of grill and fit pineapple slices tightly into skillet. Place 1 raspberry in center of each ring. Pour batter into pan; cover grill and cook 30 minutes, until cake is browned and set. Place a platter directly over skillet and carefully invert. Replace any fruit that has stuck to skillet.

PER SERVING 437 **CAL**; 24 g **FAT** (7 g **SAT**); 3 g **PRO**; 50 g **CARB**; 33 g **SUGARS**; 1 g **FIBER**; 316 mg **SODIUM**

PINEAPPLE
UPSIDE-DOWN
CAKE

FOUR WAYS WITH GRILLED FRUIT

Cooking fruit over a flame gives it great smoky flavor.

Watermelon-Jicama Salad

MAKES 8 servings **PREP** 30 minutes **GRILL** 10 minutes

- 2 **limes**
- ¼ **cup sugar**
- 2 **tbsp water**
-    **Cayenne pepper**
- 1 **seedless round watermelon**
- 1 **large jicama**
- ¼ **cup packed fresh mint, chopped**
-    **Sea salt**
-    **Lime wedges**

■ Heat grill to high. Zest and juice 2 limes.

■ In a small skillet, heat ¼ cup sugar, ¼ cup lime juice, 2 tbsp water and cayenne pepper to taste. Cook until sugar dissolves; set aside to cool.

■ Peel 1 seedless round watermelon; slice into 1-inch-thick slabs. Peel and halve 1 large jicama; cut into ¼-inch-thick slices. Dip jicama in syrup and grill 2 to 3 minutes, until well marked. Brush with syrup, flip and grill 2 more minutes. Dip watermelon in syrup and grill 1 to 2 minutes per side.

■ Cut watermelon into eighths and quarter the jicama slices. Drizzle wedges with remaining lime juice. Sprinkle with lime zest, mint, and sea salt and cayenne to taste. Serve with lime wedges.

PER SERVING 160 CAL; 0 g **FAT** (0 g **SAT**); 2 g **PRO**; 43 g **CARB**; 30 g **SUGARS**; 9 g **FIBER**; 79 mg **SODIUM**

Plums with Chicken

MAKES 4 servings **PREP** 15 minutes
GRILL 15 minutes

- 8 **cups baby spinach**
- ½ **cup sliced almonds, toasted**
- 1 **small shallot, halved and thinly sliced**
- 2 **tbsp sherry vinegar**
- 1 **tbsp Dijon mustard**
- ¼ **tsp salt**
- ¼ **tsp black pepper**
- 6 **tbsp olive oil**
- 1 **lb boneless, skinless chicken breasts**
- 4 **large plums**
- 2 **tsp olive oil**

■ Heat grill to high. Toss baby spinach with sliced almonds and shallot.

■ In a medium bowl, whisk vinegar, Dijon mustard, salt and pepper. Whisk in the 6 tbsp olive oil. Reserve ⅓ cup dressing. Add chicken breasts to remaining dressing; turn to coat.

■ Grill chicken, brushing with additional marinade, 6 to 8 minutes per side or until temperature reaches 165°. Remove from heat and keep warm.

■ Meanwhile, halve and pit 4 large plums. Brush cut sides with the 2 tsp olive oil. Grill, cut side down, 2 to 3 minutes, until well marked. Thinly slice chicken; quarter the plums. Add half the reserved dressing to spinach and toss to coat; transfer to a platter. Top with chicken and plums; drizzle with remaining dressing.

PER SERVING 489 CAL; 33 g **FAT** (4 g **SAT**); 32 g **PRO**; 15 g **CARB**; 7 g **SUGARS**; 6 g **FIBER**; 374 mg **SODIUM**

WATERMELON-JICAMA SALAD

PLUMS WITH CHICKEN

Banana Pudding

MAKES 4 servings **PREP 10 MINUTES**
COOK 15 minutes **GRILL** 5 minutes

- ½ cup sugar
- 2 tbsp water
- ¼ cup heavy cream
- 3 tbsp unsalted butter
- 1 tbsp bourbon
-    Pinch of salt
- 1 3.4 oz box instant vanilla pudding mix
- 3 bananas
- 4 1-inch-thick slices pound cake
- ¼ cup light whipped topping

BANANA PUDDING

■ Heat grill to medium-high. Melt sugar and water in a small pot over medium-high, swirling occasionally until dark amber, about 12 to 15 minutes. Remove from heat and carefully stir in heavy cream. Add 1 tbsp of the butter, the bourbon and a pinch of salt. Set caramel sauce aside to cool.

■ Prepare instant vanilla pudding according to package directions using skim milk. Halve bananas lengthwise, leaving peel on; coat cut sides with nonstick cooking spray. Grill, cut side down, 3 minutes, until well marked. Peel bananas and cut into bite-size pieces.

■ Melt remaining 2 tbsp butter and brush on cut sides of the sliced pound cake. Grill 1 to 2 minutes per side, until toasted. Cut each slice into 6 cubes.

■ In each of 4 dishes, layer 3 cubes cake and ¼ cup pudding; evenly distribute half the banana. Repeat layers. Top each with 2 tbsp light whipped topping and drizzle each with ½ tbsp caramel sauce.

PER SERVING 504 **CAL**; 19 g **FAT** (12 g **SAT**); 8 g **PRO**; 71 g **CARB**; 52 g **SUGARS**; 3 g **FIBER**; 572 mg **SODIUM**

PEACH PANZANELLA

Peach Panzanella

MAKES 6 servings **PREP** 20 minutes **COOK** 12 minutes **GRILL** 15 minutes

- 6 slices thick-cut bacon (about 10 oz)
- 4 cups packed baby arugula
- ½ cup torn fresh basil leaves
- 3 peaches
- 4 1-inch-thick slices crusty multigrain bread
- 2 tbsp red wine vinegar
- 1 tbsp honey
- 1 tsp Dijon mustard
- ¼ tsp salt
- ¼ tsp black pepper
- ¼ cup olive oil

■ Cut bacon into 8 pieces each; cook in a skillet over medium-high for 12 to 14 minutes, until crisp. Transfer with a slotted spoon to a paper-towel-lined plate, reserving 2 tbsp fat.

■ Toss baby arugula with basil leaves.

■ Heat grill to medium-high. Halve and pit peaches. Brush cut sides of peaches and both sides of bread with bacon fat. Grill bread 3 to 5 minutes per side, until well marked. Remove and cut into 1-inch cubes. Add to arugula mixture.

■ Grill peaches, cut side down, 6 to 8 minutes, until well marked. Remove and cut into 1-inch pieces. Add to arugula mixture; toss to combine.

■ In a small bowl, whisk red wine vinegar, honey, Dijon mustard, salt and pepper. Whisk in olive oil. Add dressing and bacon to bread mixture; toss to coat.

PER SERVING 454 **CAL**; 30 g **FAT** (8 g **SAT**); 26 g **PRO**; 24 g **CARB**; 12 g **SUGARS**; 4 g **FIBER**; 966 mg **SODIUM**

HEALTHY FAMILY DINNERS

Try these 7 easy grill recipes on crazy-busy nights.

BBQ BUFFALO
CHICKEN SALAD

BBQ Buffalo Chicken Salad

MAKES 4 servings **PREP** 15 minutes
GRILL 14 minutes **REST** 5 minutes

- 1 **tsp plus 2 tbsp olive oil**
- 1½ **lb boneless, skinless chicken breasts**
- ½ **tsp kosher salt**
- 2 **tbsp Buffalo wing sauce, plus more for serving**
- 3 **tbsp light sour cream**
- 1½ **tbsp water**
- 1 **tbsp light mayonnaise**
- 1 **tbsp minced fresh chives**
- 1 **tsp white wine vinegar**
- ¼ **tsp garlic powder**
- 6 **cups chopped romaine hearts**
- 1 **cup croutons**
- ¾ **cup halved cherry tomatoes**
- ¾ **cup chopped English cucumber**
- 1 **large rib celery, sliced**
- ¼ **cup crumbled blue cheese**
  Freshly ground black pepper

■ Heat grill to medium-high. Rub 1 tsp oil on chicken breasts and season with ¼ tsp salt. Grill on both sides until chicken is cooked through, 6 to 7 minutes per side.

■ Transfer chicken to a cutting board and brush with 2 tbsp wing sauce. Rest 5 minutes, then cut into slices. In a small bowl, whisk 2 tbsp oil, the sour cream, next 5 ingredients and ¼ tsp salt.

■ Toss dressing with romaine and next 4 ingredients. Divide among 4 plates, and top with sliced chicken and blue cheese. Season with pepper. Serve extra wing sauce on the side.

PER SERVING 432 **CAL**; 22 g **FAT** (7 g **SAT**); 45 g **PRO**; 13 g **CARB**; 3 g **SUGARS**; 3 g **FIBER**; 761 mg **SODIUM**

GRILLED VEGETABLE SANDWICHES WITH CREAMY HERB SPREAD

Grilled Vegetable Sandwiches with Creamy Herb Spread

MAKES 4 servings **PREP** 15 minutes **GRILL** 11 minutes

- 2 **large zucchini (about 1 lb total)**
- 1 **large sweet red pepper**
- 1 **large red onion**
- 2 **tbsp balsamic vinegar**
- 2 **tbsp plus 1 tsp olive oil**
- ⅛ **tsp plus a pinch kosher salt**
  Freshly ground black pepper
- 8 **slices sourdough bread**
- 1 **container (5.2 oz) Boursin cheese**
- 1 **cup packed arugula**

■ Heat grill to medium-high. Cut zucchini lengthwise into ⅓-inch-thick slabs. Core and cut red pepper into 8 slices. Cut onion into ⅓-inch-thick slices. Toss zucchini and pepper with 1 tbsp vinegar, 1 tsp oil, ⅛ tsp salt and the black pepper. Brush onion with 2 tsp oil.

■ Grill veggies on both sides until tender, 7 to 11 minutes. Brush bread with 1 tbsp oil. Grill until lightly toasted. Spread Boursin over 4 slices of bread. Layer veggies on top. Toss arugula with 1 tbsp vinegar, 1 tsp oil and a pinch of salt, and place over veggies. Cover sandwiches with remaining bread and cut each in half.

PER SERVING 387 **CAL**; 21 g **FAT** (6 g **SAT**); 7 g **PRO**; 42 g **CARB**; 6 g **SUGARS**; 4 g **FIBER**; 471 mg **SODIUM**

SPICE-RUBBED PORK CHOPS WITH GRILLED NECTARINES

For the same char on your chops—but done indoors— use a cast-iron skillet on your stovetop.

SHRIMP IN LETTUCE CUPS WITH MANGO SALSA AND COCONUT RICE

Spice-Rubbed Pork Chops with Grilled Nectarines

MAKES 6 servings **PREP** 10 minutes
STAND 10 minutes **GRILL** 8 minutes
REST 5 minutes

- 1 **tbsp paprika**
- 1 **tbsp brown sugar**
- 1½ **tsp garlic powder**
- ½ **tsp cayenne pepper**
- 2¼ **tsp kosher salt**
- ¼ **tsp plus ⅛ tsp black pepper**
- 6 **1-inch-thick bone-in pork chops**
- 3 **nectarines, pitted and quartered**
- 2 **tsp olive oil**
   Buttered corn on the cob

■ Heat grill to medium-high. In a small bowl, combine first 4 ingredients, 2 tsp salt and ¼ tsp black pepper. Rub into pork chops and let stand 10 minutes. Coat nectarines with oil, ¼ tsp salt and ⅛ tsp black pepper.

■ Put pork chops and nectarines on grill and cook on both sides until chops are faintly pink in center, about 4 minutes per side. Transfer chops to a platter and rest 5 minutes. Move nectarines to coolest part of grill and cover with lid until chops are ready. Serve pork chops with nectarines and corn on the cob on the side.

PER SERVING 425 **CAL**; 21 g **FAT** (8 g **SAT**); 33 g **PRO**; 28 g **CARB**; 13 g **SUGARS**; 4 g **FIBER**; 778 mg **SODIUM**

Shrimp in Lettuce Cups with Mango Salsa and Coconut Rice

MAKES 4 servings **PREP** 5 minutes **MICROWAVE** 1½ minutes **GRILL** 4 minutes

- 2 **cups precooked brown rice**
- ⅓ **cup light coconut milk**
- ¼ **tsp ground ginger**
- 1¼ **tsp sugar**
- ½ **tsp plus a pinch kosher salt**
- 1¼ **lb peeled medium raw shrimp**
- 2 **tsp toasted sesame oil**
   Juice of 1 lime
- 2 **ripe mangoes, peeled, pitted and diced**
- 2 **cups diced English cucumber**
- 3 **tbsp seasoned rice vinegar**
- 1 **large shallot, minced**
- 2 **tbsp finely chopped fresh mint**
- 1 **tbsp minced jalapeño**
- 1 **large head Bibb lettuce, leaves separated and rinsed**

■ In a microwave-safe bowl, stir first 4 ingredients and ¼ tsp kosher salt. Microwave on high for 90 seconds.

■ Heat grill to high. Toss shrimp with sesame oil, lime juice and a pinch of salt. Grill on both sides until pink and opaque, about 2 minutes per side.

■ In a medium bowl, toss mangoes with next 5 ingredients and ¼ tsp kosher salt.

■ To assemble, put rice on lettuce leaf, top with several shrimp and mango salsa, and eat like a taco.

PER SERVING 422 **CAL**; 8 g **FAT** (3 g **SAT**); 33 g **PRO**; 59 g **CARB**; 27 g **SUGARS**; 5 g **FIBER**; 580 mg **SODIUM**

INDIAN-STYLE CHICKEN
WITH CUCUMBER SALAD

Throw your naan on the grill too—all you need is a minute per side for warm, toasty bread.

Indian-Style Chicken with Cucumber Salad

MAKES 4 servings **PREP** 5 minutes **MARINATE** 10 minutes **GRILL** 14 minutes **STAND** 5 minutes

- ½   **cup plain low-fat Greek yogurt**
- 4   **tbsp fresh lime juice, plus lime wedges for serving**
- 1½ **tsp olive oil**
- 1   **clove garlic, minced**
- 1   **tsp ground coriander**
- ½   **tsp ground turmeric**
- ½   **tsp paprika**
- 1¼ **tsp salt**
- ¼   **tsp black pepper**
- 2   **lb boneless, skinless chicken thighs**
- 2   **tsp sugar**
- 1   **tbsp cider vinegar**
- ½   **small red onion, thinly sliced**
- 1   **large English cucumber, thinly sliced**
- 2   **tbsp roughly chopped fresh cilantro, plus 4 sprigs for serving**
- **Naan bread wedges**

■ Heat grill to medium-high. In a large bowl, combine yogurt, 2 tbsp lime juice, the oil, garlic, coriander, turmeric, paprika, ¾ tsp salt and the pepper.

■ Marinate chicken in yogurt sauce for at least 10 minutes or up to 4 hours. Lightly coat each thigh with nonstick cooking spray, and grill on both sides until temperature reaches 165° in center, 12 to 14 minutes.

■ In a medium bowl, combine sugar, ½ tsp salt, 2 tbsp lime juice and the vinegar. Add onion, toss several times and let stand 5 minutes. Add cucumber and cilantro. Stir well.

■ Serve chicken on a large plate with cilantro sprigs, lime wedges, cucumber salad and naan.

PER SERVING 502 **CAL**; 15 g **FAT** (4 g **SAT**); 51 g **PRO**; 37 g **CARB**; 6 g **SUGARS**; 2 g **FIBER**; 796 mg **SODIUM**

Grilled Salmon with Yogurt Dill Sauce

MAKES 4 servings **PREP** 5 minutes
COOK 15 minutes **GRILL** 14 minutes

- 1¼ **lb small red potatoes**
- 1½ **lb salmon fillet**
- 2   **tsp olive oil**
- 1   **tsp kosher salt**
- **Freshly ground black pepper**
- 1   **cup plain Greek yogurt**
- ¼   **cup finely chopped fresh dill**
- 2   **tbsp finely chopped fresh chives**
- 1   **heaping tbsp Dijon mustard**
- **Lemon wedges, for serving**

■ In a medium pot, add potatoes and cover with salted cold water by 1 inch. Bring to a boil and cook until tender, about 15 minutes. Drain.

■ Meanwhile, heat grill to medium-high. Coat salmon with oil and season with ½ tsp salt and pepper to taste.

■ Grill salmon until just cooked through, 6 to 7 minutes per side. In a small bowl, whisk yogurt, dill, chives, mustard and ½ tsp salt. Spoon sauce over salmon and potatoes, and serve lemon wedges on the side.

PER SERVING 461 **CAL**; 18 g **FAT** (4 g **SAT**); 47 g **PRO**; 25 g **CARB**; 4 g **SUGARS**; 2 g **FIBER**; 732 mg **SODIUM**

GRILLED SALMON WITH
YOGURT DILL SAUCE

For a little more spice, swap teriyaki with gochujang, a Korean hot chile paste found in the Asian section of markets.

Teriyaki Flank Steak and Vegetables

MAKES 6 servings **PREP** 10 minutes
GRILL 13 minutes **REST** 10 minutes

1¾	lb flank steak
½	tsp salt
¼	tsp freshly ground black pepper
1	bunch asparagus, trimmed
1	lb large cremini mushrooms, halved
5	tbsp teriyaki sauce, plus more for serving
4½	cups cooked white rice

■ Heat grill to medium-high. Season steak with salt and pepper.

■ Toss asparagus and mushrooms with 1 tbsp teriyaki sauce. Place steak and veggies on grill. Grill veggies until just tender, 6 to 10 minutes. Transfer to a serving plate and toss with 2 tbsp teriyaki sauce.

■ Grill steak about 5 minutes per side for medium-rare, 6 minutes per side for medium. Brush on 2 tbsp teriyaki sauce and grill 30 more seconds per side. Transfer to a carving board and rest 10 minutes. Carve steak against the grain into 1-inch-wide slices. Serve with veggies, rice and extra teriyaki sauce on the side.

PER SERVING 398 **CAL**; 7 g **FAT** (3 g **SAT**); 36 g **PRO**; 14 g **CARB**; 9 g **SUGARS**; 2 g **FIBER**; 749 mg **SODIUM**

TERIYAKI FLANK STEAK AND VEGETABLES

FLAVOR BOMBS

These rubs and marinades are for anything and everything.

Moroccan

GOOD FOR LAMB, CHICKEN, SALMON, VEGETABLES

Combine 4 tsp curry powder, 1½ tsp each ground coriander and kosher salt, 1 tsp each ground ginger and cumin, and ½ tsp each freshly ground black pepper and sugar. Rub into food 1 hour before cooking. Makes ¼ cup.

Tandoori

GOOD FOR BEEF, LAMB, CHICKEN

Whisk 1 container (6 oz) plain low-fat yogurt, ¼ cup milk, 1 tbsp lemon juice, 1 tsp each sugar, salt and paprika, ½ tsp ground coriander and ¼ tsp curry powder. Marinate food in fridge for up to 2 hours. Makes 1 cup.

Mexican

GOOD FOR BEEF, PORK, CHICKEN, SHRIMP

Combine 2 tbsp chili powder, 1 tbsp kosher salt, 2 tsp cumin, 1 tsp each garlic powder, smoked paprika and ground coriander, and ½ tsp cayenne pepper. Rub into food 1 hour before cooking. Makes ⅓ cup.

Sesame-Soy

GOOD FOR BEEF, PORK, SHRIMP

Combine ½ cup soy sauce, 1 finely chopped scallion, 2 tbsp each packed brown sugar and mirin rice wine, 1 tbsp dark sesame oil, 2 chopped cloves garlic, ½ tsp ground ginger and ¼ tsp freshly ground black pepper. Marinate food in fridge for 1 to 3 hours. Makes 1 scant cup.

Jamaican

GOOD FOR CHICKEN, FISH, VEGETABLES

Combine 2 tbsp onion powder, 2 tsp each sugar, dried thyme and salt, 1½ tsp red pepper flakes, 1 tsp freshly ground black pepper and ½ tsp each allspice and cinnamon. Rub into food 1 hour before cooking. Makes ⅓ cup.

Chimichurri

GOOD FOR BEEF, SHRIMP, VEGETABLES

In a mini chopper, combine ⅓ cup olive oil, ¼ cup red wine vinegar and ½ tsp salt, and pulse until well combined. Add 3 coarsely chopped cloves garlic, ½ cup fresh parsley leaves and 3 tbsp coarsely chopped fresh cilantro. Pulse until smooth. Marinate food in fridge for 30 minutes to 1 hour. Makes ⅔ cup.

TANDOORI

SESAME-SOY

JAMAICAN

CHIMICHURRI

MEXICAN

MOROCCAN

CLASSIC
LOBSTER ROLL,
PAGE 201

AUGUST

180

188

193

MEXICANA MAMA

Pati Jinich—cookbook author and host of PBS's *Pati's Mexican Table*— puts some spice into a summer party.

TRADITIONAL CHICKEN TOSTADAS

Sazón—the Mexican knack for seasoning—is proudly passed down from generation to generation in Mexico.

Traditional Chicken Tostadas

MAKES 6 servings **PREP** 20 minutes

- 12 **corn tostadas**
- 2 **cups warm refried beans**
- 3 **cups shredded cooked chicken**
- 1 **cup finely sliced iceberg or romaine lettuce**
- 1 **to 2 ripe avocados, halved, pitted, peeled and sliced**
- 2 **ripe tomatoes, sliced**
- 1 **cup crumbled queso fresco, Cotija cheese or farmer's cheese**
- ½ **cup Mexican crema (optional)**

■ Place tostadas on a large platter and all other ingredients in separate bowls.

■ Spread a couple tablespoons of refried beans on each tostada. Top with some chicken, lettuce, avocado and tomato. Add cheese and, if using, crema.

PER SERVING 447 **CAL**; 21 g **FAT** (7 g **SAT**); 35 g **PRO**; 33 g **CARB**; 2 g **SUGARS**; 8 g **FIBER**; 1,008 mg **SODIUM**

Quick Salsa Verde

MAKES about 2 cups **PREP** 15 minutes
COOK 12 minutes

- 2 **lb tomatillos, husked and rinsed**
- 2 **jalapeño or serrano chiles**
- 2 **cloves garlic**

QUICK SALSA VERDE

GRAPEFRUIT AND GUAVA FIZZ

- ½ **cup coarsely chopped fresh cilantro leaves and upper part of stems**
- ¼ **cup coarsely chopped onion**
- ¾ **tsp kosher or sea salt**

■ In a medium saucepan, combine first 3 ingredients. Cover generously with water and bring to a simmer over medium. Cook 10 to 12 minutes, until tomatillos are olive green and tender but not falling apart.

■ Using a slotted spoon, transfer tomatillos and garlic to a blender. Drain and stem chiles. Add 1 chile, the cilantro, onion and salt to blender; puree until smooth. Add salt to taste. If you want more heat, add remaining chile and blend again.

PER TBSP 10 **CAL**; 0 g **FAT** (0 g **SAT**); 0 g **PRO**; 2 g **CARB**; 1 g **SUGARS**; 0 g **FIBER**; 46 mg **SODIUM**

Grapefruit and Guava Fizz

MAKES 8 servings **PREP** 5 minutes

- 4 **cups guava nectar**
- 2 **cups freshly squeezed grapefruit juice, chilled**
- ¼ **cup light agave syrup**
    Cold citrus-flavored sparkling water

■ In a large pitcher, combine first 3 ingredients. Stir well to combine. Taste for sweetness and add more agave if needed. Add ice cubes to glasses. Pour juice mixture over ice and top with a splash of cold citrus-flavor sparkling water.

PER SERVING 133 **CAL**; 0 g **FAT** (0 g **SAT**); 0 g **PRO**; 34 g **CARB**; 24 g **SUGARS**; 1 g **FIBER**; 32 mg **SODIUM**

Queso Cotija, a classic crumbly dry cheese, is used in many Mexican dishes. It comes from Michoacán, the state where this salad's namesake city is located. Alternately, use mild feta.

Morelia-Style Savory Fruit Salad

MAKES 6 servings **PREP** 15 minutes

- **2 cups peeled and diced ripe mango (2 champagne mangoes)**
- **2 cups peeled, cored and diced pineapple**
- **2 cups peeled and diced jicama (1 small to medium jicama)**
- **6 tbsp finely chopped white onion**
- **1 cup freshly squeezed orange juice**
- **2 tbsp freshly squeezed lime juice**
- **Kosher or sea salt**
- **Dried ground chile piquín or Mexican dried ground chile**
- **¾ cup finely crumbled Cotija cheese, queso fresco or mild feta**

■ In a large bowl, combine first 4 ingredients. Add orange and lime juices and toss to coat. Season with salt and ground chile, and toss again. Top with cheese and a sprinkle of salt and ground chile.

PER SERVING 190 **CAL**; 5 g **FAT** (3 g **SAT**); 5 g **PRO**; 34 g **CARB**; 25 g **SUGARS**; 5 g **FIBER**; 294 mg **SODIUM**

Avocado, Roasted Asparagus and Cherry Tomato Salad

MAKES 4 servings **PREP** 25 minutes
ROAST at 425° for 19 minutes

- **1 lb asparagus**
- **2 tbsp chopped fresh basil**
- **2 tbsp chopped fresh mint**
- **2 tbsp chopped fresh sage**
- **6 tbsp olive oil**
- **¼ cup thinly sliced shallot**
- **2 tsp kosher or sea salt**
- **1 tsp freshly ground black pepper**
- **1 lb cherry tomatoes**
- **Zest of 1 lime**
- **2 tbsp freshly squeezed lime juice**
- **1 tsp Dijon mustard**
- **2 hard-boiled eggs, cut in half, yolks separated from whites, whites finely chopped**
- **2 large avocados, halved, pitted and cut into large bite-size pieces**

■ Heat oven to 425°.

■ Trim ¼ inch from bottom of asparagus. Peel the bottom 1½ to 2 inches of each stalk.

■ In a large mixing bowl, combine basil, mint, sage, ¼ cup oil, the shallot, 1½ tsp salt and the pepper. Add tomatoes, toss to coat and transfer with a slotted spoon to one side of a rimmed 18 x 13-inch sheet pan.

■ Place asparagus on other half of sheet pan. Pour remaining marinade over asparagus and toss until coated. Spread out in a single layer.

■ Roast 12 to 13 minutes, until asparagus is crisp-tender. Remove asparagus and let cool on a cutting board. Roast tomatoes another 5 to 6 minutes, until they have burst, deflated and begun to char. Let cool.

■ Using a slotted spoon, gently transfer tomatoes to a large bowl. Pour juices from pan into a blender.

■ Cut 1 inch from bottom of asparagus and add to blender. Cut remaining asparagus into 1½-inch pieces and add to tomatoes.

■ Add lime zest and juice, 2 tbsp oil, the mustard, ½ tsp salt and cooked egg yolks to blender. Puree until smooth.

■ Add avocados to asparagus and tomatoes. Add ¼ cup dressing and gently toss to coat. Add more dressing, if desired. Transfer to a platter and garnish with chopped egg whites.

PER SERVING 252 **CAL**; 23 g **FAT** (3 g **SAT**); 5 g **PRO**; 11 g **CARB**; 4 g **SUGARS**; 5 g **FIBER**; 690 mg **SODIUM**

MORELIA-STYLE SAVORY FRUIT SALAD

AVOCADO, ROASTED ASPARAGUS AND CHERRY TOMATO SALAD

Traditional Mexican barbacoa (the word from which "barbecue" is derived) refers to meats that are slow cooked over an open fire. Here, the slow cooker does the trick—with a smoky homemade chile sauce.

Barbacoa Sliders

MAKES 24 sliders **PREP** 25 minutes **COOK** 28 minutes **SLOW COOK** on HIGH for 4½ hours or LOW for 8 hours **REST** 15 minutes

ADOBO

8	**dried guajillo chiles, stemmed and seeded**
8	**dried ancho chiles, stemmed and seeded**
⅓	**cup apple cider vinegar**
1	**medium Roma tomato, quartered**
½	**cup coarsely chopped white onion**
3	**cloves garlic**
1	**tbsp dried oregano**
½	**tsp ground cinnamon**
½	**tsp ground allspice**
½	**tsp freshly ground black pepper**
5	**whole cloves, stems removed**
2½	**tsp kosher salt**
3	**tbsp vegetable oil**

SLIDERS

4	**lb beef round roast or brisket, cut into 4-inch chunks**
24	**small slider buns (brioche or challah)**
	Onion and Cabbage Slaw (optional; recipe follows)
	Pickled jalapeños (optional)

■ **Adobo.** Heat a large dry skillet over medium. Toast chiles, turning often, about 3 minutes, until colored and fragrant. Transfer to a medium saucepan, cover with water and bring to a simmer over medium. Simmer 15 minutes, until softened and rehydrated.

■ Transfer chiles and ¼ cup of the cooking liquid to a blender. Add vinegar and next 9 ingredients (through salt); puree until smooth. Rinse and dry saucepan and add oil. Heat over medium for 1 to 2 minutes, until hot but not smoking. Carefully add mixture to pan; it will sizzle and splatter at first. Stir once, cover partially and cook 6 to 8 minutes, stirring occasionally, until it darkens and mixture thickens to a paste-like consistency.

■ **Sliders.** Place beef in a large bowl and combine with adobo. (If not cooking that day, cover and place in fridge for up to 48 hours.) Transfer meat and adobo to a large slow cooker. Cover and cook on HIGH for 4½ hours or LOW for 8 hours, until meat is juicy and comes apart when pulled with a fork.

■ Rest 10 to 15 minutes before removing to a cutting board and pulling apart with forks.

■ Serve barbacoa on buns with, if desired, Onion and Cabbage Slaw and/or pickled jalapeños.

Onion and Cabbage Slaw Halve and thinly slice 1 red onion; soak in cold water for 10 to 15 minutes. Drain well. In a large bowl, toss onion, 4 cups finely shredded green cabbage, ⅓ cup each fresh orange juice and fresh lime juice, ¼ cup unseasoned rice vinegar, 2 tbsp olive oil, 1¼ tsp kosher salt and ¼ tsp freshly ground black pepper. Mix well and let stand at room temperature for 20 minutes to an hour. Cover and refrigerate.

PER SLIDER 276 CAL; 9 g FAT (2 g SAT); 21 g PRO; 27 g CARB; 4 g SUGARS; 2 g FIBER; 480 mg SODIUM

BARBACOA
SLIDERS

MANGO MOUSSE

Mango Mousse

MAKES 12 servings   PREP 15 minutes
REST 3 minutes   COOK 3 minutes
REFRIGERATE 2 hours

- 1 **cup lukewarm water**
- 1 **packet unflavored gelatin**
- 1 **can (14 oz) sweetened condensed milk**
- 4 **cups cubed mango (fresh or thawed frozen)**
- 1 **tbsp freshly squeezed lime juice**
- 2 **cups heavy cream**
- 1 **cup diced fresh mango and mixed berries**

■ Add water and gelatin to a medium heatproof bowl. Stir and let rest until gelatin blooms, about 3 minutes.

■ In a medium saucepan, bring 2 to 3 inches of water to a simmer over medium-low. Set gelatin bowl on top of pan and cook 2 to 3 minutes, stirring occasionally, until gelatin completely dissolves. Remove from heat.

■ In a blender, combine condensed milk, mango and lime juice; puree until smooth. Add gelatin and blend on low speed for a few seconds to combine. Pour into a large mixing bowl.

■ In a stand mixer fitted with whisk attachment or with a hand mixer in a very large bowl, beat cream at medium speed 3 to 4 minutes, until it holds soft peaks (be careful not to overbeat). Fold whipped cream into mango gelatin, which should have started to set a bit, until thoroughly combined.

■ Pour into individual ice cream dishes or wineglasses, cover tightly with plastic wrap, and refrigerate until completely chilled and set, at least 2 hours.

■ When ready to serve, top with diced fresh mango and berries.

PER SERVING 291 CAL; 17 g FAT (11 g SAT); 5 g PRO; 31 g CARB; 29 g SUGARS; 1 g FIBER; 53 mg SODIUM

PINEAPPLE EMPANADAS

Pineapple Empanadas

MAKES 10 empanadas   PREP 30 minutes   REFRIGERATE 1 hour   BAKE at 350° for 20 minutes

- 2 **cups all-purpose flour, plus more for dusting**
- ½ **cup granulated sugar**
- **Pinch of kosher or coarse sea salt**
- 2 **large eggs**
- 3 **tbsp sour cream**
- 1½ **sticks (12 tbsp) unsalted butter, diced**
- ½ **lb pineapple, peeled and diced (about 1½ cups)**
- ¼ **lb apricots, pitted and diced (about ¾ cup)**
- ½ **cup pecans, finely chopped**
- ¼ **cup dark brown sugar**
- 1½ **tsp cornstarch**
- 1½ **tsp freshly squeezed lime juice**
- ⅛ **tsp five-spice powder**
- **Dulce de leche (optional)**

■ Heat oven to 350°.

■ In a large mixing bowl, combine 2 cups flour, the granulated sugar and salt. In a small bowl, beat 1 egg and sour cream.

■ With your fingers, rub butter into dry ingredients until it resembles coarse meal (should be crumbly). Add egg mixture. Mix with a spatula until it forms a smooth dough. Wrap in plastic wrap and refrigerate at least 1 hour.

■ In a large bowl, combine pineapple and next 6 ingredients; mix well.

■ Generously flour a work surface and rolling pin. Roll dough to ¼-inch thickness. Cut into 4-inch rounds. Repeat with any scraps until you have used up all dough. Place 1 heaping tablespoon fruit filling in middle of each round. Beat 1 egg and brush around edges of dough; fold to make a half-moon and gently press with fingers to close edges. Use the back of a fork to seal dough without breaking it.

■ Line 2 baking sheets with parchment and divide empanadas between them. Brush tops with beaten egg.

■ Bake 20 minutes, until golden brown. Serve warm with dulce de leche, if using.

PER SERVING 351 CAL; 20 g FAT (10 g SAT); 5 g PRO; 40 g CARB; 19 g SUGARS; 2 g FIBER; 44 mg SODIUM

COLONIAL MODERN

"Drinking" vinegars came blazing into fashion a couple of years ago thanks to kombucha; shrubs are part of that same sour family tree.

Blackberry Shrub

PREP 10 minutes **CHILL** overnight

- 2 **cups blackberries, roughly chopped**
- ⅔ **cup sugar**
- ⅔ **cup white wine vinegar,**
  Seltzer
  Blackberries

■ In a glass bowl, mash the 2 cups blackberries, with sugar. Cover and refrigerate overnight. Whisk in vinegar, then press with a spatula through a fine-mesh strainer into a resealable container. Fill a glass with ice. Pour in 2 oz shrub and 5 oz seltzer. Garnish with blackberries and serve. Shrub can be stored in the fridge for up to three weeks. (The longer you refrigerate, the mellower the flavor.)

A throwback to Colonial days, shrubs are made by mixing fruit, sugar and vinegar, and served with carbonated water—or you can whip up a boozier version with rum or brandy.

FROZEN ASSETS

Ice cream sandwiches that are anything but vanilla

Spumoni

Chocolate-chocolate chip cookies

+

Cherry-almond and pistachio ice cream

=

Aloha Summer

White chocolate–macadamia nut cookies

+

Pineapple-coconut ice cream

=

Mint Condition

Brownie

+

Mint chocolate chip ice cream

=

So Berry Italian

Mini brioche bun

+

Black raspberry chocolate chip ice cream

=

Malt Shop

Chocolate chip cookies

+

Chocolate ice cream

+

Crushed malted milk balls

=

Lemony Snicket

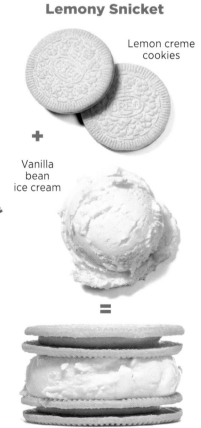

Lemon creme cookies

+

Vanilla bean ice cream

=

Strawberry Shortcake

Pound cake slices

+

Strawberry ice cream

=

Funky Monkey

Peanut butter cookies

+

Banana-chocolate swirl ice cream

=

Meet Your Matcha

Ginger cookies

+

Green tea ice cream

=

Waffle Cone 2.0

Mini waffles

+

Maple-pecan ice cream

=

Coffee Break

Biscoff cookies

+

Coffee ice cream

+

Cinnamon

=

Holy Moly

Cake doughnut

+

Cake batter ice cream

+

Chocolate sprinkles

=

FOUR WAYS WITH ALMOND MILK

This dairy-free milk isn't just for smoothies and cereal.

CHILLED CORN SOUP

TRIPLE ALMOND FRENCH TOAST

THAI-STYLE CHICKEN CURRY

Triple Almond French Toast

MAKES 4 servings **PREP** 10 minutes
COOK 12 minutes

4	eggs
¾	cup unsweetened almond milk
4	tsp sugar
1	tsp cinnamon
1	tsp almond extract
1	lb loaf challah bread
4	tbsp unsalted butter
½	cup toasted sliced almonds
6	oz raspberries
	Powdered sugar

■ Heat oven to 200°. In a shallow dish, whisk eggs, almond milk, sugar, cinnamon and almond extract. Cut eight 1-inch-thick slices challah bread.

■ In a large skillet, melt 2 tbsp of the butter. Soak 4 slices bread in egg mixture until saturated (about 15 seconds per side). Cook over medium for 2 to 3 minutes per side, until browned. Transfer to a baking sheet and place in oven to keep warm. Add the remaining 2 tbsp butter to skillet and cook remaining slices. (Or heat a nonstick griddle to 350° and cook all 8 slices at once, 2 to 3 minutes per side.)

■ Place on a serving platter and sprinkle with almonds and raspberries; dust with powdered sugar.

PER SERVING 585 **CAL**; 27 g **FAT** (9 g **SAT**); 20 g **PRO**; 65 g **CARB**; 12 g **SUGARS**; 5 g **FIBER**; 633 mg **SODIUM**

Thai-Style Chicken Curry

MAKES 4 servings **PREP** 25 minutes
COOK 25 minutes

- 2 **tbsp vegetable oil**
- 1 **cup chopped onion**
- 4 **large cloves garlic, smashed**
- 1 **2-inch piece fresh ginger, chopped**
- 1¾ **cups unsweetened almond milk**
- ¼ **cup packed fresh cilantro leaves and stems**
- 1 **tbsp fish sauce**
- ¼ **cup lime juice**
- 1 **jalapeño, roughly chopped and seeded (optional)**
- 1 **lb boneless, skinless chicken breasts**
- 2 **carrots, peeled**
- 1 **sweet red pepper**
- 2 **tsp oil**
- ¼ **tsp salt**
- ¼ **tsp black pepper**
- 1 **tbsp finely chopped fresh cilantro**
- ½ **cup toasted almonds, chopped**
- 2 **cups cooked brown rice**
  Lime wedges

■ In a large skillet, heat the 2 tbsp vegetable oil over medium-high. Cook onion, garlic and ginger for 3 to 5 minutes. Add almond milk and stir, scraping bottom of pan. Reduce heat to low, cover and simmer 5 minutes. Cool slightly.

■ Transfer to a blender; wipe out pan. Puree onion mixture with the ¼ cup cilantro, the fish sauce, lime juice and jalapeño, if desired. Cut chicken breasts, carrots and sweet red pepper into large dice. Add the 2 tsp oil to skillet and cook carrots over medium-high for 5 minutes. Add peppers, chicken, salt and black pepper; cook 5 minutes, until browned. Add sauce and simmer 5 minutes, until chicken is cooked through. Top with chopped cilantro and almonds. Serve with rice and lime wedges.

PER SERVING 532 **CAL**; 26 g **FAT** (3 g **SAT**); 34 g **PRO**; 42 g **CARB**; 7 g **SUGARS**; 6 g **FIBER**; 660 mg **SODIUM**

Chilled Corn Soup

MAKES 4 servings **PREP** 20 minutes
COOK 30 minutes **REFRIGERATE** 2 hours

- 3 **tsp olive oil**
- 5 **cups fresh corn kernels**
- 3 **scallions, chopped**
- 1 **large clove garlic, chopped**
- ½ **tsp plus ⅛ tsp salt**
- 4 **cups unsweetened almond milk**
- 12 **cooked shrimp (about ½ lb)**
- 4 **tbsp lime juice**
- 1 **tsp chopped fresh cilantro**
- ¼ **tsp black pepper**

■ In a large skillet, heat 2 tsp of the olive oil over medium-high. Add corn kernels; cook 3 minutes, until starting to brown. Add scallions and garlic; season with ¼ tsp salt and cook 5 to 7 minutes, stirring occasionally, until browned. Add almond milk and stir, scraping bottom of pan. Reduce heat to medium-low, cover and simmer 20 minutes. Allow to cool slightly.

■ Transfer half to a blender; puree with 2 tbsp of the lime juice until smooth. Strain into a large bowl. Puree and strain remaining soup; stir to combine. Cover and refrigerate at least 2 hours or overnight. When ready to serve, season with ⅛ tsp salt. Toss cooked shrimp with remaining lime juice, cilantro, remaining 1 tsp olive oil, ¼ tsp salt and pepper. Divide soup among 4 shallow bowls. Top with shrimp and 2 sliced scallions.

PER SERVING 308 **CAL**; 10 g **FAT** (1 g **SAT**); 22 g **PRO**; 39 g **CARB**; 12 g **SUGARS**; 5 g **FIBER**; 744 mg **SODIUM**

Goat Cheese Dip

MAKES 10 servings **PREP** 15 minutes
BAKE 25 minutes at 350° **BROIL** 5 minutes

- 1 **12 oz jar roasted red peppers, drained and chopped**
- 8 **oz canned artichoke hearts, chopped**
- 2 **cloves garlic, grated**
- 2½ **tbsp chopped fresh parsley**
- ¼ **tsp salt**
- ¼ **tsp black pepper**
- 10 **oz goat cheese**
- 1 **cup unsweetened almond milk**
- 2 **tbsp cornstarch**
  Toasts
  Assorted vegetables

■ Heat oven to 350°. Combine roasted red peppers, artichoke hearts, garlic, 2 tbsp of the parsley, the salt and pepper.

■ Beat goat cheese, almond milk and cornstarch until smooth. Fold in red pepper mixture.

■ Pour into an 8 x 8-inch baking dish. Bake 25 minutes, then broil 4 to 5 minutes, until browned. Sprinkle with remaining ½ tbsp chopped parsley. Serve with toasts and assorted vegetables for dipping.

Note Stir in chopped lump crabmeat or shredded cooked chicken to make this dip even heartier.

PER SERVING 100 **CAL**; 6 g **FAT** (4 g **SAT**); 6 g **PRO**; 5 g **CARB**; 1 g **SUGARS**; 2 g **FIBER**; 419 mg **SODIUM**

GOAT CHEESE DIP

HEALTHY FAMILY DINNERS

Try these 7 easy recipes on crazy-busy nights.

BUDDHA BOWL

Buddha Bowl

MAKES 4 servings **PREP** 15 minutes
COOK 20 minutes

- 1⅓ **cups uncooked white rice**
- **Pinch of salt**
- 3 **tbsp canola oil**
- 6 **very small baby bok choy (12 oz total), rinsed and halved lengthwise**
- 1 **orange bell pepper, cored, seeded and sliced**
- 1 **medium white onion, chopped**
- 2 **tsp toasted sesame oil**
- 12 **oz savory baked tofu (4 pieces)**
- 3 **tbsp bottled pad thai sauce**
- ½ **tsp sriracha sauce**
- 2 **tsp toasted sesame seeds**

■ In a lidded saucepan, bring 2⅔ cups water to a boil. Add rice and a pinch of salt. Reduce heat, cover and simmer 20 minutes.

■ Meanwhile, in a large nonstick skillet, heat 1 tbsp canola oil over medium-high. Add bok choy and cook 4 minutes, turning once. (Add a little water if browning too quickly.) Transfer to a platter.

■ Add 1 tbsp canola oil to same skillet along with bell pepper. Cook, stirring, 2 to 3 minutes. Add to platter next to bok choy.

■ Add 1 tbsp canola oil to skillet; add onion and cook 5 minutes. Remove onion to platter, add sesame oil to skillet and reduce heat to medium. Add tofu and cover skillet with foil; cook 4 minutes, turning once.

■ Whisk pad thai sauce with 1 tbsp water and the sriracha.

■ Divide rice among 4 bowls. Top with bok choy, pepper and onion. Dice tofu and add to bowls. Drizzle with sauce mixture and sprinkle with sesame seeds.

PER SERVING 484 **CAL**; 21 g **FAT** (2 g **SAT**); 19 g **PRO**; 55 g **CARB**; 7 g **SUGARS**; 3 g **FIBER**; 760 mg **SODIUM**

STUFFED ZUCCHINI

Stuffed Zucchini

MAKES 4 servings **PREP** 20 minutes **COOK** 10 minutes **BROIL** 14 minutes

- 4 **medium zucchini (28 oz total)**
- 1 **tbsp olive oil**
- ½ **tsp salt**
- ½ **tsp freshly ground black pepper**
- 1 **lb new potatoes, cut into large cubes**
- 1 **cup plain nonfat Greek yogurt**
- 4 **oz shredded cheddar**
- 1 **cup cooked fresh corn kernels**
- 1 **cup cooked shredded chicken**
- 1 **tsp chopped fresh thyme**

■ Heat broiler. Split zucchini lengthwise; scoop out and discard seeds. Place on a foil-lined rimmed baking sheet, and toss with oil and ¼ tsp each salt and pepper. Broil cut side down for 4 minutes. Flip zucchini and leave on baking sheet.

■ Meanwhile, bring a medium pot of water to a boil, add potatoes and cook 8 to 10 minutes, until tender. Drain and transfer to a large bowl. Smash potatoes with yogurt and half the cheddar. Stir in corn, chicken, thyme and ¼ tsp each salt and pepper.

■ Divide potato mixture evenly among zucchini. Top with remaining cheddar. Broil 8 to 10 minutes, until browned and heated through.

PER SERVING 379 **CAL**; 15 g **FAT** (6 g **SAT**); 29 g **PRO**; 36 g **CARB**; 9 g **SUGARS**; 4 g **FIBER**; 685 mg **SODIUM**

"Milanese" refers to the preparation of a thin scallop of meat coated in seasoned bread crumbs and quickly pan-fried until crisp. Here, it's served with whole wheat spaghetti and a salad topping of arugula, tomatoes and red onion.

Pork Milanese

MAKES 6 servings **PREP** 25 minutes **COOK** 8 minutes

- 3 tbsp red wine vinegar
- 1 tsp honey
- 1 tsp salt
- ½ tsp freshly ground black pepper
- 6 tbsp canola oil
- ½ cup all-purpose flour
- 4 large egg whites
- 1 cup seasoned bread crumbs
- 6 thin boneless pork chops (about 1½ lb total), pounded to ⅛-inch thickness
- 8 oz whole wheat spaghetti
- 3 packed cups baby arugula
- 1 cup halved cherry tomatoes
- ½ small red onion, thinly sliced

■ Bring a large pot of lightly salted water to a boil.

■ In a small bowl, whisk vinegar, honey and ¼ tsp each salt and pepper. While whisking, add 2 tbsp oil in a thin stream.

■ In a shallow dish, whisk flour, ½ tsp salt and ¼ tsp pepper. In a second dish, whisk egg whites. Place bread crumbs in a third dish.

■ Coat pork chops in flour mixture, then egg whites and bread crumbs, shaking off excess.

■ Add spaghetti to boiling water; cook per package directions, about 8 minutes. Drain.

■ Meanwhile, in a large nonstick skillet, heat 2 tbsp oil over medium-high. Add 3 cutlets; cook 2 minutes, turning once, and remove to a plate. Add 2 tbsp oil and remaining cutlets to skillet; cook 2 minutes, turning once, and remove to plate.

■ Toss arugula, tomatoes and onion in a bowl with 2 tbsp dressing. Drizzle remaining dressing over spaghetti. Divide spaghetti and cutlets among 6 plates. Top cutlets with salad and season with ¼ tsp salt.

PER SERVING 508 **CAL**; 21 g **FAT** (3 g **SAT**); 37 g **PRO**; 45 g **CARB**; 4 g **SUGARS**; 5 g **FIBER**; 741 mg **SODIUM**

PORK
MILANESE

GRILLED SAUSAGE
AND PEPPERS

Grilled Sausage and Peppers

MAKES 6 servings **PREP** 15 minutes
GRILL 20 minutes

- 1 **fennel bulb (about 1½ lb), trimmed and quartered**
- 2 **sweet red peppers, cored, seeded and cut into 4 flat pieces**
- 1 **yellow bell pepper, cored, seeded and cut into 4 flat pieces**
- 4 **large shallots, peeled and halved**
- 4 **tbsp plus 2 tsp olive oil**
- 1 **pkg (14 oz) hot and spicy chicken sausage links (not precooked)**
- 6 **plum tomatoes, halved**
- ½ **cup torn fresh basil**
- 3 **tbsp cider vinegar**
- 1 **tbsp spicy brown mustard**
- 1 **tsp sugar**
- ⅛ **tsp salt**
- 6 **pieces focaccia bread (12 oz total)**

- Heat grill to medium.

- Toss first 4 ingredients with 1 tbsp oil. Place veggies and sausages on grill and cook, covered, 20 minutes, turning every 5 minutes.

- During last 5 minutes, brush cut side of tomatoes with 2 tsp oil and grill, cut side down, 4 minutes.

- Remove veggies and sausage to a cutting board and core fennel. Chop or slice all into bite-size pieces. Transfer to a large bowl and toss with basil. In a small bowl, whisk next 4 ingredients. Whisk in 3 tbsp oil in a thin stream. Toss with sausage mixture.

- Grill bread 1 minute per side, if desired.

PER SERVING 427 **CAL**; 21 g **FAT** (4 g **SAT**); 20 g **PRO**; 42 g **CARB**; 12 g **SUGARS**; 7 g **FIBER**; 798 mg **SODIUM**

CORN AND
RICOTTA PASTA

Corn and Ricotta Pasta

MAKES 6 servings **PREP** 15 minutes **ROAST** at 400° for 20 minutes **COOK** 20 minutes

- 1½ **lb tricolor cherry tomatoes**
- 1 **tbsp plus 2 tsp olive oil**
- ¾ **tsp salt**
- ¾ **tsp black pepper**
- ½ **cup torn fresh basil**
- 1 **cup chopped white onion**
- 1½ **cups fresh corn kernels**
- 1 **lb fettuccine**
- 1 **cup part-skim ricotta**

- Heat oven to 400°.

- On a foil-lined rimmed baking sheet, toss tomatoes with 1 tbsp oil and ¼ tsp each salt and pepper. Roast 20 minutes, until lightly blistered. Toss hot tomatoes with ¼ cup basil.

- In a large skillet, heat 2 tsp oil over medium-high; add onion. Cook 3 minutes, until starting to brown. Add corn and cook 5 to 7 minutes.

- Meanwhile, bring a large pot of lightly salted water to a boil. Add fettuccine and cook according to package instructions for al dente, about 10 minutes.

- Drain pasta, reserving 1 cup cooking water. Return pasta to pot.

- Add 1 cup pasta water to corn and stir, scraping bottom of skillet. Cover, reduce heat and simmer 10 minutes. Cool mixture slightly.

- Carefully puree corn mixture with the reserved pasta water, ricotta and ½ tsp each salt and pepper. Pour sauce over pasta and stir. Transfer to a large serving bowl. Spoon tomatoes over pasta, drizzle with any juices remaining in pan and top with ¼ cup basil.

Note For extra flavor and a bit of crunch, sprinkle crumbled cooked bacon over the Corn and Ricotta Pasta.

PER SERVING 439 **CAL**; 9 g **FAT** (3 g **SAT**); 17 g **PRO**; 73 g **CARB**; 9 g **SUGARS**; 6 g **FIBER**; 339 mg **SODIUM**

CHICKEN THIGH SHAWARMA

Chicken Thigh Shawarma

MAKES 4 servings **PREP** 25 minutes **COOK** 28 minutes **REST** 5 minutes

- ¼ **cup plain nonfat Greek yogurt**
- 2 **tbsp tahini**
- 6 **cloves garlic, grated**
- 6 **tbsp lemon juice**
- 3 **tsp lemon zest**
- ¾ **tsp kosher salt**
- ¾ **tsp freshly ground black pepper**
- 2 **tsp ground cumin**
- 2 **tsp paprika**
- ½ **tsp curry powder**
- ⅛ **tsp ground cinnamon**
- 1½ **lb boneless, skinless chicken thighs**
- 1 **tbsp olive oil**
- ⅓ **cup toasted pine nuts**
- 4 **tbsp finely chopped fresh parsley**
- 2 **cups hot cooked white rice**

■ In a small bowl, combine yogurt, tahini, one-third of the garlic, 2 tbsp lemon juice and 2 tsp lemon zest; whisk in 2 tbsp water and add ⅛ tsp each salt and pepper.

■ In a small bowl, combine two-thirds of the garlic, 2 tbsp lemon juice, the cumin, paprika, curry, cinnamon and ½ tsp each salt and pepper.

■ Pat chicken dry with paper towels. In a large stainless skillet, heat ½ tbsp oil over medium-high. Add half the chicken to skillet and cook 3 to 5 minutes per side, until cooked through. Repeat with remaining oil and chicken. Transfer to a cutting board, leaving any browned bits in skillet, and rest 5 minutes. Thinly slice chicken.

■ Add ½ cup water to pan and stir, scraping bottom. Add spice mixture and cook 2 to 3 minutes, until garlic softens and sauce thickens. Return chicken to skillet. Cook, stirring constantly, until chicken is well coated and heated through, 3 to 5 minutes.

■ Stir pine nuts, 3 tbsp parsley, 2 tbsp lemon juice, 1 tsp lemon zest and ⅛ tsp each salt and pepper into rice. Top rice with chicken and sprinkle with 1 tbsp parsley. Serve with yogurt sauce.

PER SERVING 525 **CAL**; 22 g **FAT** (4 g **SAT**); 43 g **PRO**; 40 g **CARB**; 1 g **SUGARS**; 4 g **FIBER**; 535 mg **SODIUM**

Catfish Banh Mi

MAKES 4 servings **PREP** 30 minutes **ROAST** at 375° for 14 minutes

- 1 **tbsp olive oil**
- 1 **tsp garlic powder**
- 1 **tsp ground ginger**
- ¼ **tsp salt**
- 4 **catfish fillets (5 oz each)**
- ½ **cup rice vinegar**
- 1½ **tbsp sugar**
- 1 **carrot, grated**
- 2 **radishes, sliced**
- ¼ **English cucumber, julienned**
- ¼ **cup sour cream**
- ½ **tbsp sriracha sauce**
- 4 **mini baguettes, split lengthwise**
- ½ **cup fresh cilantro leaves**
- 1 **jalapeño, thinly sliced, seeded if desired**

■ Heat oven to 375°.

■ In a small bowl, combine first 4 ingredients. Place catfish fillets on a foil-lined rimmed baking sheet and rub with oil mixture. Roast 12 to 14 minutes, until temperature reaches 145°.

■ In a medium bowl, combine vinegar and sugar. Add carrot, radishes and cucumber, and toss to coat.

■ Combine sour cream and sriracha, and spread on cut side of baguette bottoms. Layer with catfish, pickled vegetables, cilantro leaves and as much jalapeño as desired. Cover with baguette tops.

PER SERVING 457 **CAL**; 12 g **FAT** (3 g **SAT**); 33 g **PRO**; 54 g **CARB**; 11 g **SUGARS**; 3 g **FIBER**; 786 mg **SODIUM**

CATFISH
BANH MI

SUMMER SMACKDOWN

Which lobster roll do you prefer, classic or buttered?

CLASSIC
LOBSTER ROLL

Classic Lobster Roll

MAKES 4 servings **PREP** 35 minutes
STEAM 8 minutes

- **2 1¼ lb lobsters***
- **¼ cup mayonnaise**
- **1 tbsp lemon juice**
- **1 tbsp chopped fresh parsley**
- **¼ tsp salt**
- **¼ tsp black pepper**
- **4 New England hot dog buns**

■ In a large, lidded stockpot fitted with a steamer, bring 2 inches of water to a boil. Add lobsters and cover pot. Steam until shells are bright red, 8 to 12 minutes. Remove to a large bowl. If serving chilled, add ice and water, and cool until cold to the touch. If serving warm, let lobsters rest in bowl until cool enough to handle. To remove meat from shells, hold tail in one hand and body in the other, and twist tail away from you at the same time as you twist body toward you. Remove meat from tail, then claws, arms and knuckles. Small kitchen shears and skewers or lobster picks are helpful.

■ In a medium bowl, mix together 2 cups lobster meat, the mayonnaise, lemon juice, parsley, salt and pepper. Fill buns with lobster mixture.

***Lobster Prep** Place lobster on a cutting board and brace its body with your nondominant hand. Insert the tip of a chef's knife into the head of the lobster about ½ inch behind the eyes. Swiftly cut straight down through head of lobster.

PER SERVING 283 **CAL**; 13 g **FAT** (2 g **SAT**); 18 g **PRO**; 23 g **CARB**; 3 g **SUGARS**; 1 g **FIBER**; 803 mg **SODIUM**

BUTTERED LOBSTER ROLL

Buttered Lobster Roll

MAKES 4 servings **PREP** 35 minutes **STEAM** 8 minutes

- **2 1¼ lb lobsters***
- **6 tbsp melted butter**
- **1 tbsp lemon juice**
- **2 tsp chopped fresh chives**
- **¼ tsp salt**
- **¼ tsp black pepper**
- **4 classic split-top hot dog buns**

■ In a large, lidded stockpot fitted with a steamer, bring 2 inches of water to a boil. Add lobsters and cover pot. Steam until shells are bright red, 8 to 12 minutes. Remove to a large bowl. If serving chilled, add ice and water, and cool until cold to the touch. If serving warm, let lobsters rest in bowl until cool enough to handle. To remove meat from shells, hold tail in one hand and body in the other, and twist tail away from you at the same time as you twist body toward you. Remove meat from tail, then claws, arms and knuckles. Small kitchen shears and skewers or lobster picks are helpful.

■ In a medium bowl, mix together 2 cups lobster meat, the melted butter, lemon juice, chives, salt and pepper. Fill buns with lobster mixture.

***Lobster Prep** Place lobster on a cutting board and brace its body with your nondominant hand. Insert the tip of a chef's knife into the head of the lobster about ½ inch behind the eyes. Swiftly cut straight down through head of lobster.

PER SERVING 341 **CAL**; 20 g **FAT** (11 g **SAT**); 18 g **PRO**; 22 g **CARB**; 3 g **SUGARS**; 1 g **FIBER**; 717 mg **SODIUM**

TEXAS-STYLE BRISKET,
PAGE 221

SEPTEMBER

208

212

221

DINNER MATRIX

In his newest cookbook, *Live to Eat*, chef Michael Psilakis shows that dinner is all in the prep. Once you've got a fridge stocked with key ingredients, the meal combinations are endless.

Garlic Confit

MAKES 3½ cups **PREP** 15 minutes
BAKE at 300° for 50 minutes

- 3 cups peeled garlic cloves
- 1 fresh bay leaf
- 8 to 10 sprigs fresh thyme
- 1 tbsp kosher salt
- 1½ tsp whole black peppercorns
- 1 cup canola oil
- 1 cup olive oil

■ Heat oven to 300°. Place garlic cloves, bay leaf, thyme, salt, and peppercorns in a heavy-bottom oven-proof pot. Pour canola oil and olive oil over to cover.

■ Cover pot, transfer to oven and bake at 300° until garlic cloves are pale gold and tender (you should be able to smash them with the back of a spoon), about 50 minutes.

■ Cool to room temperature. Transfer garlic and oil to a clean, wide-mouth resealable jar and refrigerater for up to 1 month.

PER TBSP 30 **CAL**; 2 g **FAT** (0 g **SAT**); 0 g **PRO**; 2 g **CARB**; 0 g **SUGARS**; 0 g **FIBER**; 0 mg **SODIUM**

Garlic Puree Transfer only the cloves of the Garlic Confit to a food processor and pulse until smooth.

Cucumber Yogurt Dip

MAKES 5½ cups **PREP** 15 minutes

- 3 cloves garlic, peeled
- ½ cup white vinegar or white wine vinegar
- 4 cups Greek yogurt
- 1 large English cucumber, peeled and cut into ¼-inch dice
- 3 tbsp loosely packed chopped fresh dill
- 2 tsp kosher salt
- ¼ tsp freshly ground black pepper

■ In a blender, puree the garlic and the vinegar until smooth.

■ Pour into a bowl and add Greek yogurt. Using a whisk, gently work liquid into yogurt until it is fully incorporated.

■ Fold in cucumber, fresh dill, kosher salt, and freshly ground black pepper.

■ Transfer to a container with a tight-fitting lid. Dip will keep for up to 1 week in the fridge.

PER ¼ CUP 45 **CAL**; 3 g **FAT** (1 g **SAT**); 3 g **PRO**; 14 g **CARB**; 2 g **SUGARS**; 1 g **FIBER**; 60 mg **SODIUM**

Roasted Cherry Tomatoes

MAKES 4 cups **PREP** 15 minutes
ROAST at 425° for 15 minutes

- 3 tbsp extra-virgin olive oil
- 3 cloves garlic, minced
- 1 tsp kosher salt
- ½ tsp dried oregano
  Freshly ground black pepper
- 3 pints cherry tomatoes

■ In a large bowl, combine extra-virgin olive oil, garlic, kosher salt, dried oregano, a pinch of freshly ground black pepper and cherry tomatoes. Toss to coat tomatoes.

■ Spread out on a roasting pan and roast at 425° until tomatoes start to shrivel and blister, 12 to 15 minutes.

■ Transfer tomatoes, their juices and any bits that are stuck to pan to a rigid container with a tight-fitting lid. Refrigerate for up to 1 week.

■ To freeze, label and date quart-size resealable freezer bags. Turn the top inside out and spoon tomatoes into bag. Squeeze bag to release any air and seal. Tomatoes will keep, frozen, for up to 2 months.

PER ½ CUP 70 **CAL**; 5 g **FAT** (1 g **SAT**); 2 g **PRO**; 11 g **CARB**; 2 g **SUGARS**; 2 g **FIBER**; 260 mg **SODIUM**

GARLIC CONFIT

CUCUMBER
YOGURT DIP

ROASTED
CHERRY
TOMATOES

RED WINE
VINAIGRETTE,
PAGE 206

TOMATO
SAUCE,
PAGE 206

BLANCHED
CAULIFLOWER,
PAGE 206

SWEET-AND-
SOUR PEPPERS
AND ONIONS,
PAGE 206

Red Wine Vinaigrette

Pictured on page 205.

MAKES 3 cups **PREP** 10 minutes

- ¾ **cup red wine vinegar**
- 1 **tbsp finely diced shallot**
- 2½ **tsp Dijon mustard**
- 2½ **tsp Garlic Puree (recipe, page 204)**
- ½ **tsp minced garlic**
- ½ **tsp dried oregano**
- 1 **tbsp kosher salt**
- ½ **tsp freshly ground black pepper**
- 1½ **cups canola oil**
- ¼ **cup extra-virgin olive oil**

■ Combine red wine vinegar, shallot, mustard, Garlic Puree, garlic, dried oregano, kosher salt, and freshly ground black pepper in a blender and puree on medium speed until smooth.

■ With motor running, slowly add canola oil and extra-virgin olive oil in a thin stream and blend until thoroughly incorporated.

■ Transfer to a large container with a tight-fitting lid and refrigerate. Vinaigrette will keep for up to 1 month in the fridge.

PER TBSP 70 **CAL**; 8 g **FAT** (0 g **SAT**); 0 g **PRO**; 0 g **CARB**; 0 g **SUGARS**; 0 g **FIBER**; 125 mg **SODIUM**

Blanched Cauliflower

Pictured on page 205.

MAKES 4 servings **PREP** 15 minutes **COOK** 2½ minutes

- 6 **cups cauliflower florets (from 1½ heads)**

■ Bring a large pot of salted water to a boil. Prepare an ice bath in a large bowl; line a baking sheet with paper towels.

■ Add cauliflower florets to boiling water and cook 2 to 2½ minutes, checking every 30 seconds, until a knife pierces the flesh with little effort. (You don't want cauliflower to cook all the way through because you'll be reheating it.) To test, with a slotted spoon, remove a floret and dip into ice water. Taste for doneness; it should be firm to the bite and look vibrant.

■ Using slotted spoon, transfer florets to ice water to stop cooking process. Let sit until cool, then transfer to baking sheet to dry.

■ Place in a paper-towel-lined storage container and refrigerate. Cauliflower will keep for up to 1 week in the fridge.

PER SERVING 40 **CAL**; 0 g **FAT** (0 g **SAT**); 3 g **PRO**; 8 g **CARB**; 3 g **SUGARS**; 3 g **FIBER**; 50 mg **SODIUM**

Tomato Sauce

Pictured on page 205.

MAKES 12 to 13 cups **PREP** 15 minutes **COOK** 1 hour, 35 minutes

- ⅓ **cup extra-virgin olive oil**
- 20 **small cloves garlic, peeled**
- 4 **cans (28 oz each) peeled plum tomatoes in juice**
- 6 **cups water**
- 15 **fresh basil leaves**
- 1 **tbsp plus 2 tsp kosher salt**
- ¼ **tsp freshly ground black pepper**
    Red wine vinegar, to taste

■ In a large pot, heat extra-virgin olive oil over medium-high. Add garlic cloves and cook until soft, about 5 minutes.

■ Add peeled plum tomatoes in juice and water, stir and bring to a boil. Reduce heat and simmer, uncovered, until sauce clings to a wooden spoon, about 1½ hours.

■ Stir in basil leaves and crush tomatoes with back of spoon. Season with kosher salt and freshly ground black pepper.

■ Taste and add enough red wine vinegar to achieve your desired acidity (we used 2 tsp).

■ Store, covered, in the fridge for up to 1 week or freeze up to 3 months.

PER ½ CUP 60 **CAL**; 3 g **FAT** (0 g **SAT**); 1 g **PRO**; 6 g **CARB**; 3 g **SUGARS**; 2 g **FIBER**; 370 mg **SODIUM**

Sweet-and-Sour Peppers and Onions

Pictured on page 205.

MAKES 10 cups **PREP** 15 minutes **COOK** 3 hours

- ¼ **cup canola oil**
- 4 **yellow bell peppers, cut into ¼-inch strips**
- 4 **red bell peppers, cut into ¼-inch strips**
- 3 **large yellow onions, cut into slivers**
- 15 **cloves garlic, roughly chopped**
- 6 **tbsp tomato paste**
- 1 **cup white wine vinegar**
- ½ **cup dry white wine**
- 6 **cups water**
- 2 **cups Tomato Sauce (recipe, left)**
- 2 **tbsp honey**
- 2 **tbsp kosher salt**
- ½ **tsp freshly ground black pepper**

■ In a large heavy-bottom pot, heat canola oil over medium-high. Add yellow and red bell peppers, and sauté until just softened and fragrant and peppers begin to release liquid, 5 to 8 minutes.

■ Add yellow onions and garlic. Sauté 6 to 8 minutes, until onions are soft; do not let them take on any color.

■ Add tomato paste and stir to combine. Add white wine vinegar and dry white wine, and cook 12 to 13 minutes, until liquid is reduced by half. (The larger the pan, the faster the liquid will reduce.)

■ Add water, Tomato Sauce, honey, kosher salt, and freshly ground black pepper and stir. Bring mixture to a boil, then reduce heat and simmer until liquid thickens to consistency of salsa, about 2½ hours.

■ Peppers and onions will keep, tightly covered, for 1 week in the fridge or up to 3 months in the freezer.

PER SERVING 80 **CAL**; 3.5 g **FAT** (0 g **SAT**); 1 g **PRO**; 11 g **CARB**; 5 g **SUGARS**; 2 g **FIBER**; 670 mg **SODIUM**

Modern Greek Salad

MAKES 6 servings **PREP** 30 minutes
GRILL 12 minutes **REST** 8 minutes

1½	**lb hanger steak**
	Kosher salt
	Freshly ground black pepper
4	**cups hearts of romaine, cut into ¼-inch strips and tightly packed**
3	**medium red bell peppers, diced**
2	**medium cucumbers, diced**
2	**medium tomatoes, cored and diced**
1	**large red onion, diced**
1½	**cups crumbled feta cheese**
1	**cup Greek olives, pitted and halved**
¼	**cup chopped mixed fresh herbs (parsley, mint, dill)**
½	**cup Red Wine Vinaigrette (recipe, page 206), plus more for serving**

■ Heat grill to high. Pat steak dry with paper towels. Season with salt and pepper, and grill over high heat to desired doneness, turning once, about 12 minutes for medium-rare. Transfer to a cutting board and rest at least 8 minutes. Slice steak on the diagonal into ¼-inch-thick slices.

■ In a large bowl, add romaine and next 7 ingredients and toss. Add ½ cup vinaigrette and toss to coat. Season with salt and pepper. Divide salad among 6 plates, arrange steak slices on top and drizzle with additional vinaigrette.

PER SERVING 500 **CAL**; 31 g **FAT** (8 g **SAT**); 39 g **PRO**; 15 g **CARB**; 9 g **SUGARS**; 4 g **FIBER**; 880 mg **SODIUM**

MODERN GREEK
SALAD

ISRAELI COUSCOUS WITH SHRIMP, CAULIFLOWER, PEAS AND MINT

Chicken Souvlaki

MAKES 4 servings **PREP** 15 minutes
CHILL 2 hours **GRILL** 8 minutes

> 1   lb boneless, skinless chicken breasts, cut into ½-inch cubes
> ½   cup Ladolemono (recipe, below)
> 4   sweet onion rings (¼ inch thick)
> 2   tsp canola oil
> ½   cup Cucumber Yogurt Dip (recipe, page 204) or store-bought tzatziki
> 4   rounds whole-wheat pita, warmed
> 4   or 8 slices (¼ inch thick) beefsteak tomato
> 1   roasted red pepper, drained and cut into ¼-inch-thick strips
>   Kosher salt
>   Freshly ground black pepper
> 1   cup packed arugula
> ½   lemon

■ Combine chicken with ¼ cup Ladolemono in a resealable plastic bag, shake to coat and refrigerate at least 2 hours. Toss onion rings in oil.

■ Heat a gas grill or grill pan over medium-high. Grill chicken, taking care to keep pieces from falling through grate, turning once, until cooked through and firm to the touch, 4 minutes. Meanwhile, grill onion rings until charred and softened, 4 minutes per side. Transfer to a plate. Drizzle remaining Ladolemono over chicken.

■ To assemble souvlaki, spread 2 tbsp dip down middle of each pita. Top with chicken pieces, followed by onion, tomato and red pepper. Season with salt and pepper. Top with arugula and finish with a squeeze of lemon juice. Serve warm.

PER SERVING 550 **CAL**; 27 g **FAT** (4 g **SAT**); 38 g **PRO**; 45 g **CARB**; 11 g **SUGARS**; 3 g **FIBER**; 1,020 mg **SODIUM**

Ladolemono Whisk 1 cup fresh lemon juice, 1 cup Garlic Puree (page 204), 1 tbsp Dijon mustard, 2 tbsp kosher salt, ½ tsp freshly ground black pepper, and ¼ tsp dried oregano. Slowly drizzle in 2⅓ cups extra-virgin olive oil, whisking until thoroughly incorporated. Store, tightly covered, in the fridge for up to 2 weeks.

Israeli Couscous with Shrimp, Cauliflower, Peas and Mint

MAKES 4 servings **PREP** 15 minutes **COOK** 18 minutes

> 1   cup whole-grain dry Israeli couscous
> ¼   cup canola oil
> 6   cups Blanched Cauliflower (recipe page 206)
> 20 large shrimp (15–20 per lb), peeled, deveined, tails removed, halved lengthwise
> 3   cups English peas, thawed if frozen
> ¾   cup Garlic Puree (recipe page 204)
> 12 fresh mint leaves
>   Juice of 1 lemon
>   Kosher salt
>   Freshly ground black pepper

■ Prepare couscous according to package directions.

■ Heat oil in a large skillet over medium. Add cauliflower and sear florets, turning occasionally, until golden in spots, resisting the urge to move them until parts touching skillet are properly seared, 7 to 8 minutes.

■ Add couscous, ¾ cup water, shrimp, peas, garlic puree, mint and lemon juice; season with salt and pepper. Cook 10 minutes, until shrimp are opaque and liquid is reduced by half. Serve warm.

PER SERVING 750 **CAL**; 36 g **FAT** (5 g **SAT**); 25 g **PRO**; 87 g **CARB**; 10 g **SUGARS**; 10 g **FIBER**; 1,430 mg **SODIUM**

CHICKEN
SOUVLAKI

EASY BAKE

It's 9 p.m. and you just found out your kid needs treats for school in the morning. Sigh.

MINI MARBLED
BUNDT CAKES

Mini Marbled Bundt Cakes

MAKES 24 cakes **PREP** 20 minutes
MICROWAVE 1 minute
BAKE at 350° for 20 minutes

- **2** oz semisweet baking chocolate, broken up
- **1** tsp plus ⅓ cup vegetable oil
- **1** box (16.25 oz) white cake mix
- **3** large egg whites
- **¼** cup unsweetened cocoa powder, sifted

■ Heat oven to 350°. Liberally coat two 12-indent mini Bundt pans with flour-and-oil baking spray.

■ In a small glass bowl, combine chocolate and 1 tsp oil. Microwave at 100% for 30 seconds. Stir. Microwave 30 seconds more; stir until smooth. Cool slightly.

■ In a large bowl, combine ⅓ cup oil, cake mix, water (use amount listed on cake mix box) and egg whites. Beat on low speed for 30 seconds, then on medium for 2 minutes, until there are no more lumps. Spoon 2 cups batter into a medium bowl.

■ Beat melted chocolate and cocoa into remaining batter in large bowl.

■ Working quickly, dollop some white batter and some chocolate batter into each indent of prepared Bundt pans. Swirl batters together with a knife. Tap pans on counter to release any air bubbles.

■ Bake 18 to 20 minutes, until cakes spring back when lightly pressed. Cool slightly, then gently remove cakes from pans and cool completely on wire racks.

Note: This recipe also works for cupcakes.

PER CAKE 144 **CAL**; 8 g **FAT** (2 g **SAT**); 2 g **PRO**; 16 g **CARB**; 9 g **SUGARS**; 0 g **FIBER**; 130 mg **SODIUM**

WHITE CHOCOLATE PRETZEL BROWNIES

White Chocolate Pretzel Brownies

MAKES 24 brownies **PREP** 10 minutes **BAKE** at 350° for 25 minutes

- **1** family-size box (18.4 oz) brownie mix
- **½** to ⅔ cup vegetable oil
- **3** large eggs
- **1** cup white chocolate chips
- **1** cup chopped mini pretzels

■ Heat oven to 350°. In a large bowl, combine first 3 ingredients (using amount of oil listed on brownie mix box) with ¼ cup water and stir until blended. Fold in half the white chocolate chips and chopped pretzels.

■ Spread into a greased foil-lined 13 x 9 x 2-inch pan. Sprinkle with remaining white chocolate chips and pretzels. Bake 25 minutes, until set. Cool completely and cut into squares.

PER BROWNIE 255 **CAL**; 14 g **FAT** (3 g **SAT**); 3 g **PRO**; 28 g **CARB**; 18 g **SUGARS**; 1 g **FIBER**; 142 mg **SODIUM**

KETTLE CORN

Chocolate-Covered Rice Krispies Treats

MAKES 24 bars **PREP** 15 minutes
COOK 5 minutes **MICROWAVE** 2½ minutes
STAND 1 hour

> 3 **tbsp unsalted butter**
> 1 **bag (10 oz) marshmallows**
> 6 **cups Rice Krispies cereal**
> 1 **bag (12 oz) semisweet chocolate chips**
> 2 **tsp vegetable oil**

- Line a 13 x 9-inch baking pan with foil. Coat foil with nonstick cooking spray.

- In a large pot, melt butter over low heat. Stir in marshmallows and continue heating until completely melted, about 5 minutes.

- Stir in cereal until evenly coated with marshmallow mixture. Pour into prepared pan and press in evenly with greased hands. Cool completely.

- Place chocolate and oil in a glass bowl. Microwave at 50% for 1 minute. Stir and continue to melt at 50% in 30-second increments until a few lumps remain. Stir until smooth.

- Cut cereal bar into 24 pieces. Dip one end of each in chocolate to coat, shake off excess and place on a wax-paper-lined sheet pan. Let dry 30 minutes.

- Remelt chocolate. With a spoon, drizzle remaining chocolate over dipped end of each bar. Let dry 30 minutes.

PER BAR 148 **CAL**; 6 g **FAT** (3 g **SAT**); 2 g **PRO**;
25 g **CARB**; 15 g **SUGARS**; 1 g **FIBER**;
48 mg **SODIUM**

Kettle Corn

MAKES 10½ cups **PREP** 5 minutes **COOK** 12 minutes

> ¾ **cup slivered almonds**
> ¼ **cup vegetable oil**
> ½ **cup popcorn kernels**
> ⅓ **cup granulated sugar**
> ½ **tsp salt**
> 1 **cup M&M's candies**

- In a large lidded pot, toast almonds over medium for 5 to 6 minutes, stirring frequently. Transfer to a plate and carefully wipe out pot.

- Heat oil in pot over medium. Add popcorn kernels and cover.

- Cook until a few kernels begin to pop, about 3 minutes, shaking pot, then quickly add sugar. Continue to cook, shaking pot constantly, until popping slows down to once every 2 seconds (about another 3 minutes).

- Pour popcorn into a large bowl and add almonds and salt. Toss to combine. Cool a few minutes and toss with M&M's.

PER CUP 234 **CAL**; 14 g **FAT** (3 g **SAT**); 3 g **PRO**;
25 g **CARB**; 17 g **SUGARS**; 3 g **FIBER**;
127 mg **SODIUM**

CARROT CAKE
COOKIES

Sneak veggies and fruit into classroom treats with these quick and easy Carrot Cake Cookies.

Carrot Cake Cookies

MAKES 20 cookies **PREP** 10 minutes
BAKE at 350° for 17 minutes
STAND 1 hour

- 1 **box (16.5 oz) spice or classic carrot cake mix**
- 6 **tbsp unsalted butter, melted**
- 2 **large eggs**
- 1 **cup finely shredded carrots**
- ½ **cup raisins**
- ½ **cup chopped walnuts**
- 2 **cups confectioners' sugar, sifted**

■ Heat oven to 350°. Line 2 large cookie sheets with parchment.

■ In a large bowl, combine cake mix, butter, eggs and ¼ cup water. Stir until smooth. Fold in carrots, raisins and walnuts.

■ Drop by heaping tablespoonfuls onto prepared sheets and spread to 3-inch circles. Bake 14 to 17 minutes, until set. Transfer cookies directly to a wire rack to cool; repeat with remaining batter.

■ To prepare icing, beat confectioners' sugar and 3 tbsp water in a medium bowl. Spoon onto cookies and spread to edges. Let dry at least 1 hour or overnight. Slide into glassine or wax paper treat bags.

PER COOKIE 221 **CAL**; 10 g **FAT** (3 g **SAT**); 2 g **PRO**; 30 g **CARB**; 22 g **SUGARS**; 0 g **FIBER**; 151 mg **SODIUM**

HOMEMADE MARSHMALLOWS

Homemade Marshmallows

MAKES 36 marshmallows **PREP** 15 minutes **COOK** 7 minutes **STAND** 2 hours

- ½ **cup confectioners' sugar**
- ⅓ **cup cornstarch**
- 2 **envelopes (0.25 oz each) unflavored gelatin**
- 1¼ **cups granulated sugar**
- ⅔ **cup light corn syrup**
- ⅛ **tsp salt**

■ Sift confectioners' sugar and cornstarch into a small bowl. Line a 9 x 9 x 2-inch pan with foil. Coat with nonstick cooking spray. Sift 2 tbsp confectioners' sugar mixture into pan, tilting to coat sides. Leave any excess in pan.

■ Place ⅔ cup water in a large bowl and sprinkle with gelatin. Let stand 5 minutes to soften.

■ Meanwhile, in a medium heavy-bottom saucepan, combine granulated sugar, corn syrup and salt. Cook over medium until sugar dissolves, stirring occasionally, about 7 minutes. Strain into bowl with gelatin.

■ Beat on high speed with an electric mixer until light and fluffy, about 12 minutes. Spread into prepared pan and smooth top. Dust with 2 tbsp confectioners' sugar mixture. Let stand 1 to 2 hours, until set.

■ Lift marshmallow from pan with foil. With a wet knife, cut into 4 squares. Cut each square into 9 pieces. Spread remaining confectioners' sugar mixture onto sheet pan. Toss marshmallows in sugar mixture and let stand 1 hour. Store in an airtight container at room temperature.

PER MARSHMALLOW 170 **CAL**; 0 g **FAT** (0 g **SAT**); 2 g **PRO**; 14 g **CARB**; 10 g **SUGARS**; 0 g **FIBER**; 13 mg **SODIUM**

FOUR WAYS WITH MARINARA SAUCE

A jar of pasta sauce is the foundation for dinner.

TOMATO-BAKED EGGS

Spaghetti and Meatball Skillet Pie

MAKES 6 servings **PREP** 10 minutes **COOK** 9 minutes **BAKE** at 425° for 15 minutes

- 1 **lb spaghetti**
- 1 **jar (24 oz) marinara sauce**
- 1 **bag (14 oz) frozen fully cooked mini meatballs, thawed**
- 4 **eggs, beaten**
- 6 **oz diced fresh mozzarella**
- ¼ **cup grated Parmesan**

■ In a large pot of lightly salted water, cook spaghetti for 9 minutes, until al dente.

■ Meanwhile, in a medium pot, heat marinara sauce and mini meatballs until just simmering. Stir into cooked spaghetti with eggs and fresh mozzarella.

■ Transfer to a 12-inch cast-iron skillet. Top with diced mozzarella and grated Parmesan.

■ Bake at 425° for 15 minutes, until cheese begins to brown. Cut into wedges and serve with more marinara on the side.

PER SERVING 630 **CAL**; 22 g **FAT** (9 g **SAT**); 35 g **PRO**; 70 g **CARB**; 7 g **SUGARS**; 3 g **FIBER**; 780 mg **SODIUM**

SPAGHETTI AND MEATBALL SKILLET PIE

Tomato-Baked Eggs

MAKES 4 servings **PREP** 10 minutes **BAKE** at 400° for 12 minutes

- 1 **tbsp extra-virgin olive oil**
- ½ **cup diced yellow onion**
- 2 **cloves garlic, sliced**
- 1 **jar (24 oz) marinara sauce**
- 1 **cup packed torn fresh basil**
- ¼ **tsp black pepper**
- 8 **eggs**
  Salt
  Black pepper
- 8 **tsp jarred pesto**
  Fresh basil, to garnish
  Bread (optional)

■ In a medium pot, heat extra-virgin olive oil over medium. Stir in diced yellow onion and garlic. Cook 3 to 5 minutes, until softened.

■ Stir in marinara sauce and bring to a simmer. Stir in packed torn basil and ¼ tsp. black pepper.

■ Evenly ladle sauce into four 2-cup baking dishes. Crack 2 eggs into each dish and season with a pinch each of salt and black pepper. Bake at 400° for 12 minutes, until egg whites set.

■ Drizzle jarred pesto over each and garnish with more basil. Serve with bread, if desired.

PER SERVING 310 **CAL**; 20 g **FAT** (5 g **SAT**); 18 g **PRO**; 17 g **CARB**; 10 g **SUGARS**; 1 g **FIBER**; 990 mg **SODIUM**

CHICKEN TIKKA MASALA

SPANISH-STYLE MUSSELS

Chicken Tikka Masala

MAKES 4 servings   **PREP** 10 minutes
COOK 11 minutes

- 1   **lb boneless, skinless chicken thighs**
- 2   **tsp garam masala**
- ¼   **tsp cayenne pepper**
- ⅛   **tsp salt**
- 1   **tbsp unsalted butter**
- 1   **jar (24 oz) marinara sauce**
- ¼   **cup water**
- 1   **clove garlic, grated**
- 1   **tsp sugar**
- ¼   **cup heavy cream**
- 1   **tbsp unsalted butter**
-     **Handful of fresh cilantro**
-     **Cooked basmati rice**
-     **Naan bread (optional)**

■ Dice chicken into 1-inch pieces. Toss with garam masala, cayenne pepper, and salt.

■ In a large skillet, heat 1 tbsp unsalted butter over medium-high. Stir in chicken and cook 3 minutes, until browned. Add marinara sauce, water, garlic, and sugar. Bring to a simmer.

■ Cover, reduce heat to medium-low and simmer 8 minutes, until chicken is cooked through.

■ Remove from heat and stir in heavy cream and 1 tbsp unsalted butter.

■ Garnish with a handful of cilantro. Serve with basmati rice and, if desired, naan bread.

PER SERVING 500 **CAL**; 18 g **FAT** (8 g **SAT**); 30 g **PRO**; 53 g **CARB**; 10 g **SUGARS**; 0 g **FIBER**; 850 mg **SODIUM**

Spanish-Style Mussels

MAKES 6 servings   **PREP** 15 minutes   **COOK** 12 minutes

- 4   **lb mussels**
- 1   **tbsp extra-virgin olive oil**
- 2   **oz cured Spanish chorizo, casing removed and diced**
- 8   **cloves garlic, sliced**
- 1   **large shallot, minced**
- 2   **tsp smoked paprika**
- ⅓   **cup dry red wine**
- 2   **cups marinara sauce**
- ½   **cup chopped fresh parsley**
-     **Baguette (optional)**

■ Place mussels in a large bowl of lightly salted cold water. Debeard each mussel by pulling the seaweed-like string between the shells. (If a mussel is open, tap it on the counter. If shell closes, keep it; otherwise discard.)

■ In a large, lidded pot, heat extra-virgin olive oil over medium. Add Spanish chorizo, garlic, shallot and paprika. Cook 3 minutes, until garlic is softened. Pour in wine and simmer 1 minute. Add marinara sauce and bring to a simmer.

■ Drain mussels and carefully stir into pot. Cover and cook 8 minutes or until shells open and mussels are cooked through.

■ Stir in parsley. Discard any mussels that did not open. Serve with baguette slices, if desired.

PER SERVING 250 **CAL**; 8 g **FAT** (2 g **SAT**); 18 g **PRO**; 23 g **CARB**; 5 g **SUGARS**; 1 g **FIBER**; 1,060 mg **SODIUM**

HEALTHY FAMILY DINNERS

Come home to these satisfying suppers—straight from the slow cooker.

PORK TACOS
WITH SPICY
SLAW

Pork Tacos with Spicy Slaw

MAKES 8 servings **PREP** 20 minutes
COOK 12 minutes
SLOW COOK on HIGH for 6 hours

- ¾ cup cider vinegar
- 8 cloves garlic
- 1 4-inch piece fresh ginger, peeled and chopped
- 6 scallions, chopped
- 1½ tbsp sriracha
- 1 tsp salt
- 1 bag (14 oz) coleslaw mix
- 1 boneless pork shoulder (about 3 lb)
- ½ tsp ground black pepper
- 2 tbsp canola oil
- 1 medium white onion, chopped
- 1 can (14.5 oz) chicken broth
- 16 corn tortillas, warmed

■ In a blender, combine ½ cup vinegar, 4 cloves garlic, ginger, scallions, sriracha and ½ tsp salt. Puree until smooth. Pour half over coleslaw mix. Add ¼ cup vinegar to slaw and stir to combine. Cover and refrigerate until pork is ready.

■ Pat pork dry with paper towels. Sprinkle all over with ½ tsp each salt and pepper. In a large skillet, heat oil over medium-high. Cook pork 8 to 12 minutes, turning, until evenly browned on all sides. Transfer to a 5-quart slow cooker.

■ Smash 4 cloves garlic and add to slow cooker, along with onion, broth and remaining vinegar mixture. Cover and cook on HIGH for 6 hours, until falling apart.

■ Transfer pork to a large bowl and discard fat layer. Shred pork. Using a slotted spoon, add onion to pork, discarding garlic cloves. Strain cooking liquid into a de-fatting cup and allow to separate. Pour 1 cup de-fatted cooking liquid over pork and toss well. Divide among warm tortillas and top with slaw.

PER SERVING 522 **CAL**; 27 g **FAT** (7 g **SAT**); 36 g **PRO**; 31 g **CARB**; 6 g **SUGARS**; 5 g **FIBER**; 560 mg **SODIUM**

ZUCCHINI LASAGNA

Zucchini Lasagna

MAKES 8 servings **PREP** 10 minutes **COOK** 10 minutes
SLOW COOK on HIGH for 3½ to 4 hours or LOW for 5 to 5½ hours **REST** 30 minutes

- 1 tbsp olive oil
- 1 lb ground turkey
- ¼ tsp salt
- 1 small white onion, chopped
- 3 cloves garlic, grated
- 1 jar (24 oz) marinara sauce
- ¼ tsp crushed red pepper
- 9 lasagna noodles (not no-boil), broken into pieces
- 1 lb zucchini, trimmed and sliced ¼ inch thick on the bias
- 1 bag (7 oz) 2% shredded Italian cheese blend
- ⅓ cup packed fresh basil, chopped

■ In a large skillet, heat oil over medium-high. Add turkey and salt; cook 4 to 5 minutes, until cooked through. Transfer turkey to a plate and increase heat to high. Add onion and garlic to skillet and cook 4 to 5 minutes, until translucent and tender. Return turkey to skillet and add marinara and crushed red pepper. Stir to combine and remove from heat.

■ Line a 5-quart slow cooker with a plastic liner; coat liner with cooking spray. Layer a third of the meat sauce, a third of the noodles and a third each of the zucchini, cheese and basil. Repeat layering twice, arranging top zucchini layer in a circular pattern and reserving the final third of the basil.

■ Cook on HIGH for 3½ to 4 hours or LOW for 5 to 5½ hours. Rest 15 to 30 minutes. Sprinkle with remaining basil, slice and serve.

PER SERVING 342 **CAL**; 13 g **FAT** (5 g **SAT**); 24 g **PRO**; 33 g **CARB**; 7 g **SUGARS**; 3 g **FIBER**; 698 mg **SODIUM**

40-CLOVE GARLIC
CHICKEN

It's a lot of garlic, but garlic mellows and sweetens as it cooks. Look for the large containers of peeled garlic to make this recipe fast to prep.

TEXAS-STYLE
BRISKET

40-Clove Garlic Chicken

MAKES 6 servings **PREP** 10 minutes
COOK 8 minutes per batch, plus 2 minutes
SLOW COOK on LOW for 4 hours

- **40** cloves garlic, peeled
- **3** lb bone-in, skinless chicken thighs
- **1** tsp salt
- **½** tsp freshly ground black pepper
- **2** tbsp canola oil
- **1** cup unsalted chicken broth
- **¼** cup dry white wine
- **6** sprigs fresh thyme, plus more, chopped, for serving
- **4** tsp cornstarch
- **3** cups cooked brown and wild rice blend
- Cooked broccoli rabe

■ Sprinkle garlic into a 5-quart slow cooker. Pat chicken dry with paper towels. Sprinkle all over with ½ tsp each salt and pepper. In a large skillet, heat oil over medium-high. Working in batches, cook chicken 3 to 4 minutes per side, until browned.

■ Transfer chicken to slow cooker. Add broth, wine, thyme and ½ tsp salt.

■ Cook on LOW for 4 hours. Discard thyme stems. With a slotted spoon, transfer chicken and garlic to a large platter; cover with foil and keep warm.

■ Pour cooking liquid into a small saucepan and bring to a simmer. Combine cornstarch with 4 tsp water and stir into saucepan; boil 2 minutes. Pour sauce over chicken and sprinkle with chopped thyme. Serve with rice and broccoli rabe.

PER SERVING 583 **CAL**; 18 g **FAT** (3 g **SAT**);
53 g **PRO**; 51 g **CARB**; 0 g **SUGARS**; 6 g **FIBER**;
745 mg **SODIUM**

Texas-Style Brisket

MAKES 8 servings **PREP** 25 minutes **COOK** 24 minutes
SLOW COOK on HIGH for 6 hours or LOW for 9 hours **BROIL** 8 minutes

- **¾** cup low-sodium beef broth
- **2** tbsp tomato paste
- **1** tbsp cider vinegar
- **2** large chipotles in adobo, seeded for less heat if desired, finely chopped (about 2 tbsp)
- **½** tsp ground cumin
- **½** tsp ancho chile powder
- **½** tsp chili powder
- **26** oz prepared polenta
- **1** tsp salt
- **1** tsp ground black pepper
- **1** cup finely diced red onion
- **4** cloves garlic, grated
- **3** lb beef brisket, cut into 2-inch chunks
- **4** tsp vegetable oil
- **4** scallions, chopped
- Cooked collard greens

■ In a 5-quart slow cooker, whisk first 7 ingredients plus ½ cup crumbled polenta (about a 1-inch slice) and ¼ tsp each salt and pepper. Stir in onion and garlic.

■ Pat brisket dry with paper towels and toss with ½ tsp each salt and pepper. Heat a large skillet over medium-high; add 2 tsp oil. Add half the brisket and cook 6 to 12 minutes, turning frequently, until browned all over; add to slow cooker. Repeat with remaining oil and brisket. Cook on HIGH for 6 hours or LOW for 9 hours.

■ Strain cooking liquid into a de-fatting cup and allow to separate. Transfer meat (and any solids clinging to it) to a bowl. Pour de-fatted liquid over meat and toss well to combine.

■ Meanwhile, heat broiler. Line a baking sheet with foil and coat lightly with cooking spray. Slice remaining polenta into 24 (⅓-inch) rounds. Place on baking sheet and sprinkle with ¼ tsp each salt and pepper. Broil 6 to 8 minutes, until browned.

■ Divide polenta evenly among 8 shallow bowls. Top with meat and sprinkle with scallions. Serve with warm collard greens.

PER SERVING 354 **CAL**; 13 g **FAT** (4 g **SAT**);
39 g **PRO**; 19 g **CARB**; 3 g **SUGARS**; 2 g **FIBER**;
710 mg **SODIUM**

MOROCCAN
CHICKPEAS

When served with a hearty and fiber-rich kale salad, this classic creamy soup makes a satisfying supper.

Potato-Leek Soup

MAKES 4 servings PREP 15 minutes
COOK 8 minutes SLOW COOK on HIGH for
4 hours or LOW for 5 hours

- **2 tbsp unsalted butter**
- **1 lb leeks, white and pale green parts only, thinly sliced and rinsed well (about 2 cups)**
- **1½ lb russet potatoes, peeled and chopped**
- **3 cups unsalted chicken stock**
- **6 sprigs fresh thyme**
- **2 bay leaves**
- **1 tsp salt**
- **1 tbsp finely chopped fresh chives**
- **Coarsely ground black pepper**
- **Kale salad**

■ In a large skillet, melt butter over medium. Add leeks and cook about 8 minutes, until softened but not browned.

■ Transfer to a 5-quart slow cooker. Stir in potatoes and next 4 ingredients. Cook on HIGH for 4 hours or LOW for 5 hours. Discard thyme stems and bay leaves. Let cool slightly.

■ Using an immersion blender, puree until smooth. Sprinkle with chives and pepper, and serve with kale salad on the side.

PER SERVING 254 CAL; 7 g FAT (4 g SAT);
10 g PRO; 40 g CARB; 4 g SUGARS; 4 g FIBER;
672 mg SODIUM

Moroccan Chickpeas

MAKES 4 servings PREP 30 minutes SLOW COOK on HIGH for 4 hours or LOW for 6 hours

- **2 cups diced carrots**
- **2 cups diced yellow onion**
- **3 cloves garlic, finely chopped**
- **1 2-inch piece fresh ginger, peeled and finely chopped**
- **2 cans (8 oz each) tomato sauce**
- **2 cans (15.5 oz each) chickpeas, drained and rinsed**
- **3 oz (packed ½ cup) dried apricots, chopped**
- **½ tsp ground coriander**
- **½ tsp ground cumin**
- **¼ tsp ground cinnamon**
- **¼ tsp salt**
- **⅛ tsp cayenne pepper**

- **1 tbsp lemon juice**
- **2 cups hot cooked couscous**
- **1 tbsp roughly chopped fresh parsley**

■ In a 5-quart slow cooker, layer first 4 ingredients. Pour in tomato sauce.

■ Toss chickpeas and apricots with next 5 ingredients. Add to slow cooker and cook on HIGH for 4 hours or LOW for 6 hours.

■ Stir in lemon juice. Serve over couscous and sprinkle with parsley.

PER SERVING 264 CAL; 3 g FAT (0 g SAT);
10 g PRO; 53 g CARB; 17 g SUGARS; 10 g FIBER;
493 mg SODIUM

POTATO-LEEK
SOUP

HUMMUS SKULL
PLATTER, PAGE 233

OCTOBER

228

239

244

HEALTHY FAMILY DINNERS

Using your noodle is always a good thing!

COCONUT
CURRY NOODLE
SOUP

Coconut Curry Noodle Soup

MAKES 4 servings **PREP** 15 minutes
COOK 23 minutes

- 1 **tbsp vegetable oil**
- 1 **2-inch piece fresh ginger, peeled and grated**
- 1 **large shallot, peeled and grated**
- 4 **cloves garlic, grated**
- 1 **tbsp red curry paste**
- ½ **tsp turmeric**
- 1 **tbsp all-purpose flour**
- 2 **cups unsalted chicken broth**
- 1 **can (14.5 oz) light coconut milk**
- 1 **lb boneless, skinless chicken thighs, sliced in half**
- 1 **tbsp fish sauce**
- 1 **tbsp packed brown sugar**
- 1 **tbsp lime juice**
- 12 **oz fresh linguine or fettuccine, cooked and drained**

  Bean sprouts, fresh cilantro, sliced shallots, crispy chow mein noodles, lime wedges and chili oil (optional)

■ In a medium pot, heat oil over medium-high. Add ginger, shallot and garlic, cooking 1 to 2 minutes. Stir in curry paste, turmeric and flour; cook 1 minute. Whisk in broth and coconut milk, scraping up browned bits from bottom of pan. Bring to a boil, add chicken and reduce heat to a low simmer. Cover and simmer 20 minutes, until chicken is cooked through.

■ Remove chicken with tongs and shred into large pieces. Whisk in fish sauce, brown sugar and lime juice. Return chicken to pot.

■ Divide noodles evenly among 4 shallow bowls and ladle soup on top. Sprinkle with sprouts, cilantro, shallots, crispy noodles, lime and chili oil, if using.

PER SERVING 600 **CAL**; 15 g **FAT** (7 g **SAT**); 38 g **PRO**; 77 g **CARB**; 10 g **SUGARS**; 1 g **FIBER**; 790 mg **SODIUM**

LAMB BOLOGNESE

Lamb Bolognese

MAKES 6 servings **PREP** 15 minutes **COOK** 43 minutes

- 2 **tbsp extra-virgin olive oil**
- 2 **stalks celery, finely diced**
- 1 **large carrot, peeled and finely diced**
- 1 **small white onion, finely diced**
- 3 **cloves garlic, sliced**
- 2 **tbsp chopped fresh rosemary**
- 1 **lb ground lamb**
- ¼ **tsp ground nutmeg**
- 1 **cup milk**
- ½ **cup dry red wine**
- 1 **can (14.5 oz) diced tomatoes**
- 1 **cup crushed tomatoes**
- ½ **tsp salt**
- ½ **tsp black pepper**
- 12 **oz papardelle, cooked and drained**

  Ricotta (optional)

■ In a medium pot, heat 1 tbsp oil over medium. Stir in next 5 ingredients. Cook 5 minutes, stirring a couple times. Stir in another 1 tbsp oil, lamb and nutmeg. Cook 5 minutes, stirring several times, until meat is no longer pink.

■ Increase heat to medium-high and pour in milk. Simmer until almost evaporated, about 5 minutes. Add wine and cook until evaporated, about 3 minutes. Stir in tomatoes; bring to a simmer and reduce heat to medium-low. Cook 25 minutes, uncovered, stirring as needed, until thickened. Season with salt and pepper.

■ Serve Bolognese over papardelle with a dollop of ricotta, if using.

PER SERVING 450 **CAL**; 13 g **FAT** (5 g **SAT**); 26 g **PRO**; 53 g **CARB**; 8 g **SUGARS**; 4 g **FIBER**; 460 mg **SODIUM**

MISO-GLAZED SALMON
AND SOBA BOWL

Sichuan peppercorns can leave a pleasant, tingly feeling on the tongue. Look for this Chinese spice near other Asian ingredients.

Sichuan Pork and Cabbage Noodles

MAKES 4 servings **PREP** 15 minutes
COOK 14 minutes

- 1 pkg (8.8 oz) thin rice noodles (such as Thai Kitchen)
- 1 cup unsalted chicken stock
- ¼ cup low-sodium soy sauce
- ¼ cup rice vinegar
- 1 tbsp light brown sugar
- 1 tbsp vegetable oil
- 1 3-inch piece ginger, peeled and sliced
- 4 cloves garlic, sliced
- ¾ lb ground pork
- 2 tsp Sichuan peppercorns, crushed
- 4 cups sliced napa cabbage
- 8 oz sliced shiitake mushrooms
- ½ cup sliced scallions

■ Cook rice noodles according to package directions, about 8 minutes. Drain, reserving ½ cup water. Rinse noodles under cold water until cool; set aside. In a small bowl, whisk stock, soy sauce, vinegar and sugar.

■ Meanwhile, in a large skillet, heat oil over medium-high. Stir in ginger and garlic. Cook 2 minutes and remove to a plate with a slotted spoon. Stir in pork and peppercorns. Cook 5 minutes, stirring a couple times, until pork is browned. Mix in cabbage and mushrooms; cook 5 to 7 minutes, until starting to brown. Pour in reserved noodle water and stock-soy mixture. Stir ginger and garlic back into skillet. Pour over noodles in a large bowl and toss. Scatter scallions on top.

PER SERVING 470 **CAL**; 9 g **FAT** (2 g **SAT**);
33 g **PRO**; 63 g **CARB**; 5 g **SUGARS**; 3 g **FIBER**;
710 mg **SODIUM**

Miso-Glazed Salmon and Soba Bowl

MAKES 4 servings **PREP** 15 minutes **ROAST** at 450° for 15 minutes **COOK** 15 minutes

- 1 pkg (8 oz) soba noodles
- 3 tbsp miso paste
- 3 tbsp rice vinegar
- 2 tsp sesame oil
- 2 tsp molasses
- 1 lb salmon fillet
- 2 tbsp extra-virgin olive oil
- 1 large eggplant (about 1 lb), cut into ¾-inch cubes
- 1 pkg (5 oz) baby spinach
- ¼ tsp salt
- 4 tsp toasted sesame seeds

■ Heat oven to 450°. Bring a large pot of salted water to a boil. Add soba and cook according to package directions, about 8 minutes. Drain, reserving ½ cup soba water, and rinse under cold water until cool.

■ Meanwhile, whisk miso paste, 3 tbsp water, vinegar, sesame oil and molasses until smooth. Place salmon on a foil-lined baking sheet and brush with 1 tbsp miso mixture. Roast 15 minutes. Set aside to cool slightly, then flake.

■ In a large skillet, heat olive oil over medium-high. Add eggplant and cook 4 to 6 minutes, stirring, until tender. Add spinach, tossing to wilt. Season with salt. Pour in reserved soba water and remaining miso mixture, scraping bottom of pan. Simmer 1 minute. Toss in a large bowl with soba and sesame seeds, then fold in salmon.

PER SERVING 550 **CAL**; 20 g **FAT** (3 g **SAT**);
36 g **PRO**; 59 g **CARB**; 10 g **SUGARS**; 4 g **FIBER**;
640 mg **SODIUM**

SICHUAN PORK AND
CABBAGE NOODLES

SHRIMP AND BROCCOLI
RABE FUSILLI

Shrimp and Broccoli Rabe Fusilli

MAKES 6 servings **PREP** 15 minutes
COOK 14 minutes

- **3 medium lemons**
- **1 lb long fusilli pasta**
- **1 lb broccoli rabe, trimmed and chopped into 1-inch pieces**
- **3 tbsp extra-virgin olive oil**
- **½ tsp sugar**
- **½ tsp salt**
- **1 lb shrimp, peeled and deveined**
- **¼ tsp black pepper**
- **¼ cup grated Parmesan**

■ Bring a large pot of salted water to a boil. Zest and juice 2 lemons. Cut ends off 3rd lemon, then quarter and seed. Thinly slice each quarter into triangles. Add to boiling water and cook 2 minutes. With a slotted spoon, remove to a paper-towel-lined plate and blot dry. Add pasta and cook 10 minutes. During last 3 minutes, add broccoli rabe. Drain both, reserving 1 cup pasta water.

■ Meanwhile, in a large skillet, heat 1 tbsp oil over medium-high. Stir in lemon pieces, sugar and ¼ tsp salt. Cook 5 minutes, until starting to brown. Transfer to a plate.

■ Add another 1 tbsp oil to skillet. Stir in shrimp, lemon zest and ¼ tsp each salt and pepper. Cook 2 minutes, until pink. Stir in pasta, broccoli rabe, lemon pieces, ½ cup pasta water, lemon juice, Parmesan and 1 tbsp olive oil. Stir in more pasta water, if desired.

PER SERVING 450 **CAL**; 11 g **FAT** (2 g **SAT**); 23 g **PRO**; 63 g **CARB**; 5 g **SUGARS**; 2 g **FIBER**; 730 mg **SODIUM**

SWEET POTATO NOODLE CARBONARA

Sweet Potato Noodle Carbonara

MAKES 4 servings **PREP** 15 minutes **BAKE** at 400° for 12 minutes
MICROWAVE 30 seconds **COOK** 5 minutes

- **3 lb sweet potatoes, peeled**
- **2 tbsp extra-virgin olive oil**
- **¾ tsp freshly cracked black pepper**
- **½ tsp salt**
- **3 tbsp heavy cream**
- **2 whole eggs plus 2 yolks**
- **¼ cup grated Parmesan**
- **¼ cup chopped parsley**
- **2 slices thick-cut bacon, diced**

■ Heat oven to 400°. Peel sweet potatoes and trim ends. Spiral cut with a small to medium blade. Toss with oil and ¼ tsp each pepper and salt. Place on 2 rimmed baking sheets and roast 12 minutes, stirring once.

■ Meanwhile, microwave heavy cream in a glass bowl at 100% for 30 seconds. In a bowl, whisk whole eggs, yolks, cheese, parsley, ½ tsp pepper and ¼ tsp salt.

■ In a large skillet, cook bacon until crispy, about 5 minutes. Add sweet potato noodles and toss gently; remove skillet from heat. Whisk warm cream into egg mixture, then slowly mix into skillet, stirring constantly to cook eggs but keep them from scrambling. Serve immediately.

PER SERVING 470 **CAL**; 23 g **FAT** (9 g **SAT**); 14 g **PRO**; 51 g **CARB**; 11 g **SUGARS**; 8 g **FIBER**; 680 mg **SODIUM**

NO TRICKS...SO MANY TREATS

You'll get much delight—and no fright—from these fun Halloween foods!

SPOOKY BAT COOKIES

This wide-ranging Halloween menu features food and drink for every taste and age (including both kid-friendly and adult beverages), so the whole gang can dress up and enjoy the fun!

Spooky Bat Cookies

MAKES 3½ dozen **PREP** 20 minutes
BAKE at 375° for 12 minutes

- **1** **batch dough from Skeleton Cookies (recipe, page 239)**
- **3** **cups confectioners' sugar**
- **3** **tbsp meringue powder or powdered egg whites**
  Purple food coloring
  Purple sparkling sugar
  Edible eyeballs

■ Prepare and refrigerate dough from Skeleton Cookies. Heat oven to 375°. Roll dough to ¼-inch thickness. Using a 3½-inch bat cookie cutter, cut out shapes. Transfer to 2 large baking sheets and bake at 375° for 12 minutes. Cool completely on a wire rack.

■ To prepare icing, beat confectioners' sugar and meringue powder with 4 tbsp water until good frosting consistency. Thin with a little more water, if needed. Tint with purple food coloring and spread onto cooled cookies. Dip in purple sparkling sugar and use a small dot of icing to attach edible eyeballs. Let dry.

PER COOKIE 132 **CAL**; 5 g **FAT** (3 g **SAT**); 2 g **PRO**; 22 g **CARB**; 15 g **SUGARS**; 1 g **FIBER**; 24 mg **SODIUM**

HUMMUS SKULL PLATTER

Hummus Skull Platter

MAKES 8 servings **PREP** 20 minutes

- **1** **Family-size container (17.6 oz) hummus**
  Assorted vegetables: beet slices, radish slices, black olives, fresh chives, mini sweet peppers, Kirby cucumber slices, baby carrots
  Sliced almonds

■ On a large platter, spread hummus in the shape of a skull (about 10 inches long and 8 inches across the cheek area).

■ For eyes, use 2 thin red beet slices topped with 2 thin radish slices and the end slices from a pitted black olive. Create eyelashes with halved pitted black olive slices. For the nose, use a thin beet slice cut into a heart shape. Make a mouth from sliced almonds and a piece of chives. We also used sliced mini sweet peppers, sliced Kirby cucumbers and sliced baby carrots for other features and as decoration.

■ Arrange more of these vegetables plus halved radishes around skull for dipping.

Note To make ahead, spread hummus on platter and prep veggies, but keep separate. Assemble just before serving.

PER SERVING 189 **CAL**; 12 g **FAT** (2 g **SAT**); 6 g **PRO**; 15 g **CARB**; 4 g **SUGARS**; 4 g **FIBER**; 309 mg **SODIUM**

SALUMI AND EYEBALL PLATTER

REDRUM COCKTAIL

These spooky eyeballs are not only fun to "look at," but super-simple to make from tiny balls of fresh mozzarella and black and green olives.

DARK-AS-MIDNIGHT CLUSTERS

Salumi and Eyeball Platter

MAKES 6 servings **PREP** 15 minutes

- **1   pkg (6 oz) assorted cured meats (such as capicola, Salumi and prosciutto)**
- **2   oz prosciutto**
- **1   pkg (6 oz) BelGioioso fresh mozzarella snacking cheese**
- **Black or green olives**

■ Arrange assorted cured meats plus prosciutto on a cutting board. Unwrap mozzarella snacking cheese and thread onto toothpicks, 2 per pick. Thinly slice olives. Place a slice on each piece of cheese to resemble an eyeball.

PER SERVING 190 **CAL**; 14 g **FAT** (7 g **SAT**); 14 g **PRO**; 0 g **CARB**; 0 g **SUGARS**; 0 g **FIBER**; 733 mg **SODIUM**

Redrum Cocktail

MAKES 6 servings **PREP** 5 minutes

- **Ice**
- **9   oz light rum**
- **1   lime**
- **3   cans (11.5 oz each) blood orange sparkling soda (such as San Pellegrino Aranciata Rossa)**

■ Fill 6 glasses with ice. Add 1½ oz light rum and a squeeze of lime juice to each glass. Pour ½ can sparkling soda into each glass.

PER SERVING 142 **CAL**; 0 g **FAT** (0 g **SAT**); 0 g **PRO**; 12 g **CARB**; 12 g **SUGARS**; 0 g **FIBER**; 6 mg **SODIUM**

Dark-as-Midnight Clusters

MAKES 3½ dozen **PREP** 5 minutes
COOK 5 minutes **STAND** 1 hour

- **⅔   cup hazelnuts, chopped**
- **1   bag (10 oz) bittersweet chocolate chips**
- **1   cup puffed rice cereal**
- **¾   cup dried tart cherries**
- **¾   cup roasted salted pumpkin seeds (pepitas)**
- **Maldon sea salt flakes**

■ Add hazelnuts to a medium skillet over medium-high. Toast, stirring occasionally, 3 to 4 minutes. Reduce

CAULIFLOWER MAC AND CHEESE

heat to low and add chocolate chips. Cook, stirring constantly, 1 minute or until melted. Transfer to a large bowl and add puffed rice cereal, cherries, and pumpkin seeds, stirring until all ingredients are well combined. Drop mixture by tablespoonfuls into miniature muffin cup liners; you should get about 3½ dozen clusters. Sprinkle each cluster with Maldon sea salt flakes and let set at least 1 hour, until dry to the touch.

PER CLUSTER 73 **CAL**; 5 g **FAT** (2 g **SAT**); 1 g **PRO**; 6 g **CARB**; 4 g **SUGARS**; 0 g **FIBER**; 53 mg **SODIUM**

Cauliflower Mac and Cheese

MAKES 12 servings **PREP** 25 minutes
COOK 10 minutes **BAKE** 20 minutes at 350°

- **8   oz macaroni**
- **6   cups golden or white cauliflower florets**
- **¼   cup unsalted butter**
- **¼   cup finely chopped onion**
- **¼   cup all-purpose flour**
- **3   cups whole milk**
- **¾   tsp salt**
- **½   tsp freshly ground black pepper**
- **10   oz sharp cheddar cheese**
- **¾   cup Goldfish crackers**

■ Bring a large pot of lightly salted water to a boil. Cook macaroni according to package directions, adding cauliflower during last 3 minutes. Drain and cover to keep warm. Meanwhile, in a medium saucepan, melt butter over medium. Add onion; cook 3 minutes. Add all-purpose flour; cook 1 minute. While whisking, add whole milk, salt and pepper. Bring to a simmer and cook 1 minute. Remove from heat. Shred sharp cheddar and whisk into milk mixture. Stir into macaroni and cauliflower. Grease a 13 x 9 x 2-inch baking dish and add macaroni and cheese. Crush Goldfish crackers and scatter on top. Bake at 350° for 20 minutes.

Note To make ahead, prepare mac and cheese, but don't top with crackers. Refrigerate, covered. Uncover, top with crackers and bake at 350° for 30 minutes until hot.

PER SERVING 299 **CAL**; 16 g **FAT** (9 g **SAT**); 12 g **PRO**; 27 g **CARB**; 5 g **SUGARS**; 2 g **FIBER**; 394 mg **SODIUM**

Frankensmoothie

MAKES 6 servings **PREP** 10 minutes

- 1 **avocado, pitted and peeled**
- 1 **cup seedless green grapes**
- 2 **kiwis, trimmed and peeled**
- 3½ **cups cold bottled limeade**
  Green food coloring (optional)

■ In a blender combine avocado, grapes, kiwis, limeade and 4 drops green food coloring, if using. Puree until smooth. With a permanent marker, decorate 6 plastic tumblers to resemble Frankenstein. Divide smoothie among tumblers.

PER SERVING 139 **CAL**; 4 g **FAT** (1 g **SAT**); 1 g **PRO**; 28 g **CARB**; 22 g **SUGARS**; 2 g **FIBER**; 12 mg **SODIUM**

FRANKENSMOOTHIE

Turkey Cheeseburger Mummy Faces

MAKES 8 servings **PREP** 30 minutes
COOK 5 minutes **BAKE** 18 minutes at 375°

- 2 **tbsp vegetable oil**
- 1 **lb ground turkey**
- 2 **tbsp dried minced onion**
- ¼ **cup yellow mustard**
- 3 **tbsp ketchup**
- 1 **cup shredded mozzarella**
- 2 **tubes (16.3 oz each) large refrigerated biscuits**
  Black olives, pitted
- 1 **egg, beaten**

■ In a large skillet, heat vegetable oil over medium-high. Add ground turkey and dried minced onion. Cook 5 minutes, breaking apart with a spoon and adding yellow mustard and ketchup near end of cook time. Remove from heat and stir in mozzarella.

■ Roll out 4 large refrigerated biscuits to 6-inch circles and transfer to a large baking sheet. Spread heaping ⅓ cup turkey mixture onto each biscuit round. Roll out remaining 4 biscuits and cut into thin strips (a pizza cutter works well for this). Slice a few black olives into rounds and add 2 slices on top of turkey mixture to resemble eyes. Arrange 1 biscuit of thin strips over filling to resemble

TURKEY CHEESEBURGER MUMMY FACES

bandages and brush with beaten egg. Repeat with a second tube of large refrigerated biscuits and remaining filling, olive slices and egg. Bake at 375° for 18 minutes.

Note To make ahead, assemble and bake mummies. Wrap in foil and refrigerate. Warm in 250° oven for 10 minutes until heated through.

PER SERVING 483 **CAL**; 20 g **FAT** (7 g **SAT**); 24 g **PRO**; 53 g **CARB**; 10 g **SUGARS**; 2 g **FIBER**; 1,186 mg **SODIUM**

Chicken Artichoke Puffs

MAKES 24 servings **PREP** 20 minutes
BAKE 18 minutes at 400°

- **2** boxes (17.3 oz each) puff pastry
- **1** cup chopped cooked chicken
- **3** tbsp jarred pesto, plus more for serving
- **1** jar (6 oz) marinated artichoke heart quarters
- **1** egg, beaten

■ Thaw puff pastry. In a large bowl, combine chicken with 3 tbsp jarred pesto. Drain and chop artichoke and add to bowl, stirring to combine well.

■ Unfold 1 pastry sheet and roll out slightly. With a 2¾-inch pumpkin cookie cutter, cut out 12 pumpkins. Repeat with second sheet. Place 12 pumpkins on a baking sheet and brush with beaten egg.

■ Top each with 1 tbsp chicken mixture. Place a second pumpkin over each mound of filling and press edges to seal. Repeat with 2 remaining sheets pastry and filling. Score top of each to resemble pumpkin ridges; brush all with egg. Bake at 400° for 15 to 18 minutes. Serve with more pesto alongside.

Note To make ahead, assemble puffs through sealing and freeze in a single layer. Brush with egg and bake straight from frozen, extending baking time by 5 minutes.

PER SERVING 199 **CAL**; 13 g **FAT** (3 g **SAT**); 5 g **PRO**; 15 g **CARB**; 1 g **SUGARS**; 1 g **FIBER**; 277 mg **SODIUM**

CHICKEN ARTICHOKE PUFFS

HORCHATA

Chipotle Queso

MAKES 12 servings **PREP** 10 minutes
COOK 8 minutes **MICROWAVE** 1 minute

- **8 oz shredded Monterey Jack**
- **1 tsp cornstarch**
- **8 oz Velveeta cheese, cubed**
- **1 cup milk**
- **1 chipotle chile in adobo sauce, chopped, plus 1 tbsp adobo sauce**
- **24 corn tortillas**
- **½ avocado, diced**
- **½ cup cherry tomatoes, chopped**

■ In a medium bowl, toss Monterey Jack with cornstarch. Transfer to a medium saucepan with Velveeta cheese and milk. Heat over medium, stirring until melted, 5 to 8 minutes.

■ Stir in chipotle chile and adobo sauce, then transfer to a dish. Wrap tortillas in damp paper towels; microwave 1 minute or until warm. Top queso with avocado and cherry tomatoes.

PER SERVING 259 **CAL**; 13 g **FAT** (6 g **SAT**); 10 g **PRO**; 26 g **CARB**; 5 g **SUGARS**; 4 g **FIBER**; 438 mg **SODIUM**

CHIPOTLE QUESO

Horchata

MAKES 6 servings **PREP** 15 minutes **SOAK** 3 hours

- **1 cup long grain white rice**
- **½ tsp ground cinnamon**
- **1 cup rice milk**
- **½ cup sugar**
- **6 cinnamon sticks**

■ Combine 5 cups water and the rice in a high-power blender. Blend on medium-high speed until rice begins to break up. Pour into a large bowl and add 1½ cups water and the ground cinnamon. Cover with plastic wrap and let soak at least 3 hours.

■ Stir mixture; transfer half to blender and blend until fairly smooth. Strain into a pitcher and repeat with remaining rice mixture. Stir in rice milk and sugar.

■ Refrigerate until chilled. Serve over ice with a cinnamon stick as garnish.

PER SERVING 139 **CAL**; 0 g **FAT** (0 g **SAT**); 2 g **PRO**; 33 g **CARB**; 19 g **SUGARS**; 0 g **FIBER**; 17 mg **SODIUM**

SKELETON COOKIES

Mini Taco Bites

MAKES 36 servings **PREP** 5 minutes
COOK 5 minutes **MICROWAVE** 1 minute
BAKE 5 minutes at 375°

- ½ **lb ground beef**
- 1 **tbsp chili powder**
- 1 **tsp onion powder**
- ½ **tsp ground cumin**
- ¼ **tsp salt**
- 1 **cup canned refried beans**
- 1 **bag multigrain mini tortilla chip cups (such as Tostitos Scoops)**

  Garnish: cherry tomato slices, sour cream, sliced scallions

■ Heat a large nonstick skillet over medium-high. Add ground beef, chili powder, onion powder, cumin and salt. Cook 3 to 5 minutes, breaking apart with a spoon.

■ Meanwhile, microwave refried beans at 100% for 1 minute and stir until loose. Transfer to a resealable plastic bag.

■ Spread 36 tortilla chip cups on a baking sheet. Snip a corner from bag with refried beans and add about 1 tsp to each tortilla cup. Divide meat evenly among cups and bake at 375° for 5 minutes. Remove from oven and top each with a cherry tomato slice, a small spoonful of sour cream, and some sliced scallions.

PER SERVING 39 **CAL**; 2 g **FAT** (1 g **SAT**);
2 g **PRO**; 3 g **CARB**; 0 g **SUGARS**; 1 g **FIBER**;
69 mg **SODIUM**

Skeleton Cookies

MAKES 3 dozen **PREP** 20 minutes **CHILL** 2 hours **BAKE** 12 minutes at 375°

- 1 **cup softened unsalted butter (2 sticks)**
- 1¼ **cups granulated sugar**
- 1 **large egg**
- 1 **tsp vanilla extract**
- 2¾ **cups all-purpose flour**
- ½ **cup unsweetened cocoa powder**
- ¼ **tsp salt**
- ¼ **cup milk**
- 3 **cups confectioners' sugar**
- 3 **tbsp meringue powder or powdered egg whites**

■ Beat butter with granulated sugar until creamy. Beat in egg and vanilla extract. Whisk in flour, cocoa powder and salt, and beat on low, alternating with milk. Gather dough together, divide in half, wrap in plastic and refrigerate 2 hours or overnight.

■ Roll dough to ¼-inch thickness. Use a 3½- to 4-inch gingerbread cutter to cut out cookies. Repeat with all dough. Bake at 375° for 12 minutes. Cool on a wire rack. To decorate, beat confectioners' sugar, meringue powder and 4 to 5 tbsp water until stiff. Transfer to a piping bag fitted with a small writing tip. Pipe skeletons onto cooled cookies. Let dry.

PER COOKIE 154 **CAL**; 6 g **FAT** (3 g **SAT**);
2 g **PRO**; 25 g **CARB**; 17 g **SUGARS**; 1 g **FIBER**;
27 mg **SODIUM**

MINI TACO BITES

OATS 4 WAYS

Brighten up your breakfast, lunch or dinner with this fall favorite.

SPINACH RIS-OAT-TO

Bacon-Cheddar Cakes

MAKES 6 servings **PREP** 10 minutes
COOK 5 minutes **COOL** 15 minutes
BAKE at 350° for 40 minutes

- 1½ **cups old-fashioned rolled oats**
- 1½ **cups milk**
- ½ **tsp salt**
- ½ **tsp freshly ground black pepper**
- 1 **cup shredded cheddar cheese**
- ⅓ **cup chopped cooked bacon**
- 1 **scallion, sliced**
- ¼ **cup sour cream**
- 1 **tsp water**
- ¼ **tsp garlic salt**
- 1 **scallion, thinly sliced**
- 1 **tbsp chives, thinly sliced, plus more for garnish**

■ Line a baking sheet with parchment. In a medium saucepan, bring oats, milk, salt and pepper to a boil over medium-high. Reduce heat to medium-low, cover and simmer 5 minutes, stirring occasionally, until oats are tender. Let cool about 15 minutes, then stir in cheddar, bacon and sliced scallion.

■ Drop heaping tablespoonfuls of mixture onto prepared baking sheet. With moistened fingers, flatten each mound into a 2-inch patty.

■ Bake at 350° for 40 minutes, flipping halfway through, until golden brown. Stir together sour cream, water, garlic salt, thinly sliced scallion and chives. Sprinkle cakes with more chives and serve with sour cream dip.

PER SERVING 220 **CAL**; 12 g **FAT** (6 g **SAT**); 10 g **PRO**; 18 g **CARB**; 4 g **SUGARS**; 2 g **FIBER**; 441 mg **SODIUM**

Spinach Ris-oat-to

MAKES 4 servings **PREP** 10 minutes
COOK 36 minutes

- 5 **cups low-sodium vegetable broth**
- 2 **tbsp unsalted butter**
- 1 **small shallot, finely chopped**
- 1 **cup steel-cut oats**
- 1 **pkg (10 oz) frozen chopped spinach, thawed and squeezed dry**
- ½ **cup grated Parmesan**
- ¾ **tsp salt**
- ¼ **tsp freshly ground black pepper**
-   **Shaved parmesan**

■ In a medium pot, bring broth to a boil over medium-high, then immediately reduce heat and keep warm over medium-low, partially covered.

■ Meanwhile, in a medium saucepan, melt butter over medium-low; stir in shallot and cook 2 minutes. Add oats and cook 1 minute, until fragrant. Add 1 cup warm broth and simmer 3 minutes, until mostly absorbed. Add ½ cup broth at a time, about every 3 minutes, stirring after each addition and as needed, until oats are softened and sauce is thick but soupy, about 30 minutes. Stir in spinach.

■ Remove from heat; add the grated Parmesan, salt and pepper. Stir in more broth if needed to maintain loose texture. Spoon into 4 dishes and top with shaved Parmesan.

PER SERVING 310 **CAL**; 12 g **FAT** (6 g **SAT**); 13 g **PRO**; 39 g **CARB**; 4 g **SUGARS**; 9 g **FIBER**; 846 mg **SODIUM**

BACON-CHEDDAR CAKES

**GLUTEN-FREE
CHICKEN FINGERS**

Un-fried Ice Cream

MAKES 2 cups coating **PREP** 5 minutes
COOK 2 minutes **BAKE** at 325° for 45 minutes
COOL 10 minutes

- ½ **cup sugar**
- ¼ **cup water**
- ⅛ **tsp salt**
- 2 **cups old-fashioned rolled oats**
-    **Ice cream**
-    **Chocolate syrup**
-    **Light whipped topping**
-    **Sprinkles**

■ Line a rimmed baking sheet with parchment. In a small pot, heat sugar, water and salt over medium for 2 minutes, until sugar is dissolved. Pour over oats in a large bowl and stir with a rubber spatula to coat well.

■ Transfer to prepared baking sheet and spread in a single layer. Bake at 325° for 45 minutes, stirring every 15 minutes, until browned and dry. Let cool completely, about 10 minutes. Transfer to a medium bowl and break up any clumps.

■ Roll scoops of ice cream in oats until completely covered. Serve drizzled with chocolate syrup and topped with light whipped topping and sprinkles.

PER SERVING 176 **CAL**; 6 g **FAT** (3 g **SAT**); 3 g **PRO**; 28 g **CARB**; 18 g **SUGARS**; 1 g **FIBER**; 58 mg **SODIUM**

Gluten-Free Chicken Fingers

MAKES 4 servings **PREP** 15 minutes
FRY 6 minutes per batch **KEEP WARM** at 200°

- ½ **cup almond flour**
- 3 **eggs**
- 1½ **cups old-fashioned rolled oats**
- 1½ **tsp salt**
- 1½ **tsp onion powder**
- ¾ **tsp garlic powder**
- ¾ **tsp dried thyme**
- ¾ **tsp freshly ground black pepper**
- 1 **lb boneless, skinless chicken breasts**
- 2 **cups canola oil**
- ¼ **cup apricot preserves**
- ¼ **cup Dijon mustard**
- 1 **tbsp water**

■ In a shallow dish, add almond flour. In a second dish, beat eggs.

■ In a food processor, pulse oats with salt, onion powder, garlic powder, dried thyme and black pepper until finely ground. Pour into a third dish.

■ Pound chicken breasts to an even ¼-inch thickness. Cut into 3 x 1-inch strips. Dip in flour, then egg, then oats, shaking off excess. Transfer to a baking sheet.

■ In a large skillet, heat oil. Working in batches, fry chicken 6 minutes, turning halfway through, until golden brown. Transfer first batch to a clean baking sheet and place in a 200° oven to keep warm while frying remaining chicken.

■ Mix apricot preserves and Dijon mustard with the water. Serve chicken with apricot sauce.

PER SERVING 447 **CAL**; 28 g **FAT** (3 g **SAT**); 24 g **PRO**; 23 g **CARB**; 7 g **SUGARS**; 3 g **FIBER**; 900 mg **SODIUM**

**UN-FRIED
ICE CREAM**

TV DINNERS

Here's a behind-the-scenes look at the *MasterChef* chicken-and-potatoes challenge. See how the winning dishes were created!

SPICE-RUBBED CHICKEN LEGS WITH DUCK FAT POTATOES AND APPLE PUREE

This multifaceted meal may look fancy—and it is—but it's based on simple, inexpensive ingredients like chicken legs, potatoes, and apples. It's perfect for a dinner party on a crisp fall evening.

Spice-Rubbed Chicken Legs with Duck Fat Potatoes and Apple Puree

MAKES 4 servings **PREP** 1 hour **BRINE** 30 minutes **COOK** 34 minutes **ROAST** at 425° for 10 minutes

- **8 chicken drumsticks (about 1¾ lb total)**
- **Brine**
- **Duck Fat Potatoes**
- **Honey Sauce**
- **Spice Mix**
- **2 tbsp unsalted butter**
- **2 tbsp duck fat (lard or vegetable shortening may be substituted)**
- **6 thyme sprigs**
- **Juice from 1 lemon (about 4 tbsp)**
- **3 cloves garlic, chopped**
- **2 tbsp minced shallots**
- **Apple Puree**
- **1 cup diced pancetta**
- **12 fresh sage leaves**

■ Place chicken in a large bowl or stockpot. Add Brine and let sit at least 30 minutes.

■ Meanwhile, prepare Duck Fat Potatoes (but don't brown them) and Honey Sauce.

■ Remove chicken from brine, rinse well, pat dry and rub all over with Spice Mix. Heat oven to 425°. In a pan, melt butter and duck fat over medium-high. Add thyme, lemon juice, garlic and shallots, followed by chicken. Sear each side, spooning butter mixture over chicken as it cooks, about

3 minutes per side. Remove to a rimmed baking sheet and roast 10 minutes, until cooked through.

■ Meanwhile, prepare Apple Puree and brown the potatoes.

■ In a saucepan, cook pancetta over medium-high until crispy, about 3 minutes. Remove to a paper towel. Add sage and fry until crispy, about 1 minute.

■ On each of 4 plates, place about ⅓ cup apple puree, 2 drumsticks and 4 potatoes. Sprinkle with pancetta and sage, and spoon a good amount of sauce over all.

Brine Whisk ⅔ cup packed light brown sugar and ½ cup kosher salt into 1 gallon cold water.

Duck Fat Potatoes Peel 8 Yukon gold potatoes, and cut each into two 1-inch-thick rounds. In a large sauté pan, melt 2 tbsp unsalted butter over medium. Toss in 2 sprigs each fresh dill and rosemary, 3 sprigs fresh thyme and 1½ cups chicken stock. Bring to a boil, add potatoes and cook 5 to 6 minutes. Drain, discarding herbs and stock. In a large cast-iron skillet, heat ½ cup duck fat (or lard or shortening) over medium-high. Brown potatoes, about 5 minutes, and season with ½ tbsp Himalayan sea salt and ½ tsp freshly ground black pepper.

Honey Sauce In a medium saucepan, heat 1 tbsp olive oil over medium. Add 2 tbsp chopped shallots, 1 minced clove garlic and 1 tbsp chopped fresh thyme. Cook 5 minutes, until softened but not browned. Add ¾ cup honey, 2 tbsp balsamic vinegar and 1 tsp paprika; whisk to combine. Cook 5 minutes, until slightly reduced. Stir in 2 tbsp unsalted butter and 1 tbsp demi-glace (such as More Than Gourmet). Season with ½ tsp sea salt and freshly ground black pepper to taste.

Spice Mix In a small bowl, combine ¼ cup each kosher salt and paprika, 2 tbsp each coarsely ground black pepper and dried sage, and 1 tbsp each ground cumin and coriander.

Apple Puree In a saucepan, combine 4 cups water, juice of 2 lemons and 3 sprigs fresh rosemary over medium. Add 1 lb peeled, diced Granny Smith apples and cook 3 minutes, until tender. In another pan, heat ¼ cup heavy cream and 2 tbsp unsalted butter. Drain apples and transfer to a blender (discard rosemary). Add some cream mixture plus a pinch of ground cinnamon and nutmeg. Blend, adding more cream mixture if too thick. Strain through a mesh strainer if lumpy.

What are chicharrones, you ask? Paper-thin pieces of chicken skin that are seasoned and roasted at high temperature until crispy—yum!

Stuffed Chicken Roulade with Chicharrones, Pommes Soufflés and Red Wine–Pasilla Sauce

MAKES 4 servings **PREP** 2 hours **ROAST** at 450° for 25 minutes **COOK** 1 hour 20 minutes **FRY** 2 minutes **BAKE** at 350° for 42 minutes **REST** 5 minutes

- 4 **boneless, skin-on chicken thighs**
   Chicharrones
   Red Wine-Pasilla Sauce
   Pommes Soufflés
   Stained-Glass Chips
- 1 **poblano chile**
- 1 **ear corn on the cob, shucked**
- 2 **tbsp vegetable oil**
- 1½ **cups mixed wild mushrooms, sliced**
- ¼ **cup finely diced yellow onion**
- 1 **tbsp chopped fresh oregano**
- ¼ **cup grated Oaxaca cheese**
- 1 **tbsp Cotija cheese**
   Salt and black pepper
   Butcher's twine
   Microgreens, snipped fresh chives and edible flowers (for garnish)

■ **Chicharrones** Heat oven to 450°. Carefully remove skin from chicken thighs. Place skin between 2 pieces of plastic wrap on a cutting board and pound with bottom of a skillet until flattened. Season with salt and pepper and place between 2 baking sheets covered with nonstick foil. Place a cast-iron skillet (or heavy, oven-safe object) on top to flatten chicken skin. Roast 25 minutes or until golden brown. Transfer with tongs to a wire rack to cool.

■ **Red Wine-Pasilla Sauce** Meanwhile, in a small pot, toast 2 dried pasilla or guajillo chiles over medium for 2 minutes, turning once. Add 2 cups dry red wine and simmer until

reduced by half, about 25 minutes. Pour in 1 cup unsalted chicken stock and simmer until reduced by half, about 20 minutes. Add 1 tbsp demi-glace and 1 tsp lemon juice; reduce until sauce coats the back of a spoon, about 15 minutes. Pour sauce through a fine-mesh strainer into another pot and stir in 1 tbsp cold unsalted butter. Cover and set aside.

■ **Pommes Soufflés** In a medium heavy-bottom pot, heat 2 cups vegetable oil to 300°. Peel 1 Yukon gold potato. Slice off edges to make a cube. Cut into ⅛-inch slices, then cut slices into 2 x ½-inch rectangles. Pat dry and fry at 300° for 1 minute. Remove with a slotted spoon to a paper-towel-lined plate. Increase oil temperature to 375°. Fry 1 minute more, until puffed and barely browned.

■ **Stained-Glass Chips** Reduce oven temperature to 350°. Melt 2 tbsp unsalted butter. Peel 1 Yukon gold potato and thinly slice on a mandoline. Line a baking sheet with parchment and brush with melted butter. Place potato slices on parchment and brush with melted butter. Place 1 or 2 microgreen leaves on at least 8 slices, then place a similarly sized potato slice on top of each and press together. Brush tops with more butter, then season with salt and pepper. Cover with another piece of parchment and place another baking sheet on top. Weigh down with a cast-iron pan or heavy, oven-safe object. Bake about 15 minutes, rotating pan halfway through. Remove potatoes to a baking sheet fitted with a wire rack. Bake until

golden brown and crispy, about 15 minutes more. Remove from oven and set aside.

■ **Stuffed Chicken Roulade** Heat oven to 350°. Roast poblano and corn over an open flame on the grill or stove, turning with tongs, for 3 to 5 minutes, until charred. Transfer poblano to a bowl and cover with plastic for 5 minutes. Peel off skin, remove seeds and finely dice. Cut kernels from cob.

■ Heat a medium skillet over medium-high. Add 1 tbsp oil and stir in mushrooms; cook 5 minutes. Stir in onion; cook 3 to 5 minutes, until softened. Stir in poblano, corn and oregano. Remove from heat and fold in Oaxaca and Cotija cheese; season to taste with salt and pepper.

■ Place chicken thighs between 2 pieces of plastic wrap on a cutting board and pound until ⅛ inch thick. Season with salt and pepper. Spoon 2 tbsp poblano-corn mixture on one end of each thigh. Roll each thigh tightly and tie several times with butcher's twine.

■ In a large skillet, heat 1 tbsp oil over medium-high. Brown thighs on all sides for 3 to 5 minutes. Transfer to a baking sheet and bake 12 minutes, until temperature reaches 165°. Rest 5 minutes.

■ Snip off butcher's twine. Slice roulade in half. Serve with chicharrones, sauce, pommes soufflés and chips, reheating as needed. Garnish with microgreens, chives and flowers.

STUFFED CHICKEN ROULADE WITH
CHICHARRONES, POMMES SOUFFLÉS
AND RED WINE–PASILLA SAUCE

APPLE-CHEDDAR
SLAB PIE, PAGE 269

NOVEMBER

253

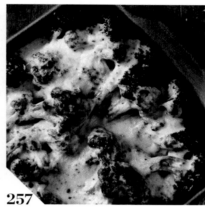

257

270

HEALTHY FAMILY DINNERS

One and done: Sheet-pan suppers keep it simple.

SHRIMP WITH
ASPARAGUS AND
POLENTA, PAGE 254

EYE ROUND ROAST WITH
POTATOES AND BLISTERED
GREEN BEANS, PAGE 250

EYE ROUND ROAST WITH POTATOES AND BLISTERED GREEN BEANS

Eye Round Roast with Potatoes and Blistered Green Beans

MAKES 6 servings **PREP** 15 minutes **ROAST** at 425° for 25 minutes, then at 375° for 25 minutes
REST 10 minutes

- 1½ **tsp salt**
- ½ **tsp freshly ground black pepper**
- 1 **tsp onion powder**
- 1 **tsp garlic powder**
- 1¾ **lb assorted small potatoes, quartered**
- 2 **large red onions, peeled and cut into wedges**
- 3 **tbsp olive oil**
- 2 **tsp fresh thyme, chopped**
- 1 **boneless beef eye round roast (about 2 lb)**
- 1 **lb green beans, trimmed**
- ¾ **cup sour cream**
- 2 **tbsp prepared horseradish**

■ Heat oven to 425°. In a small bowl, combine first 4 ingredients.

■ Place potatoes and onions in a large bowl and toss with 2 tbsp oil, the thyme and 1 tsp spice mix. Spread onto a sheet pan. Rub 2 tsp spice mix all over roast and add to pan, pushing veggies out of the way. Roast 25 minutes.

■ Meanwhile, toss green beans with 1 tbsp oil and remaining spice mix.

■ Stir veggies on pan and push together, making space for green beans. Add beans to pan and reduce oven temp to 375°. Return pan to oven and roast 20 to 25 minutes, until veggies are tender and beef reaches 125° for medium-rare. Rest beef for 10 minutes before slicing. Combine sour cream and horseradish; serve alongside beef.

PER SERVING 493 **CAL**; 20 g **FAT** (7 g **SAT**); 43 g **PRO**; 37 g **CARB**; 7 g **SUGARS**; 7 g **FIBER**; 733 mg **SODIUM**

Roasted Kale and Butternut Squash

MAKES 4 servings **PREP** 15 minutes
ROAST at 450° for 40 minutes

- 1½ **lb butternut squash cubes**
- 4 **tbsp olive oil**
- ¾ **tsp salt**
- ½ **tsp freshly ground black pepper**
- 8 **cups packed chopped kale**
- 1 **tsp chopped fresh oregano**
- 1 **can (15 oz) butter beans, drained and rinsed**
- 1 **pkg (8.8 oz) heat-and-eat white rice**
- 2 **oz feta cheese, crumbled (½ cup)**
- 2 **tbsp bottled balsamic glaze**

■ Heat oven to 450°. Toss squash on a sheet pan with 2 tbsp oil, ½ tsp salt and ¼ tsp pepper. Spread in a single layer and roast 20 to 25 minutes.

■ Meanwhile, in an extra-large bowl, toss kale with 2 tbsp oil, ¼ tsp each salt and pepper, and the oregano. Stir in butter beans.

■ Stir squash and push to one side of pan. Add kale-bean mixture to other side, mounding slightly. Roast 15 minutes.

■ Microwave rice per package directions. Transfer kale, beans and squash to a large bowl; gently stir in rice and crumbled feta. Drizzle with balsamic glaze and toss. Serve warm.

PER SERVING 417 **CAL**; 19 g **FAT** (4 g **SAT**); 11 g **PRO**; 56 g **CARB**; 9 g **SUGARS**; 12 g **FIBER**; 782 mg **SODIUM**

ROASTED KALE AND
BUTTERNUT SQUASH

PARMESAN CHICKEN
THIGHS AND VEGGIES

Parmesan Chicken Thighs and Veggies

MAKES 4 servings **PREP** 20 minutes
ROAST at 425° for 30 minutes
BROIL 3 minutes

- 1¼ lb Brussels sprouts, trimmed and halved
- 1 lb carrots, peeled and cut on the diagonal into ¼-inch-thick slices, or use 1 lb carrot chips
- 2 tbsp olive oil
- 2 tbsp white wine vinegar
- 1 tbsp Dijon mustard
- ½ tsp salt
- ½ tsp freshly ground black pepper
- 4 bone-in chicken thighs (about 2 lb)
- ⅓ cup grated Parmesan

■ Heat oven to 425°. Place Brussels sprouts and carrots on a sheet pan. In a medium bowl, whisk next 5 ingredients. Brush 1 tbsp mustard mixture onto each thigh and dip fleshy side into Parmesan until it adheres.

■ Toss veggies with remaining mustard mixture. Spread in a single layer on pan, add chicken and roast 20 minutes. Stir veggies and roast 10 minutes.

■ Broil 3 minutes, until chicken browns slightly.

PER SERVING 447 **CAL**; 21 g **FAT** (6 g **SAT**); 41 g **PRO**; 22 g **CARB**; 8 g **SUGARS**; 8 g **FIBER**; 794 mg **SODIUM**

PORK WITH CAULIFLOWER AND MASHED SWEET POTATOES

Pork with Cauliflower and Mashed Sweet Potatoes

MAKES 6 servings **PREP** 15 minutes **BAKE** at 425° for 1 hour 20 minutes **REST** 10 minutes

- 1 bone-in pork rib roast (about 3¼ lb)
- 1 tbsp plus 1 tsp olive oil
- 3 cloves garlic, minced
- 2 tsp chopped fresh rosemary
- 1½ tsp salt
- 1¼ tsp freshly ground black pepper
- 8 cups golden or white cauliflower florets
- 2 large sweet potatoes (about 2 lb), halved lengthwise
- ⅓ cup milk

■ Heat oven to 425°. Rub pork with 1 tsp oil, two-thirds of the garlic, 1 tsp rosemary, ¾ tsp salt and ½ tsp pepper. Place on a sheet pan and roast 35 minutes.

■ Meanwhile, toss cauliflower with 1 tbsp oil, remaining garlic, 1 tsp rosemary and ¼ tsp each salt and pepper.

■ Remove pan from oven and carefully add cauliflower and sweet potatoes, cut side up. Roast 45 minutes, until pork reaches 130° and veggies are tender. Rest pork for 10 minutes.

■ Scoop flesh from potatoes; mash with milk and ½ tsp each salt and pepper. Slice pork and serve with sweet potatoes and cauliflower.

PER SERVING 461 **CAL**; 21 g **FAT** (5 g **SAT**); 38 g **PRO**; 30 g **CARB**; 8 g **SUGARS**; 6 g **FIBER**; 781 mg **SODIUM**

SHRIMP WITH
ASPARAGUS AND
POLENTA

Shrimp with Asparagus and Polenta

MAKES 4 servings **PREP** 10 minutes **BROIL** 10 minutes

- **1** **tube (18 oz) polenta, cut into 12 slices**
- **1** **bunch (1 lb) asparagus, trimmed**
- **4** **tbsp olive oil**
- **¼** **tsp salt**
- **¼** **tsp freshly ground black pepper**
- **2** **lemons, halved**
- **1½** **lb jumbo tail-on shrimp**
- **2** **tbsp chopped fresh parsley**
- **1** **tbsp capers**
  Lemon- or garlic-infused oil, for drizzling (optional)

■ Heat broiler. Line a sheet pan with foil and coat with nonstick cooking spray. Spread polenta slices on one half of prepared pan. Toss asparagus with 2 tbsp oil and ⅛ tsp each salt and pepper. Spread on other half of pan. Juice ½ lemon. Place remaining lemon halves on pan near asparagus. Broil 5 minutes.

■ Toss shrimp with 2 tbsp oil, the lemon juice, parsley, capers and ⅛ tsp each salt and pepper.

■ Remove polenta to a platter and spread shrimp on pan in its place. Broil 4 to 5 minutes, turning once. Spoon shrimp over polenta and drizzle with flavored oil, if using. Serve with roasted lemons and asparagus on the side.

PER SERVING 380 **CAL**; 15 g **FAT** (2 g **SAT**); 39 g **PRO**; 24 g **CARB**; 3 g **SUGARS**; 4 g **FIBER**; 797 mg **SODIUM**

Chicken Scarapiello

MAKES 5 servings **PREP** 20 minutes
ROAST at 425° for 35 minutes

- **2** **red bell peppers, cut into 1-inch pieces**
- **1** **green bell pepper, cut into 1-inch pieces**
- **1** **cup grape tomatoes**
- **1** **medium fennel bulb, trimmed, cored and sliced ¼ inch thick**
- **5** **cloves garlic, halved**
- **2** **tbsp olive oil**
- **½** **tsp freshly ground black pepper**
- **¼** **tsp plus ⅛ tsp salt**
- **10** **bone-in chicken pieces (breasts, thighs and drumsticks; about 2½ lb)**
- **½** **tsp dried Italian seasoning**
- **4** **links chicken sausage (not precooked; about 12 oz)**
  Sourdough or Italian bread (optional)

■ Heat oven to 425°. Toss first 5 ingredients with 1 tbsp oil, ¼ tsp pepper and ⅛ tsp salt, and spread onto a sheet pan. Toss chicken with 1 tbsp oil, ¼ tsp pepper, ¼ tsp salt and the Italian seasoning. Add to pan along with sausages.

■ Roast 35 minutes, turning sausages halfway through.

■ Cut sausages on the diagonal into ½-inch-thick slices. Divide veggies and sausage among 5 plates, and top each with 2 pieces of chicken. Serve with bread, if desired.

PER SERVING (calculated without skin)
471 **CAL**; 24 g **FAT** (6 g **SAT**); 52 g **PRO**; 14 g **CARB**; 6 g **SUGARS**; 4 g **FIBER**; 787 mg **SODIUM**

CHICKEN
SCARAPIELLO

SIDE EFFECTS

This Thanksgiving, take a trip around the globe in 10 dishes.

CURRIED CRANBERRY
CHUTNEY

SWEET POTATO
BISCUITS

BROCCOLI
CACIO E PEPE

These accompaniments to the Thanksgiving turkey are based on classic holiday favorites, but with a worldly twist—such as a bit of spice, a sprinkle of cheese, or a touch of coconut.

Curried Cranberry Chutney

MAKES 12 servings **PREP** 10 minutes
COOK 31 minutes

- 1 tbsp vegetable oil
- 1 medium shallot, grated
- 1 4-inch piece fresh ginger, peeled and grated
- 3 cloves garlic, grated
- 2 tbsp curry powder
- ½ tsp ground cardamom
- 2 bags (12 oz each) fresh cranberries
- 1¼ cups packed light brown sugar
- ¼ cup apple cider vinegar
- ¾ tsp salt
- 1 cup raisins

■ In a medium pot, heat oil over medium. Stir in next 5 ingredients. Cook 30 seconds to 1 minute. Stir in cranberries, sugar, vinegar, ½ cup water and the salt. Bring to a simmer. Reduce heat to low and cook 20 minutes, uncovered. Stir in raisins and cook 10 minutes, until thickened.

PER SERVING 180 **CAL**; 2 g **FAT** (0 g **SAT**); 1 g **PRO**; 41 g **CARB**; 35 g **SUGARS**; 3 g **FIBER**; 160 mg **SODIUM**

Sweet Potato Biscuits

MAKES 16 biscuits **PREP** 20 minutes
BAKE at 425° for 12 minutes

- 3 cups all-purpose flour
- 1 tbsp baking powder
- ½ tsp baking soda
- 1½ tsp salt
- 6 tbsp unsalted butter, cut into small cubes and chilled
- 1 cup canned sweet potato puree
- ¾ cup buttermilk

■ Heat oven to 425°. In a large bowl, sift first 4 ingredients.

■ Using your hands, rub butter cubes into flour mixture until pea-size pieces form. Whisk sweet potato puree and buttermilk, then add to flour-butter mixture. Combine with a fork until just blended, and turn onto a lightly floured surface.

■ Knead dough 1 minute and roll to ½-inch thickness. (Do not overwork or biscuits will be tough.) Use a 2½-inch-round biscuit cutter to cut 16 circles, re-rolling dough scraps as necessary. On 2 baking sheets, place dough circles 2 inches apart.

■ Bake 10 to 12 minutes, until just beginning to brown.

PER BISCUIT 160 **CAL**; 5 g **FAT** (3 g **SAT**); 4 g **PRO**; 25 g **CARB**; 2 g **SUGARS**; 1 g **FIBER**; 420 mg **SODIUM**

Broccoli Cacio e Pepe

MAKES 8 servings **PREP** 10 minutes
COOK 9 minutes **BAKE** at 425° for 15 minutes
BROIL 3 minutes

- 3 lb broccoli (2 to 3 bunches)
- 3 tbsp unsalted butter
- 3 tbsp all-purpose flour
- 3 cups whole milk
- 1½ cups shredded Parmesan
- 2 tsp freshly cracked black pepper
- ½ tsp salt

■ Heat oven to 425°. Bring a large pot of salted water to a boil. Quarter broccoli stalks lengthwise. Add to boiling water and simmer 3 minutes. Drain.

■ In a medium pot, melt butter over medium. Stir in flour and cook 1 minute. Whisk in milk. Bring to a simmer and cook 5 minutes. Remove from heat and stir in Parmesan, pepper and salt.

■ Transfer broccoli to a 13 x 9-inch baking dish. Pour sauce on top and bake 15 minutes. Broil 2 to 3 minutes, until cheese sauce begins to brown.

PER SERVING 200 **CAL**; 12 g **FAT** (7 g **SAT**); 11 g **PRO**; 15 g **CARB**; 6 g **SUGARS**; 3 g **FIBER**; 490 mg **SODIUM**

ANCHO CHILE–LIME
BRUSSELS SPROUTS

- Place potatoes in a lidded pot. Fill with cold water until potatoes are covered by 1 inch. Cover pot and bring to a boil. Reduce heat to a simmer and cook 10 minutes, until fork-tender.

- Meanwhile, heat a sauté pan over medium. Cook chorizo 3 to 5 minutes, until crispy.

- Drain potatoes and return to pot immediately; mash. Stir in three-fourths of the crispy chorizo, the buttermilk, butter and salt. Scatter remaining chorizo and cilantro on top.

PER SERVING 250 CAL; 10 g FAT (5 g SAT); 7 g PRO; 34 g CARB; 4 g SUGARS; 3 g FIBER; 500 mg SODIUM

Jamaican Coconut Collard Greens

MAKES 12 servings PREP 10 minutes
COOK 24 minutes

- 1   tbsp coconut or olive oil
- 1   cup chopped white onion
- 1   habanero chile, stemmed and sliced
- 2   tsp chopped fresh thyme
- 1   tbsp all-purpose flour
- 2   cans (13.5 oz each) coconut milk
- 2   bags (16 oz each) fresh chopped collard greens
- 1½ tsp salt
- ⅛   to ¼ tsp ground nutmeg
- ¼   cup unsweetened coconut flakes, toasted

- In a large pot, heat oil over medium-high. Stir in onion, chile and thyme. Cook 3 minutes. Add flour and cook 1 minute. Whisk in coconut milk. Bring to a simmer and cook 3 minutes.

- Stir in collard greens. Cover and cook 2 minutes. Using tongs, mix in wilted leaves. Reduce heat to medium and cook 15 minutes, covered, mixing a couple more times. Stir in salt and nutmeg. Transfer to a bowl and scatter toasted coconut on top.

PER SERVING 180 CAL; 16 g FAT (14 g SAT); 4 g PRO; 9 g CARB; 1 g SUGARS; 4 g FIBER; 310 mg SODIUM

Ancho Chile-Lime Brussels Sprouts

MAKES 8 servings PREP 15 minutes
ROAST at 425° for 20 minutes

- 2½ lb Brussels sprouts
- ¼   cup extra-virgin olive oil
- 2   tsp ancho chile powder
- ¾   tsp salt
- ¼   cup pumpkin seeds (pepitas)
- ½   cup roughly chopped fresh cilantro
- 2   tbsp crumbled Cotija or grated Parmesan cheese
- 3   tbsp lime juice

- Heat oven to 425°.

- Trim Brussels sprouts and halve. On a rimmed baking sheet, toss with 3 tbsp oil, the chile powder and ½ tsp salt. Roast 15 minutes. Stir in pumpkin seeds, 1 tbsp oil and ¼ tsp salt. Roast 5 minutes, until tender.

- Toss Brussels sprouts with cilantro, cheese and lime juice.

PER SERVING 140 CAL; 9 g FAT (2 g SAT); 6 g PRO; 12 g CARB; 3 g SUGARS; 5 g FIBER; 300 mg SODIUM

Spanish-Style Mashed Potatoes with Chorizo

MAKES 8 servings PREP 15 minutes
COOK 10 minutes

- 3   lb Yukon gold potatoes, peeled and cut into 1-inch chunks
- 4   oz Spanish-style cured chorizo, casing removed, diced
- 1½ cups buttermilk
- 2   tbsp unsalted butter
- ¾   tsp salt
    Fresh cilantro, for garnish

**SPANISH-STYLE
MASHED POTATOES
WITH CHORIZO**

**JAMAICAN COCONUT
COLLARD GREENS**

ZA'ATAR-ROASTED
CARROTS WITH
YOGURT

PERSIAN
CAULIFLOWER RICE

Labneh (Middle Eastern strained yogurt) is similar to Greek yogurt but thicker in consistency and richer in flavor.

Za'atar-Roasted Carrots with Yogurt

MAKES 8 servings **PREP** 15 minutes
ROAST at 425° for 30 minutes

- **2 lb multicolor carrots (½ to ¾ inch thick), peeled and tops trimmed**
- **2 tbsp extra-virgin olive oil**
- **2½ tsp za'atar (Middle Eastern spice blend)**
- **¾ tsp salt**
- **¼ cup shelled pistachios, roughly chopped**
- **1 tsp lemon juice**
- **1 container (5.3 oz) labneh, plain skyr or Greek yogurt**

■ Heat oven to 425°. Toss carrots with oil, 2 tsp za'atar and ½ tsp salt. Roast 25 minutes, shaking pan halfway through. Add pistachios and roast 3 to 5 minutes, until nuts are lightly browned.

■ Carefully toss carrots and pistachios with lemon juice and ⅛ tsp salt.

■ Mix labneh with ⅛ tsp salt and spread in center of plate. Top with carrots and sprinkle with ½ tsp za'atar.

PER SERVING 120 **CAL**; 6 g **FAT** (1 g **SAT**); 4 g **PRO**; 12 g **CARB**; 8 g **SUGARS**; 3 g **FIBER**; 280 mg **SODIUM**

Persian Cauliflower Rice

MAKES 8 servings **PREP** 5 minutes **COOK** 7 minutes

- **3 tbsp unsalted butter**
- **1½ tsp ras el hanout (Moroccan spice blend, found in spice aisle)**
- **½ tsp ground turmeric**
- **2 bags (12 oz each) cauliflower rice, thawed if frozen**
- **¾ tsp salt**
- **½ cup pomegranate seeds**
- **¼ cup chopped parsley**
- **½ cup chopped toasted walnuts**

■ In a large sauté pan, melt butter over medium-high. Stir in ras el hanout and turmeric. Add cauliflower; cook 5 to 7 minutes, stirring, until pieces start to brown. Stir in salt, pomegranate seeds, parsley and walnuts.

PER SERVING 120 **CAL**; 10 g **FAT** (3 g **SAT**); 3 g **PRO**; 7 g **CARB**; 3 g **SUGARS**; 3 g **FIBER**; 230 mg **SODIUM**

THAI-STYLE SQUASH

Thai-Style Squash

MAKES 8 servings **PREP** 15 minutes **ROAST** at 425° for 30 minutes

- 2 **to 3 acorn squash (3 lb total)**
- ¼ **cup packed light brown sugar**
- 2 **tbsp vegetable oil**
- 2 **tbsp fish sauce**
- 1 **tbsp balsamic vinegar**
- 2 **tbsp lime juice**
- ¼ **tsp salt**
- ⅓ **cup fresh mint, chopped**
- 2 **scallions, sliced**

■ Heat oven to 425°. Trim tops and bottoms from squash. Halve squash and scoop out seeds and pulp. Slice into 1-inch-thick wedges.

■ In a large bowl, whisk sugar, oil, fish sauce, vinegar and 1 tbsp lime juice. Toss squash in bowl to coat. Place on 2 foil-lined rimmed baking sheets and roast 20 minutes. Flip, drizzle with marinade, and roast 10 minutes, until squash is tender and browned.

■ Season squash with salt and 1 tbsp lime juice. Transfer to a platter and scatter mint and scallions on top.

PER SERVING 130 **CAL**; 4 g **FAT** (1 g **SAT**); 2 g **PRO**; 25 g **CARB**; 7 g **SUGARS**; 6 g **FIBER**; 440 mg **SODIUM**

Miso is a rich, salty condiment made from fermented soybeans. There are three types: white, yellow and red. White miso is the mildest.

Miso-Sesame Green Beans

MAKES 8 servings **PREP** 15 minutes **COOK** 10 minutes

- 1½ **lb green beans, trimmed**
- 2 **tbsp unsalted butter**
- 8 **oz sliced shiitake mushrooms**
- 4 **cloves garlic, sliced**
- 1 **tbsp sesame oil**
- ⅛ **tsp salt**
- 2 **tbsp white miso paste**
- 2 **tbsp rice vinegar**
- 2 **tbsp toasted sesame seeds**

■ Bring a large pot of salted water to a boil. Add beans and simmer 3 minutes, until crisp-tender. Drain and transfer to a bowl filled with ice water to cool.

■ Meanwhile, in a large sauté pan, melt butter over medium-high. Add mushrooms and cook 8 minutes, stirring every couple minutes, until browned. Stir in garlic, sesame oil and salt. Cook 2 minutes.

■ In a small bowl, whisk miso paste, vinegar and 2 tbsp water. Pour into skillet with beans and stir until warm. Stir in sesame seeds and serve warm.

PER SERVING 100 **CAL**; 6 g **FAT** (3 g **SAT**); 3 g **PRO**; 11 g **CARB**; 4 g **SUGARS**; 4 g **FIBER**; 180 mg **SODIUM**

MISO-SESAME
GREEN BEANS

10 TOTALLY TOTABLE TREATS

Kick your fall baking into high gear with these sweets perfect for sharing.

**SALTED CARAMEL
BLONDIE BITES**

Salted Caramel Blondie Bites

MAKES 36 bites **PREP** 20 minutes
COOK 10 minutes **BAKE** at 350° for 40 minutes
COOL 30 minutes

- 1½ **cups all-purpose flour**
- ½ **tsp baking powder**
- ¼ **tsp salt**
- ¾ **cup (1½ sticks) unsalted butter, melted**
- 1 **cup packed dark brown sugar**
- 2 **large eggs**
- 1 **tsp vanilla extract**
- 7 **oz soft caramel candies, unwrapped**
- ¾ **cup heavy cream**
- 1 **tsp flaky sea salt, plus more for sprinkling**

■ Heat oven to 350°. Line an 8 x 8-inch pan with nonstick aluminum foil; coat with nonstick cooking spray.

■ Combine flour, baking powder and salt. In a large bowl, beat butter and sugar with an electric mixer until fluffy. Working in batches, beat flour mixture into butter mixture, alternating with 1 egg at a time, mixing well between additions. Beat in vanilla. Spread batter in prepared pan.

■ In a medium nonstick saucepan, cook caramels and heavy cream over medium-low until melted, about 10 minutes. Remove from heat; stir in sea salt.

■ Pour caramel over batter. With a small knife, swirl caramel into batter as much as possible. Smooth top. Sprinkle with a pinch of sea salt. Bake 40 minutes, until a toothpick inserted in center comes out clean.

■ Cool 30 minutes in pan on a wire rack, then run a knife around edge of blondie. Use foil to lift blondie onto rack to cool completely. Carefully peel away foil. Cut into 36 bites.

PER BITE 115 **CAL**; 6 g **FAT** (4 g **SAT**); 1 g **PRO**; 14 g **CARB**; 9 g **SUGARS**; 0 g **FIBER**; 107 mg **SODIUM**

SHOOFLY PIE

Shoofly Pie

MAKES 8 servings **PREP** 10 minutes **BAKE** at 350° for 1 hour

- 1 **9-inch unbaked piecrust**
- 1 **cup all-purpose flour**
- ⅔ **cup packed dark brown sugar**
- 4 **tbsp cold unsalted butter**
- ¼ **tsp salt**
- 1 **large egg**
- 1 **cup molasses**
- ¾ **cup boiling water**
- ¾ **tsp baking soda**

■ Heat oven to 350°. Line a 9-inch glass pie plate with piecrust and place on a baking sheet.

■ In a food processor, pulse next 4 ingredients until coarse crumbs form. Reserve ½ cup.

■ In a large bowl, lightly beat egg. Add molasses and blend well with a wooden spoon.

■ In a small bowl, combine boiling water and baking soda; blend into molasses mixture. Add crumb mixture and mix well. Pour into piecrust and top with reserved crumbs.

■ Bake 1 hour. Transfer to a rack to cool completely. (Filling will firm as it cools.)

■ Cut into 8 slices and serve.

PER SERVING 392 **CAL**; 13 g **FAT** (6 g **SAT**); 3 g **PRO**; 70 g **CARB**; 46 g **SUGARS**; 0 g **FIBER**; 382 mg **SODIUM**

CHOCOLATE–PEANUT BUTTER MOUSSE CUPS

Chocolate-Peanut Butter Mousse Cups

MAKES 60 mousse cups **PREP** 5 minutes
MICROWAVE 2 minutes

- 1 **cup semisweet chocolate chips, plus more, chopped, for sprinkling**
- 1 **cup creamy peanut butter**
- 1½ **cups heavy cream**
- 60 **mini phyllo shells (four 1.9 oz pkg)**
  Peanut butter chips, chopped, for sprinkling

■ Place chocolate chips in a large microwave-safe bowl. Heat in 30-second increments until completely melted. Stir in peanut butter until well combined; set aside.

■ In a medium bowl, beat cream with an electric mixer until stiff peaks form.

■ Gently fold whipped cream into chocolate mixture. Transfer to a resealable plastic bag. Use immediately, or chill in refrigerator up to overnight and leave on counter for at least 1 hour before using.

■ When ready to serve, pipe mousse into phyllo shells and sprinkle with chopped chocolate and peanut butter chips.

Tote Tip Leave the phyllo cups in the box and then pipe the mousse right before serving.

PER MOUSSE CUP 82 **CAL**; 6 g **FAT** (3 g **SAT**); 2 g **PRO**; 7 g **CARB**; 3 g **SUGARS**; 0 g **FIBER**; 40 mg **SODIUM**

Maple Polenta Cakes

MAKES 12 servings **PREP** 10 minutes
BAKE at 350° for 20 minutes **COOL** 10 minutes

- ¾ **cup (1½ sticks) unsalted butter, at room temperature**
- ½ **cup granulated sugar**
- ½ **cup packed light brown sugar**
- 2 **cups almond flour**
- ¾ **cup very fine cornmeal (such as Goya fine yellow cornmeal)**
- 1½ **tsp baking powder**
- 3 **eggs**
  Grade A maple syrup, for brushing

■ Heat oven to 350°. Coat a 12-cup muffin pan with cooking spray with flour (or grease and flour pan).

■ In a large bowl, combine butter and sugars. With an electric mixer, beat until light and fluffy.

■ In a medium bowl, whisk almond flour, cornmeal and baking powder. Working in batches, beat cornmeal mixture into butter mixture, alternating with 1 egg at a time, mixing well between additions. Divide batter evenly among muffin cups.

■ Bake 20 minutes, until golden. Transfer to a rack and cool about 10 minutes. Run a thin knife around edges to loosen and brush tops with maple syrup. Let cool completely before removing from pan and serving.

PER SERVING 326 **CAL**; 22 g **FAT** (8 g **SAT**); 7 g **PRO**; 29 g **CARB**; 17 g **SUGARS**; 3 g **FIBER**; 26 mg **SODIUM**

MAPLE POLENTA
CAKES

APPLE-CHEDDAR
SLAB PIE

Apple-Cheddar Slab Pie

MAKES 12 servings **PREP** 30 minutes
BAKE at 400° for 35 minutes

- **2 refrigerated piecrusts**
- **¾ cup shredded plus 4 oz finely diced extra-sharp cheddar cheese**
- **3 lb Granny Smith apples**
- **¾ cup granulated sugar**
- **2 tbsp fresh lemon juice**
- **⅛ tsp salt**
- **½ cup all-purpose flour**
- **½ cup rolled oats**
- **½ cup packed light brown sugar**
- **4 tbsp unsalted butter, cubed**
- **1 large egg, beaten**

■ Heat oven to 400°. Lightly flour a work surface. Unroll 1 piecrust and sprinkle with shredded cheddar. Top with second crust and roll out to a 17 x 12-inch rectangle. Place in a rimmed 15 x 10-inch baking sheet. Refrigerate while preparing filling.

■ Peel, core and halve apples; cut into ¼-inch-thick slices. In a large bowl, toss slices with granulated sugar, lemon juice, salt and ¼ cup flour. Remove piecrust from fridge and pour filling inside, spreading evenly. Sprinkle with diced cheddar.

■ In a food processor, pulse oats, brown sugar, butter and ¼ cup flour until crumbly. Sprinkle evenly over pie. Fold edges of crust over filling and brush with egg.

■ Bake 35 minutes, until browned. Cool at least 45 minutes before slicing into squares and serving.

PER SERVING 395 **CAL**; 18 g **FAT** (9 g **SAT**); 7 g **PRO**; 55 g **CARB**; 28 g **SUGARS**; 4 g **FIBER**; 310 mg **SODIUM**

RICE PUDDING WITH ALMONDS AND CIDER SYRUP

Rice Pudding with Almonds and Cider Syrup

MAKES 12 servings **PREP** 5 minutes **COOK** 20 minutes **CHILL** 4 hours or overnight

- **5½ cups milk**
- **1 cup long grain white rice**
- **⅔ cup sugar**
- **¼ tsp salt**
- **½ tsp almond extract**
- **½ tsp ground cinnamon**
- **½ cup sliced almonds, toasted**
  Apple cider syrup (such as Stonewall Kitchen) or dark honey, for drizzling

■ In a 3-quart heavy-bottom saucepan, stir first 4 ingredients. Bring to a boil; cover and simmer on low, stirring occasionally, 20 minutes or until rice is tender. Stir in almond extract and cinnamon.

■ Transfer to a large container, press plastic wrap directly onto surface and cool 30 minutes. Refrigerate 4 hours or overnight. Serve chilled or at room temperature, topped with almonds and syrup or honey.

Tote Tip Transport in a sealed container; transfer to your serving bowl and garnish on site.

PER SERVING 180 **CAL**; 6 g **FAT** (2 g **SAT**); 5 g **PRO**; 28 g **CARB**; 15 g **SUGARS**; 0 g **FIBER**; 98 mg **SODIUM**

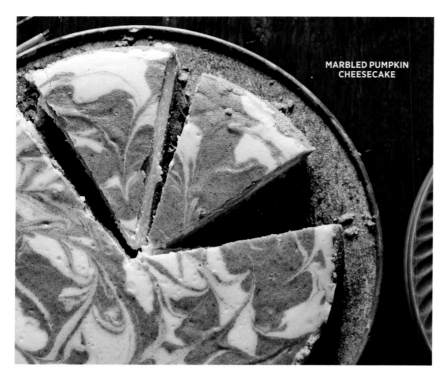

MARBLED PUMPKIN CHEESECAKE

Marbled Pumpkin Cheesecake

MAKES 12 servings **PREP** 25 minutes **BAKE** at 325° for 55 minutes **CHILL** 6 hours or overnight

CRUST

- **45** vanilla wafer cookies, crushed (about 1½ cups)
- **3** tbsp sugar
- **4** tbsp unsalted butter, melted

FILLING

- **1½** lb cream cheese, at room temperature
- **⅔** cup sugar
- **5** tsp cornstarch
- **¼** tsp salt
- **4** large eggs, at room temperature
- **1** tsp vanilla extract
- **½** cup pumpkin puree (not pumpkin pie filling)
- **2** tsp pumpkin pie spice

■ Heat oven to 325°. Wrap outside of a 9-inch springform pan with aluminum foil. Put a kettle of water on to boil.

■ **Crust:** In a medium bowl, combine cookie crumbs, sugar and melted butter until crumbs are evenly moistened. Press into bottom of springform pan.

■ **Filling:** With an electric mixer, beat first 4 ingredients for 2 minutes, until smooth and creamy.

■ Add eggs to mixer one at a time, beating well after each. Beat in vanilla. Transfer 1 cup filling to a medium bowl; pour remaining filling into prepared pan.

■ Stir pumpkin puree and pie spice into reserved filling. Drop mixture in evenly spaced dollops over top of plain filling. With tip of a small knife, swirl dollops to create a marbled look.

■ Place springform pan in a large roasting pan on oven rack. Pour boiling water into roasting pan until it reaches halfway up side of springform pan. Bake 50 to 55 minutes, until edges are set and center shakes slightly.

■ Transfer springform pan to a wire rack and carefully remove foil. Run a thin knife around edge of cake. Cool completely in pan on rack. Cover and refrigerate 6 hours or overnight.

■ To serve, remove side of pan and cut into 12 slices.

PER SERVING 371 CAL; 28 g FAT (15 g SAT); 6 g PRO; 26 g CARB; 19 g SUGARS; 0 g FIBER; 305 mg SODIUM

Pumpkin Whoopie Pies

MAKES 16 whoopie pies **PREP** 10 minutes
BAKE at 350° for 20 minutes

COOKIES

- **1** box (16.5 oz) spice cake mix
- **1** can (15 oz) pumpkin puree (not pumpkin pie filling)

FILLING

- **½** cup (1 stick) unsalted butter, at room temperature
- **½** cup confectioners' sugar, sifted
- **1** cup marshmallow crème
- **1** tsp vanilla extract

■ Heat oven to 350°. Line 2 rimmed baking sheets with parchment paper.

■ **Cookies:** Beat cake mix and pumpkin puree until well combined. Drop by 2 tablespoonfuls, 2 inches apart, onto prepared baking sheets to form 32 mounds. With moistened fingers, lightly flatten tops.

■ Bake 20 minutes, until a toothpick inserted in center comes out clean. Cool on sheets 15 minutes, then transfer to racks to cool completely.

■ **Filling:** In bowl of a stand mixer fitted with whisk attachment, beat butter and confectioners' sugar until fluffy. Add marshmallow crème; beat until well combined. Add vanilla and beat 20 seconds.

■ Sandwich cookies together, flat side to flat side, with 1 tbsp filling.

Tote Tip Zip the cookies into a plastic bag and place the filling in a container. You can assemble pies on site.

PER WHOOPIE PIE 208 CAL; 7 g FAT (4 g SAT); 2 g PRO; 34 g CARB; 22 g SUGARS; 1 g FIBER; 225 mg SODIUM

SWEET POTATO
BREAD PUDDING

Sweet Potato Bread Pudding

MAKES 12 servings **PREP** 10 minutes
SOAK 40 minutes **BAKE** at 350° for 55 minutes
COOL 15 minutes

- **2 tbsp unsalted butter, melted and cooled, plus more for greasing**
- **5 large eggs**
- **1 cup packed light brown sugar**
- **1 tsp rum extract**
- **½ tsp ground cinnamon**
- **¼ tsp ground nutmeg**
- **2 cups half-and-half**
- **1 can (15 oz) sweet potato puree**
- **1 cup chopped pecans**
- **8 cups 1-inch cubes day-old baguette, plus 1 oz torn baguette**
- **Confectioners' sugar, for dusting**

- Heat oven to 350°. Grease a 13 x 9-inch baking dish with butter.

- In a large bowl, whisk melted butter and next 5 ingredients. Whisk in half-and-half and sweet potato puree. Stir in pecans and cubed bread, blending thoroughly. Cover surface with plastic wrap and place a heavy bowl on top. Let soak 40 minutes, stirring halfway.

- In a food processor, pulse torn bread until small crumbs form. Sprinkle into bottom of prepared baking dish.

- Pour filling into baking dish. Bake 55 minutes, until just firm. Transfer to a rack and cool 15 minutes. Dust with confectioners' sugar. Serve warm.

PER SERVING 325 **CAL**; 15 g **FAT** (5 g **SAT**); 8 g **PRO**; 43 g **CARB**; 20 g **SUGARS**; 2 g **FIBER**; 233 mg **SODIUM**

CRANBERRY-ORANGE BISCOTTI

Cranberry-Orange Biscotti

MAKES 16 biscotti **PREP** 10 minutes **BAKE** at 375° for 25 minutes, then at 325° for 24 minutes

- **2¼ cups all-purpose flour**
- **1½ tsp baking powder**
- **⅛ tsp salt**
- **½ cup (1 stick) unsalted butter, at room temperature**
- **½ cup packed light brown sugar**
- **2 large eggs**
- **1 tsp vanilla extract**
- **½ cup dried cranberries**
- **Zest of 2 oranges, plus 4 tsp fresh orange juice**
- **¾ cup confectioners' sugar**

- Heat oven to 375°. Line a baking sheet with parchment. In a medium bowl, combine flour, baking powder and salt. In a large bowl, beat butter and brown sugar with an electric mixer until creamy, about 2 minutes. Beat in eggs, one at a time, then vanilla. Slowly beat in flour mixture. Fold in cranberries and half the zest. Gather dough into a ball and divide in half.

- Using floured hands, shape each portion into a 7 x 3-inch log. Place on prepared baking sheet.

- Bake 25 minutes, until lightly browned. Transfer loaves to a wire rack to cool, about 15 minutes. Lower oven temp to 325°.

- With a serrated knife, slice loaves diagonally into ¾-inch-thick slices (8 slices each). Place cut side down on baking sheet. Bake 12 minutes, then turn over and bake 12 minutes more. Transfer biscotti to rack and let cool completely.

- In a small bowl, combine confectioners' sugar, orange juice and remaining zest. Drizzle over biscotti and let set at least 1 hour.

PER BISCOTTI 171 **CAL**; 7 g **FAT** (4 g **SAT**); 3 g **PRO**; 26 g **CARB**; 12 g **SUGARS**; 1 g **FIBER**; 74 mg **SODIUM**

CHRISTMAS TREE
PULL-APART BREAD,
PAGE 290

DECEMBER

277

290

297

HEALTHY FAMILY DINNERS

Although the Italian Christmas Eve Feast of the Seven Fishes serves seven courses in one meal, these 7 fish dishes are easy dinner ideas to get you through this crazy-busy month.

ROASTED HALIBUT WITH
SWEET POTATO FRIES
AND GREEN BEANS

Roasted Halibut with Sweet Potato Fries and Green Beans

MAKES 4 servings **PREP** 20 minutes
ROAST at 425° for 32 minutes **COOK** 6 minutes

- 1½ **lb sweet potatoes, scrubbed and cut into wedges**
- 2 **tbsp vegetable oil**
- ¾ **tsp plus ⅛ tsp salt**
- ½ **tsp freshly ground black pepper**
- 4 **tbsp unsalted butter**
- 2 **tsp fresh thyme leaves**
- 1 **tsp fresh lemon zest**
- 4 **pieces halibut or sea bass (1¼ lb total)**
- 1 **lb green beans, trimmed**

■ Heat oven to 425°. Toss sweet potato wedges with oil and ¼ tsp each salt and pepper. Spread on a rimmed sheet pan and roast 20 minutes.

■ Meanwhile, melt 2 tbsp butter. Stir in thyme and lemon zest. Bring a large pot of lightly salted water to a boil.

■ Remove pan from oven and stir potato wedges. Push to one side of pan, but keep in a single layer. Add fish to pan and brush with herb butter. Season with ¼ tsp salt and ⅛ tsp pepper. Return to oven and roast 10 to 12 minutes, until fish flakes easily with a fork.

■ Add green beans to boiling water and cook 4 minutes. Drain and return to pot. Add 2 tbsp butter and ¼ plus ⅛ tsp salt and ⅛ tsp pepper. Cook over medium for 2 minutes, until butter melts and coats green beans.

■ Serve fish with sweet potato wedges and green beans.

PER SERVING 437 **CAL**; 21 g **FAT** (9 g **SAT**); 31 g **PRO**; 34 g **CARB**; 9 g **SUGARS**; 7 g **FIBER**; 748 mg **SODIUM**

VERACRUZ-STYLE TILAPIA

Veracruz-Style Tilapia

MAKES 4 servings **PREP** 15 minutes **COOK** 13 minutes **BAKE** at 350° for 20 minutes

- 4 **tbsp olive oil**
- 2 **red bell peppers, cored and cut into thin strips**
- 1 **large onion, halved and sliced**
- 1 **can (14.5 oz) stewed tomatoes**
- 8 **oz yellow or red cherry tomatoes (or a mix of both), halved**
- 4 **cloves garlic, chopped**
- ¼ **cup pepperoncini, sliced**
- ½ **tsp plus a pinch salt**
- ¼ **tsp plus ⅛ tsp freshly ground black pepper**
- 4 **small tilapia fillets (about 1½ lb total)**
- 2 **tbsp fresh lime juice**
- ¼ **cup fresh cilantro, coarsely chopped**

■ Heat oven to 350°. In a large lidded skillet, heat 3 tbsp oil over medium. Add red peppers and onion and sauté 7 minutes. Stir in stewed tomatoes, cherry tomatoes, garlic, pepperoncini, ½ tsp salt and ¼ tsp pepper. Cover and cook 6 minutes, stirring occasionally.

■ Spoon half the pepper mixture into a 13 x 9 x 2-inch baking dish. Top with tilapia. Drizzle lime juice over fish and sprinkle with half the cilantro, a pinch of salt and ⅛ tsp pepper. Top with remaining pepper mixture and bake 20 minutes or until fish flakes easily with a fork.

■ Top with remaining cilantro and drizzle with 1 tbsp olive oil before serving.

PER SERVING 428 **CAL**; 18 g **FAT** (4 g **SAT**); 47 g **PRO**; 20 g **CARB**; 9 g **SUGARS**; 4 g **FIBER**; 803 mg **SODIUM**

Look for clams that are 2 to 2½ inches at their widest point. They may be labeled either littlenecks or cherrystones, depending on their size, but these belong to the same species. Larger clams, such as chowders or steamers, will take longer to cook and are best for other uses.

Clams Rockefeller Pasta

MAKES 6 servings **PREP** 15 minutes **COOK** 21 minutes

1 tbsp unsalted butter
¼ cup seasoned bread crumbs
1 lb orecchiette pasta
4 oz bacon, chopped
1 cup diced onion
3 cloves garlic, sliced
5 oz fresh baby spinach
½ cup clam juice
½ cup dry white wine
2 lb littleneck clams, scrubbed
¼ cup heavy cream

■ Bring a large pot of lightly salted water to a boil.

■ In a small skillet, melt butter over medium. Add bread crumbs and stir, cooking until browned, 2 minutes. Remove from heat.

■ Add pasta to boiling water and cook 10 minutes. Drain.

■ Meanwhile, cook bacon in a large lidded stainless-steel sauté pan over medium until crisp, 6 minutes. Remove with a slotted spoon and discard all but 2 tbsp bacon fat from pan. Add onion and cook 4 minutes. Stir in garlic and cook 1 minute.

■ Stir spinach, clam juice and wine into pan, then add clams. Cover and cook 8 minutes or until clams open; discard any that do not. Add cream to pan.

■ In a large bowl, combine contents of pan with pasta, bacon and bread crumbs.

PER SERVING 526 **CAL**; 21 g **FAT** (10 g **SAT**); 26 g **PRO**; 60 g **CARB**; 4 g **SUGARS**; 1 g **FIBER**; 725 mg **SODIUM**

CLAMS
ROCKEFELLER
PASTA

KALE CAESAR WITH SHRIMP

COD
CHOWDER

Kale Caesar with Shrimp

MAKES 4 servings **PREP** 25 minutes
BROIL 2 minutes **COOK** 5 minutes

- **5 tbsp extra-virgin olive oil**
- **5 tbsp fresh lemon juice**
- **5 tbsp grated Parmesan**
- **2 oil-packed anchovy fillets, drained**
- **1 tsp Dijon mustard**
- **1 clove garlic**
- **1¼ lb colossal shrimp (with tails on; about 12 shrimp)**
- **Pinch salt**
- **4 diagonally cut ½-inch-thick slices of baguette (about 3 oz total)**
- **12 oz Lacinato kale (tough stems discarded), cleaned and halved**

■ Heat broiler. In a mini chopper or the small bowl of a food processor, combine 4 tbsp oil, 3 tbsp each lemon juice and Parmesan, the anchovies, mustard and garlic. Pulse until blended and smooth.

■ Toss shrimp with 1 tbsp oil, 2 tbsp lemon juice and pinch of salt. Place bread on a baking sheet. Spritz with nonstick olive oil spray and sprinkle each slice with ½ tbsp Parmesan. Broil 2 minutes.

■ Meanwhile, heat a large stainless-steel skillet over medium-high to high. Add shrimp; cook 2 to 3 minutes. Flip and cook 2 minutes, until cooked through.

■ Toss kale with half the dressing. Divide among 4 plates, top with shrimp and drizzle with remaining dressing. Serve with Parmesan-topped toasts.

PER SERVING 505 **CAL**; 21 g **FAT** (4 g **SAT**); 40 g **PRO**; 43 g **CARB**; 0 g **SUGARS**; 4 g **FIBER**; 808 mg **SODIUM**

Cod Chowder

MAKES 6 servings **PREP** 20 minutes **COOK** 23 minutes

- **3 tbsp unsalted butter**
- **1 large onion, diced**
- **2 large carrots, peeled and diced**
- **2 ribs celery, diced**
- **1 tsp salt**
- **¼ tsp freshly ground black pepper**
- **3 cloves garlic, sliced**
- **½ cup all-purpose flour**
- **1 box (32 oz) seafood stock**
- **3 cups whole milk**
- **1¼ lb russet potatoes, peeled and diced**
- **3 sprigs fresh thyme, plus more for garnish (optional)**
- **1½ to 1¾ lb skinless cod fillet, cut into 1-inch pieces**

■ Heat butter in a large stockpot over medium. Add onion, carrots, celery, salt and pepper, and cook, stirring occasionally, 5 minutes.

■ Stir in garlic and cook 2 minutes. Sprinkle with flour and cook 1 minute.

■ Whisk in stock and milk. Stir in potatoes and thyme sprigs. Increase heat to medium-high and bring to a boil. Reduce to medium-low and simmer 10 minutes. Stir in cod, cover and cook 5 minutes, until fish is opaque. Remove thyme stems and serve.

PER SERVING 386 **CAL**; 12 g **FAT** (6 g **SAT**); 32 g **PRO**; 38 g **CARB**; 9 g **SUGARS**; 3 g **FIBER**; 788 mg **SODIUM**

PASTA PUTTANESCA

If fresh scallops are unavailable, look for bags of frozen ones—just thaw completely. Before seasoning scallops, locate and remove the small, tough muscle that might still be attached to one side.

Sea Scallops with Broccoli Rice

MAKES 4 servings **PREP** 15 minutes
COOK 31 minutes

- 4   **tbsp unsalted butter**
- ⅓   **cup finely chopped onion**
- 2   **cloves garlic, minced**
- 1   **cup Arborio rice**
- ½   **tsp plus ⅛ tsp salt**
- ¼   **tsp freshly ground black pepper**
- 3   **cups small broccoli florets**
- 1   **lb large sea scallops (about 16)**
- ½   **cup grated Parmesan**
- 2   **tbsp chopped fresh flat-leaf parsley**

■ In a large lidded pot, heat 2 tbsp butter over medium. Add onion and cook 3 minutes. Stir in garlic and cook 2 minutes. Add rice and cook 1 minute, stirring to coat with butter.

■ Add 3 cups water, ½ tsp salt and ⅛ tsp pepper. Cover and simmer over medium-low 15 minutes.

■ Uncover, stir and add broccoli florets. Partially cover and cook 10 minutes.

■ Meanwhile, in a large stainless-steel skillet, melt 2 tbsp butter over medium-high. Pat scallops dry with paper towels and season with ⅛ tsp each salt and pepper. Cook 2 minutes, flip and cook 1 to 2 minutes.

■ Stir Parmesan into rice mixture. Divide among 4 shallow bowls and top each with 4 scallops. Sprinkle with parsley and serve.

PER SERVING 501 **CAL**; 16 g **FAT** (8 g **SAT**); 46 g **PRO**; 46 g **CARB**; 1 g **SUGARS**; 3 g **FIBER**; 817 mg **SODIUM**

Pasta Puttanesca

MAKES 6 servings **PREP** 15 minutes **COOK** 25 minutes

- 4   **tbsp extra-virgin olive oil**
- 1   **large shallot, peeled and minced**
- 4   **cloves garlic, sliced**
- 6   **to 8 oil-packed anchovy fillets, drained and chopped (or 1½ to 2 tbsp anchovy paste)**
- 1   **lb linguine**
- 1   **can (28 oz) crushed tomatoes**
- 1   **tbsp sugar**
- ½   **tsp salt**
- ¼   **tsp freshly cracked black pepper**
- ¼   **cup sliced green olives**
- 2   **tbsp capers, drained**
- 1   **cup fresh basil leaves, torn**

■ Bring a large pot of lightly salted water to a boil. Heat oil in a large lidded stainless-steel skillet over medium. Add shallot and garlic, and cook, stirring, 3 minutes. Add anchovies and reduce heat to medium-low. Cook 4 minutes, breaking apart with a spoon.

■ Meanwhile, add linguine to boiling water and cook 9 to 10 minutes. Drain.

■ Stir crushed tomatoes, sugar, salt and pepper into skillet. Cover and simmer 10 minutes, adding olives and capers after 5 minutes. Stir in basil and remove from heat.

■ Add cooked linguine to sauce and toss to coat. Serve warm.

PER SERVING 444 **CAL**; 12 g **FAT** (2 g **SAT**); 13 g **PRO**; 72 g **CARB**; 12 g **SUGARS**; 6 g **FIBER**; 793 mg **SODIUM**

SEA SCALLOPS WITH
BROCCOLI RICE

DOUBLE TAKE

No matter your hosting style—buttoned-up or laid-back—we've got the holiday party for you.

POMEGRANATE-GLAZED PRIME RIB

Fancy, not fussy

Pomegranate-Glazed Prime Rib

MAKES 12 servings **PREP** 15 minutes
STAND 1 hour 25 minutes **ROAST** at 450° for 30 minutes, then at 350° for 1 hour

- 1 **3-rib standing beef rib roast (about 6 lb)**
- 2 **tbsp unsalted butter, softened**
- 1 **tbsp kosher salt**
- 1 **tsp freshly cracked black pepper**
- ⅓ **cup pomegranate molasses, plus more for serving**
- 2 **tsp packed light brown sugar**
- 1 **cup pomegranate seeds**
-    **Fresh parsley**

■ Place roast in a baking pan fitted with a wire rack. Pat dry. Let stand at room temp for 1 hour.

■ Heat oven to 450°. Rub beef, especially cut sides, with butter. Season all over with salt and pepper. Roast 30 minutes. Reduce oven temp to 350° and roast 30 minutes. Carefully remove from oven. Combine molasses, brown sugar and 1 tbsp water; brush over beef. Roast another 30 minutes or until internal temperature reaches 125°.

■ Let rest 25 minutes (temp will rise to 135°). Slice, and garnish with pomegranate seeds and parsley. Serve with more molasses on the side.

PER SERVING 526 **CAL**; 40 g **FAT** (17 g **SAT**); 33 g **PRO**; 8 g **CARB**; 6 g **SUGARS**; 1 g **FIBER**; 566 mg **SODIUM**

Garlicky Broccoli Rabe

MAKES 8 servings **PREP** 5 minutes
COOK 8 minutes

- 2 **bunches (2 lb total) broccoli rabe**
- ¼ **cup extra-virgin olive oil**
- 6 **cloves garlic, sliced**
- ¼ **to ½ tsp red pepper flakes**
- ¼ **tsp salt**
- 1 **lemon, halved**

■ Bring a large pot of salted water to a boil. Add broccoli rabe and boil 2 minutes. Drain.

TRUFFLED POTATO GRATIN

GARLICKY BROCCOLI RABE

■ Heat a large skillet over medium-high. Add 2 tbsp oil, half the garlic and half the red pepper flakes; cook 1 minute. Add half the broccoli rabe and ⅛ tsp salt; sauté 2 minutes. Transfer to a platter. Repeat with remaining oil, garlic, red pepper flakes, salt and broccoli rabe. Squeeze lemon over top.

PER SERVING 89 **CAL**; 7 g **FAT** (1 g **SAT**); 4 g **PRO**; 4 g **CARB**; 1 g **SUGARS**; 3 g **FIBER**; 111 mg **SODIUM**

Truffled Potato Gratin

MAKES 12 servings **PREP** 20 minutes
BAKE at 350° for 50 minutes **STAND** 10 minutes

- 2 **cups heavy cream**
- 4 **cloves garlic, sliced**
- 1 **medium shallot, minced**
- 1 **tbsp chopped fresh thyme**
- 1¼ **tsp salt**
- ½ **tsp freshly cracked black pepper**
- 3 **lb russet potatoes**
- 2 **cups grated truffle cheese (such as Piccolo Truffle) or Gouda**

■ Heat oven to 350°. In a small pot, combine first 6 ingredients and bring to a simmer. Cover and remove from heat.

■ Meanwhile, peel potatoes. Using a mandoline, cut into ¹⁄₁₆-inch-thick slices. Layer half the slices in a 13 x 9-inch baking dish. Scatter 1 cup cheese over top. Layer remaining potatoes, pour cream evenly over top and press with a spatula to compress into dish. Scatter 1 cup cheese over top. Bake 45 to 50 minutes, until golden brown, bubbly and knife-tender. Let stand 10 minutes before serving.

PER SERVING 296 **CAL**; 20 g **FAT** (13 g **SAT**); 8 g **PRO**; 21 g **CARB**; 2 g **SUGARS**; 2 g **FIBER**; 533 mg **SODIUM**

LAYERED LEMON CREPE CAKE

Layered Lemon Crepe Cake

MAKES 16 servings   **PREP** 30 minutes
CHILL 4 hours

- 2½   cups heavy cream, chilled
- 2   jars (11 oz each) lemon curd
- 24   packaged 10-inch crepes
- ½   lemon, thinly sliced

■ In a large bowl, beat 2 cups cream to stiff peaks. Fold in lemon curd.

■ Place 1 crepe on a cake stand. Spread ¼ cup lemon cream on crepe, leaving a ½-inch border. Top with another crepe and repeat layering; do not spread cream on top layer. Refrigerate 4 hours.

■ Beat ½ cup cream to stiff peaks and mound on top of cake in center. Garnish with lemon slices.

PER SERVING 372 **CAL**; 20 g **FAT** (12 g **SAT**);
7 g **PRO**; 43 g **CARB**; 29 g **SUGARS**; 0 g **FIBER**;
408 mg **SODIUM**

Pomegranate Gimlet

MAKES 8 servings   **PREP** 30 minutes

- ½   cup sugar
- ½   cup water
- 1   cup lime juice
- 1½   cups gin
- 1   cup pomegranate juice
    Pomegranate seeds
    Lime wedges or zest

■ In a small pot, cook sugar and water until sugar is dissolved. Stir in lime juice and cool. Once cooled, mix with gin and pomegranate juice. For a high-end look, combine in a cocktail shaker with ice and strain into coupé glasses. For a simpler sipper, pour over ice in tall glasses. Garnish with pomegranate seeds, lime wedges or zest.

Maple-Baked Brie with Cherries and Pecans

MAKES 8 servings   **PREP** 5 minutes
BAKE at 350° for 14 minutes

- 1   wheel (7 oz) Brie or Camembert
- ⅓   cup pecan halves
- ⅓   cup dried tart cherries
- ¼   cup maple syrup
- 1   tsp chopped fresh rosemary
- ¼   tsp freshly cracked black pepper
- ⅛   tsp salt
    Baguette, for serving

■ Heat oven to 350°. Unwrap cheese from any packaging and place in center of a cast-iron or ceramic baking dish. Bake 7 minutes.

■ Meanwhile, in a bowl, combine next 6 ingredients. Carefully remove baking dish from oven and over and pour around cheese. Return to oven and bake 7 minutes more. Serve warm with baguette alongside.

PER SERVING 160 **CAL**; 10 g **FAT** (5 g **SAT**);
6 g **PRO**; 13 g **CARB**; 11 g **SUGARS**; 1 g **FIBER**;
195 mg **SODIUM**

POMEGRANATE GIMLET

MAPLE-BAKED BRIE
WITH CHERRIES AND
PECANS

CHICKEN, BEEF AND LAMB KOFTAS
WITH HARISSA-YOGURT AND
MINT-SCALLION SAUCES

Casual cheer

Chicken, Beef and Lamb Koftas with Harissa-Yogurt and Mint-Scallion Sauces

MAKES 8 servings **PREP** 25 minutes
BROIL 13 minutes

1	lb ground chicken
1	lb ground beef
1	lb ground lamb
1	tbsp ground coriander
1½	tsp ground cumin
1½	tsp garlic powder
1½	tsp freshly cracked black pepper
1½	tsp salt
¼	tsp allspice
1	cup fresh mint, chopped
24	8-inch skewers (soaked for 1 hour if wooden)
2	tbsp extra-virgin olive oil
	Harissa-Yogurt Sauce (recipe, below right)
	Mint-Scallion Sauce (recipe, below right)

■ Heat broiler and place 2 racks in center of oven. Line 2 baking sheets with aluminum foil.

■ Place chicken, beef and lamb in 3 separate bowls. In a small bowl, combine next 6 ingredients and divide evenly among bowls. Divide mint evenly among bowls. Mix each until well combined.

■ Starting with chicken, form meat around skewers into 8 oblong koftas (about 2 oz each). Place on a baking sheet and refrigerate while forming beef and lamb koftas. Brush all 24 koftas on both sides with oil.

■ Transfer baking sheets to oven and broil 5 minutes. Carefully remove pans from oven and rotate from top to bottom and front to back. Broil another 5 minutes, then transfer beef and lamb to a platter. Broil chicken 2 to 3 minutes, until temperature reaches 165°. Serve with sauces.

PER SERVING 330 **CAL**; 22 g **FAT** (7 g **SAT**); 30 g **PRO**; 2 g **CARB**; 0 g **SUGARS**; 1 g **FIBER**; 540 mg **SODIUM**

HOT CHOCOLATE

Harissa-Yogurt Sauce In a bowl, stir 1 cup plain Greek yogurt, 2 tbsp water, 1 tbsp each harissa paste and lemon juice, ½ tsp lemon zest and ¼ tsp salt until smooth.

PER 2 TBSP SERVING 35 **CAL**; 2 g **FAT** (1 g **SAT**); 3 g **PRO**; 2 g **CARB**; 1 g **SUGARS**; 0 g **FIBER**; 100 mg **SODIUM**

Mint-Scallion Sauce In a food processor, combine 2 cups packed fresh mint, 2 roughly chopped scallions, 1 large clove garlic, 2 tbsp lemon juice and ½ tsp salt. While processor is running, add ½ cup extra-virgin olive oil in a thin stream and process until smooth.

PER 2 TBSP SERVING 127 **CAL**; 14 g **FAT** (2 g **SAT**); 0 g **PRO**; 2 g **CARB**; 0 g **SUGARS**; 1 g **FIBER**; 149 mg **SODIUM**

Hot Chocolate

MAKES 12 servings **PREP** 15 minutes

2	cups nonfat dry milk
1	cup malted milk powder
1	cup instant chocolate milk powder
⅓	cup unsweetened cocoa powder
⅓	cup sugar
12	cups water

■ In a large pot, mix nonfat dry milk, malted milk powder, instant chocolate milk powder, unsweetened cocoa powder and sugar. Sift into a large bowl. Sift back into pot. Whisk in water; bring just to a simmer.

SPINACH-
BACON BITES

Spinach-Bacon Bites

MAKES 12 servings PREP 15 minutes
COOK 8 minutes BAKE at 375° for 35 minutes

- 3 pkg (10 oz each) frozen chopped spinach, thawed
- 8 oz bacon, diced
- 1 cup all-purpose flour
- 4 eggs
- 1 cup milk
- 1 tsp baking powder
- 1 tsp salt
- ½ tsp ground black pepper
- 4 scallions, sliced
- 8 oz pepper Jack cheese, shredded

■ Heat oven to 375°. Place spinach in a clean kitchen towel and squeeze over sink to remove as much liquid as possible.

■ Heat a skillet over medium. Add bacon and cook 6 to 8 minutes, until crispy. Remove to a plate, reserving 2 tbsp bacon fat.

■ Brush a 13 x 9-inch baking dish with 1 tbsp bacon fat. In a large bowl, mix 1 tbsp bacon fat with flour and next 5 ingredients until well combined. Stir in

spinach, scallions, cheese and bacon. Spread into greased baking dish. Bake 30 to 35 minutes, until top starts to turn golden brown.

■ Cool slightly, then cut into triangles. Serve warm or at room temperature.

PER SERVING 238 CAL; 16 g FAT (7 g SAT); 14 g PRO; 14 g CARB; 2 g SUGARS; 3 g FIBER; 519 mg SODIUM

Chocolate-Mint Mini Cakes

MAKES 48 mini cakes PREP 30 minutes
BAKE at 350° for 14 minutes per batch

MINI CAKES

- 1 box (15.25 oz) chocolate cake mix
- 1 cup buttermilk

FROSTING AND TOPPING

- 6 cups confectioners' sugar
- 1½ cups (3 sticks) unsalted butter, softened
- 2 tbsp milk
- ½ tsp peppermint extract
- ¼ tsp salt
- 24 peppermint candies, crushed

■ Heat oven to 350°. Coat 2 mini muffin pans with nonstick spray.

■ **Mini Cakes** Prepare batter according to package directions, replacing water with buttermilk. Scoop half the batter evenly into pans, filling each two-thirds full. Bake 12 to 14 minutes, until a toothpick inserted in center comes out clean. Cool 5 minutes, then remove to a rack. Repeat with remaining batter. Once cool, slice in half crosswise.

■ **Frosting and Topping** In a large bowl, beat first 5 ingredients on low for 1 minute. Increase speed to high and beat 4 minutes, until fluffy. Transfer to a piping bag fitted with a large star tip.

■ Pipe 1 tsp frosting on bottom half of each cake. Add tops; pipe on more frosting. Scatter crushed peppermints on top.

PER MINI CAKE 181 CAL; 9 g FAT (4 g SAT); 1 g PRO; 25 g CARB; 21 g SUGARS; 0 g FIBER; 103 mg SODIUM

Christmas Tree Pull-Apart Bread

MAKES 8 servings PREP 25 minutes
STAND 30 minutes BAKE at 450° for 15 minutes

- 1 lb refrigerated pizza dough
- 8 oz mozzarella, cut into 32 pieces
- 1 egg, beaten
- 2 tbsp unsalted butter, melted
- 3 tbsp grated Parmesan
- 1 tsp garlic salt
- ⅓ cup chopped fresh basil
- 1 cup marinara sauce, warmed

■ Place dough in a bowl coated with olive oil. Cover with a towel or plastic wrap and let stand at room temperature for at least 30 minutes.

■ Heat oven to 450°. Transfer dough to a lightly floured surface and cut into 32 equal pieces. Form dough balls around mozzarella and arrange in a Christmas tree pattern (photo opposite) on a baking sheet lined with parchment paper. Brush dough with egg and pour melted butter over top. Combine Parmesan and garlic salt; sprinkle over dough. Bake 15 minutes, until golden brown.

■ Slide parchment onto a serving platter. Scatter basil on top and serve with marinara alongside.

PER SERVING 259 CAL; 11 g FAT (5 g SAT); 11 g PRO; 28 g CARB; 3 g SUGARS; 2 g FIBER; 1,073 mg SODIUM

CHOCOLATE-MINT
MINI CAKES

CHRISTMAS TREE
PULL-APART BREAD

COOKIE MASTERS

These sweet treats from master bakers are the ultimate holiday cookies.

GLUTEN-FREE CHOCOLATE CRINKLES

Gluten-Free Chocolate Crinkles

MAKES 4 dozen cookies **PREP** 30 minutes
CHILL 2 hours or overnight
BAKE at 350° for 12 minutes per batch
COOL 5 minutes per batch

- ½ cup (1 stick) salted butter, cut into tablespoons
- 4 oz unsweetened chocolate, finely chopped
- 2 tsp pure vanilla extract
- 1 tsp instant espresso powder
- 1¼ cups almond flour or finely ground slivered almonds
- ½ cup potato starch
- ½ cup white or brown rice flour
- ¼ cup coconut flour
- ¼ cup natural or Dutch-process cocoa powder
- 2 tsp baking powder
- 1½ cups plus ⅓ cup granulated sugar
- 4 large eggs, at room temperature
- 1 cup semisweet chocolate chips
- ⅓ cup confectioners' sugar

■ Position racks in top third and center of oven and heat to 350°. Line 2 large rimmed baking sheets with parchment paper.

■ In a small saucepan, melt butter over medium. Remove from heat, add chopped chocolate and let stand 2 minutes to soften. Whisk until chocolate is melted and smooth. Whisk in vanilla and espresso powder. Let cool until tepid.

■ In a medium bowl, whisk next 6 ingredients. In a large bowl, beat 1½ cups granulated sugar and eggs until pale yellow and thick, about 3 minutes. Beat in cooled chocolate mixture.

■ Using a wooden spoon, gradually stir in almond flour mixture. Stir in chocolate chips. Cover bowl with plastic and refrigerate until easy to handle, at least 2 hours or overnight.

■ Add ⅓ cup granulated sugar to a bowl and the confectioners' sugar to a second bowl. Roll heaping tablespoonfuls of dough into balls. Roll each ball first in granulated sugar, then in confectioners' sugar. Place 3 inches apart on prepared baking sheets.

■ Bake just until edges are firm and tops are cracked, 10 to 12 minutes. Cookies should be soft and cake like; do not overbake. Let cool in pans 5 minutes. Transfer cookies to a wire rack to cool completely. Repeat with remaining dough, using cooled baking sheets.

PER COOKIE 110 **CAL**; 6 g **FAT** (3 g **SAT**); 2 g **PRO**; 13 g **CARB**; 8 g **SUGARS**; 1 g **FIBER**; 42 mg **SODIUM**

Cornflake-Chocolate Chip-Peppermint Cookies

MAKES 18 cookies **PREP** 30 minutes
CHILL 2 hours **BAKE** at 375° for 18 minutes per batch

- 1 cup (2 sticks) unsalted butter, at room temperature
- 1¼ cups granulated sugar
- ⅔ cup packed light brown sugar
- 1 large egg
- 1 tsp peppermint extract
- 1½ cups all-purpose flour
- ½ tsp baking powder
- ½ tsp baking soda
- 1½ tsp kosher salt
  Cornflake Crunch (recipe, below right)
- ⅔ cup mini chocolate chips
- 40 peppermint candies (or 18 candy canes), finely crushed
- 1¼ cups mini marshmallows

■ With an electric mixer, beat butter and sugars on medium-high speed 2 to 3 minutes. Scrape down bowl, add egg and peppermint extract, and beat 7 to 8 minutes.

■ Reduce speed to low and add next 4 ingredients; beat until well combined. Beat in Cornflake Crunch, chocolate chips and peppermints, then beat in marshmallows until just incorporated.

■ Using a ⅓-cup measure, drop dough onto a baking sheet. Pat dough flat and refrigerate 1 to 2 hours, until chilled.

■ Heat oven to 375°. Line 2 baking sheets with parchment paper.

CORNFLAKE-CHOCOLATE CHIP-PEPPERMINT COOKIES

■ Place chilled cookies at least 4 inches apart on prepared baking sheets (no more than 4 cookies per sheet). Bake 1 or 2 sheets at a time, 18 minutes per batch. Cookies will crackle and spread. Cool completely on sheets. Repeat with remaining dough and cooled baking sheets.

PER COOKIE 365 **CAL**; 18 g **FAT** (11 g **SAT**); 3 g **PRO**; 55 g **CARB**; 37 g **SUGARS**; 1 g **FIBER**; 392 mg **SODIUM**

Cornflake Crunch Crush 5 cups cornflakes in a medium bowl until they're one-fourth their original size. Add ½ cup milk powder, 3 tbsp sugar and 1 tsp kosher salt; toss to mix. Melt 9 tbsp unsalted butter; add to cereal mixture and toss to coat, creating small clusters. Spread clusters on a parchment-paper-lined rimmed sheet pan and bake at 275° for 20 minutes. Clusters should look toasted, smell buttery and crunch gently when cooled slightly. Cool completely before using. (If not using right away, Cornflake Crunch will keep for 1 week in an airtight container at room temperature or for 1 month in the fridge or freezer.)

SUGAR 'N' SPICE COOKIES

Sugar 'n' Spice Cookies

MAKES 4½ dozen cookies **PREP** 15 minutes
BAKE at 375° for 10 minutes per batch

- 2   **cups all-purpose flour**
- 2   **tsp baking soda**
- 1   **tsp ground cinnamon**
- ¾   **tsp ground cloves**
- ¾   **tsp ground ginger**
- ¼   **tsp salt**
- ¾   **cup (1½ sticks) unsalted butter**
- 1   **cup granulated sugar, plus more for coating**
- 1   **large egg**
- ¼   **cup molasses**

■ Heat oven to 375°. Grease 2 baking sheets.

■ In a medium bowl, combine first 6 ingredients.

■ In a large bowl, beat butter, sugar and egg with an electric mixer on medium speed until pale and creamy, about 5 minutes. Add molasses and beat thoroughly. Add dry ingredients and beat on low until dough is moist and well combined.

■ Form dough into 1-inch balls (about 1 heaping teaspoon each), then roll them in granulated sugar. Place balls 2 inches apart on prepared baking sheets. Bake 10 minutes.

■ Let cool on sheets 5 minutes, then transfer to wire racks to cool completely.

PER COOKIE 62 **CAL**; 3 g **FAT** (2 g **SAT**); 1 g **PRO**; 9 g **CARB**; 5 g **SUGARS**; 0 g **FIBER**; 60 mg **SODIUM**

Red Velvet Black-and-White Cookies

MAKES about 30 cookies
PREP 15 minutes **STAND** 45 minutes
BAKE at 350° for 10 minutes per batch

- 2¼   **cups all-purpose flour**
- 2   **tbsp unsweetened cocoa powder**
- 1   **tsp baking soda**
- ¾   **tsp kosher salt**
- ½   **cup (1 stick) unsalted butter, at room temperature**
- 1   **cup granulated sugar**
- 1   **large egg plus 1 large egg yolk**
- 1   **tbsp red food coloring**
- 1½   **tsp pure vanilla extract**
- ¾   **cup buttermilk**
      Cream Cheese Frosting (recipe, right)
      Chocolate Glaze (recipe, right)

■ Place a rack in center of oven and heat to 350°. Line 2 baking sheets with parchment paper.

■ In a medium bowl, whisk flour, cocoa powder, baking soda and salt.

■ With an electric mixer, beat butter and sugar on medium speed until light and fluffy, about 5 minutes. Add egg and yolk; beat 1 minute. Stop mixer and scrape down bowl. Add food coloring and vanilla, and beat on medium until well incorporated.

■ Add half the flour mixture and beat on low. Add buttermilk in a slow stream while beating on low. Add remaining flour mixture and beat on low until well mixed. Let batter rest 15 minutes.

■ Drop batter by heaping tablespoonfuls, 2 inches apart, onto prepared baking sheets. Bake 1 sheet at a time until dry on top and slightly firm to the touch, about 10 minutes. Remove from oven and cool on sheet 5 minutes. Transfer to a wire rack and cool completely before frosting.

■ To frost, turn cookies bottom side up and gently wipe off any crumbs. Using 2 separate butter knives, cover half of each cookie with Cream Cheese Frosting and the other half with Chocolate Glaze. Allow to set for about 30 minutes. Wrap individually or store in an airtight container with parchment paper separating any layers.

Cream Cheese Frosting Beat 4 oz softened cream cheese on medium speed until as smooth as possible, 1 to 2 minutes. Add ¼ cup (½ stick) softened unsalted butter and beat on medium until smooth, about 3 minutes. Add 1 cup sifted confectioners' sugar. Blend until incorporated. Add 1 tsp vanilla and ½ cup sifted confectioners' sugar. Beat on medium-high until frosting is smooth and silky.

Chocolate Glaze In a heatproof bowl, combine 5 tbsp softened unsalted butter and 8 oz semisweet chocolate chips. Set bowl over a pan of simmering water so that water does not hit bottom of bowl. Stir until melted and smooth, 5 to 6 minutes. Remove bowl from pan. Stir in ¼ cup light corn syrup and a pinch of kosher salt. Cool slightly before glazing cookies.

PER COOKIE 143 **CAL**; 7 g **FAT** (4 g **SAT**); 2 g **PRO**; 19 g **CARB**; 11 g **SUGARS**; 1 g **FIBER**; 116 mg **SODIUM**

RED VELVET BLACK-AND-WHITE COOKIES

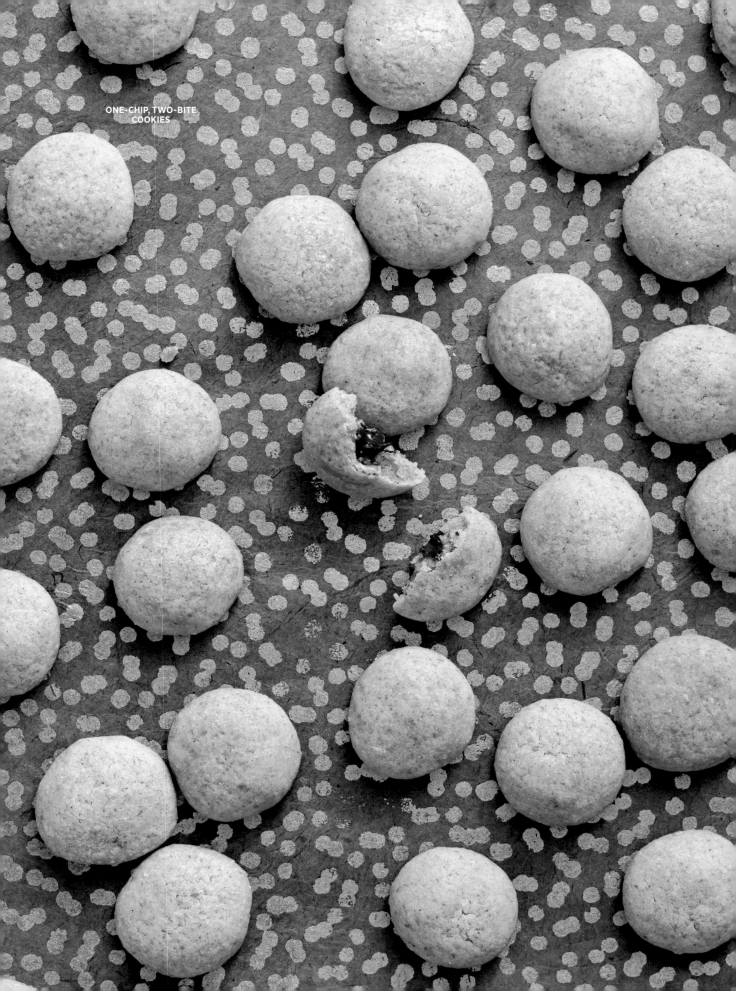

One-Chip, Two-Bite Cookies

MAKES about 60 cookies **PREP** 15 minutes
CHILL 2 hours **BAKE** at 400° for 7 minutes
per batch **REST** 5 minutes per batch

- 1¼ **cups all-purpose flour**
- ⅓ **cup whole wheat flour**
- ⅛ **tsp ground cinnamon**
- ½ **cup (1 stick) unsalted butter, cut into chunks, at room temperature**
- ½ **cup granulated sugar**
- ⅓ **cup plus 1 tbsp packed light brown sugar**
- ½ **tsp fine sea salt**
- 1 **large egg, at room temperature**
- 1 **tsp pure vanilla extract**
  About 60 chocolate chips

■ Place a rack in center of oven and heat to 400°. Line 2 baking sheets with parchment paper.

■ Whisk together both flours and the cinnamon.

■ With an electric mixer, beat butter, both sugars and the salt on medium speed until smooth, about 3 minutes. Add egg and beat 1 minute, then blend in vanilla.

■ Turn off mixer, add dry ingredients all at once and pulse to begin blending. Beat on low until dough comes together and flour is incorporated. You can use dough now, but it will be easier to work with if you wrap it and refrigerate at least 2 hours.

■ For each cookie, scoop out a level teaspoon of dough, roll it between your palms into a ball, press 1 chip into dough and then roll again to hide chip and reshape ball. Place balls 1 inch apart on baking sheets.

■ Bake 1 sheet at a time 6 to 7 minutes, until pale golden brown (cookies will still be soft). Transfer sheet to a rack and let rest about 5 minutes before lifting cookies onto rack to cool until just warm or room temperature.

PER COOKIE 42 **CAL**; 2 g **FAT** (1 g **SAT**);
1 g **PRO**; 6 g **CARB**; 3 g **SUGARS**; 0 g **FIBER**;
21 mg **SODIUM**

Snowflakes

MAKES 20 cookies **PREP** 10 minutes
CHILL 2 hours **BAKE** at 350° for 12 minutes
per batch **DRY** 1 hour

- 1¾ **cups all-purpose flour**
- ½ **tsp baking powder**
- ¼ **tsp salt**
- ½ **cup (1 stick) unsalted butter, at room temperature**
- ¾ **cup granulated sugar**
- 1 **large egg plus 1 large egg yolk**
- 1 **tsp vanilla extract**
  Royal Icing (recipe, right)
  Sparkling sugar, silver dragées or other decorations

■ Whisk flour, baking powder and salt in a small bowl. Beat butter, sugar, egg, egg yolk and vanilla in a large bowl until blended. Stir in flour mixture. Gather into a ball; wrap in plastic. Refrigerate 2 hours.

■ Heat oven to 350°. Roll out dough with a lightly floured rolling pin on a floured surface to ⅜-inch thickness. Cut with assorted-size snowflake cookie cutters. Place on ungreased baking sheets, 1½ inches apart. Bake 10 to 12 minutes, until just browned at edges. Remove cookies to a wire rack to cool.

■ Spread some of the cookies with thinned Royal Icing; let dry. Pipe designs onto cookies with thicker icing; sprinkle with sugar or top with silver dragées. Let icing dry 1 hour before stacking cookies.

PER COOKIE 178 **CAL**; 5 g **FAT** (3 g **SAT**);
2 g **PRO**; 32 g **CARB**; 23 g **SUGARS**; 0 g **FIBER**;
43 mg **SODIUM**

Royal Icing In a medium bowl, combine 3 cups confectioners' sugar, 2 tbsp meringue powder and 2 tbsp cool water. Beat on high with an electric mixer 5 minutes, adding more water as needed for good piping consistency. Divide in half; transfer one half to a pastry bag fitted with a small writing tip. Thin remaining half with a little water (to make a base coat).

Note Look for meringue powder in Michaels stores, or order from *wilton.com*.

SNOWFLAKES

INDEX